DEADLY ENCOUNTER

Isaac Davis, a sophomore at the University of South Florida, lay on a futon in his living room watching television. He had taken the day off from school to recuperate from the flu.

Suddenly there were three loud thuds against his door. On the fourth blow, the door splintered off its hinges and came crashing into his apartment. A woman carrying a gun stumbled in. Following her was a man who had a gun that appeared to be a military weapon.

Davis turned and ran.

"He's in here," Paula said.

"Get him," Chino ordered.

Paula caught him in the bedroom and marched him into the living room. Chino grabbed Davis and pushed him to the smashed door. At the door Chino looked around Davis's shoulder and yelled, "I have a hostage!"

Then he unleashed several volleys of gunfire before moving away from the door. Chino paced and said, "Oh boy. I've done something really bad. I think I killed a cop.

"Come on," Chino said.

Chino led Davis around the apartment to look out the windows. Davis peeked out. He had never seen so many policemen, some of whom were wearing what looked like combat gear.

Chino paced and said again, "We did something really, really bad!"

D0171570

LOVE ME
OR I'LL
KILL YOU

LEE BUTCHER

PINNACLE BOOKS
Kensington Publishing Corp.
http://www.kensingtonbooks.com

Some names have been changed to protect the privacy of individuals connected to this story.

PINNACLE BOOKS are published by

Kensington Publishing Corp.
850 Third Avenue
New York, NY 10022

All Kensington Titles, Imprints, and Distributed Lines are available at special quantity discounts for bulk purchases for sales promotions, premiums, fund-raising, and educational or institutional use. Special book excerpts or customized printings can also be created to fit specific needs. For details, write or phone the office of the Kensington special sales manager: Kensington Publishing Corp., 850 Third Avenue, New York, NY 10022, attn: Special Sales Department, Phone: 1-800-221-2647.

Pinnacle and the P logo Reg. U.S. Pat. & TM Off.

ISBN-13: 978-0-7860-1778-2
ISBN-10: 0-7860-1778-3

First Printing: February 2007

10 9 8 7 6 5 4 3 2 1

Printed in the United States of America

Acknowledgments

Many people helped me in writing this book. Mark Ober, Hillsborough County state attorney, was especially generous with his time and resources. He helped me understand some of the finer points of law in this case. Thanks, Mark. Deeann Athan is one of the most passionate defense attorneys I have ever met. She was also generous with her time and insights into this case. Thank you, Deeann. Anne Sheer Weiner, Florida assistant attorney general, went far beyond the call of duty to make sure I had invaluable research materials. Thanks, Anne. My gratitude also goes to the Tampa Police Department, Detective Roberto Batista, and Lieutenant Joe Durkin. Thanks also to Anna Vargas, at the Florida State Attorney's Office, and to Bonnie Fruchey, who helped proof the manuscript. Thanks to Robin Menendez, of the Hillsborough County State Attorney's Office. Thank you, Ron Kolwak, of the *Tampa Tribune*. Most special thanks to my editor at Kensington Books, Michaela Hamilton, who was so kind, encouraging, and inspiring. Thank you, Michaela—and thanks to Jeremie Ruby-Strauss, another fine editor at Kensington.

Prologue

The police were closing in on Nestor "Chino" DeJesus and his girlfriend, Paula Gutierrez. Rage coursed through Chino's blood as he ran across the hot asphalt parking lot of the Crossings Apartment Complex in Tampa, Florida. Only an hour earlier, they had robbed a branch bank of the Bank of America, less than a mile away.

The cops, those snakes, would never take him alive. He had a MAC-11 submachine gun and he would go down in a blaze of glory, taking as many cops with him as he could. Where in the hell was Paula? They had run out of the building together, but, as usual, she had screwed up and wasn't there. She was always screwing things up. He was furious with her. Where was she?

They had been inside his mother's apartment when he heard the police helicopter thundering overhead. The cops had an army looking for them. Chino yelled at Paula.

"Let's go!"

And then he ran out the door and down the stairs from the second floor. Several cops had arrived and

patrol cars, with flashing blue-and-white lights, were
starting to surround the complex.

Chino ran across the sizzling-hot parking lot and
found no way out. He needed a car. Less than an
hour ago, when he and Paula robbed the bank, he
had ditched his yellow Nissan Xterra SUV because
it was too easy to spot. Now he needed a car to
escape from the cops and didn't have one.

Remembering that there was a veteran's cemetery across Cleveland Street, Chino turned and
headed that way. There were trees and shrubs in
the cemetery that he could hide behind while he figured out a way to make his getaway. The July air was
hot and muggy, like being in a sauna, and Chino
struggled to get enough oxygen. Although he was six
feet tall and weighed two hundred pounds, he was
a heavy smoker and pot user and was badly out
of shape.

At last, he made it into the cemetery. There were
live oaks, bushes, and other trees among the head-
stones, where veterans were buried. Chino looked
for a way that he could work himself away from the
cops without being spotted. Then he saw a cop, a
woman, heading toward him.

He hated cops! He hated almost everyone and
everything. The world had never given him a
break and everybody was out to get him. Thinking
about it enraged him. Now the cop had spotted
him. Chino turned and ran back through the
cemetery and across Cleveland to the Crossings
parking lot. More cop cars were arriving, but he
didn't think anyone had spotted him except the
policewoman.

He needed a car. Chino looked around and saw the
man who lived next to his apartment come out the

door with his keys in his hand. Chino ran toward him, driven by desperation and rage.

As he ran up the outside stairs, he saw Paula in the large courtyard, which was dominated by a huge swimming pool. She was screaming and wore an expression of terror as she ran erratically in the courtyard. First this way, then that, going nowhere, just pumping her legs and flailing her arms.

Chino snatched the keys from the hand of his startled neighbor Mark Kokojan and started to run down the stairs.

"Hey! What are you doing?" Kokojan shouted. "Give me back my keys."

Chino kept going and Kokojan ran after him.

"Paula!" Chino shouted. "Paula! Come on! Let's go!"

Chino's voice seemed to cut through whatever haze Paula was in and she obeyed—as she always did. She was much too afraid of him not to. He beat her for no reason at all, except that she was no good, and could never please him. It was her own fault. Several times he had threatened to kill her, their daughter, and everyone in her family.

She had tried to leave him a dozen times, but she always came back. "The only way you're leaving me is in a body bag," he told her.

She heard his voice command her and she ran after him, trailing Kokojan. Paula didn't hear the sirens screaming. Everything seemed to be happening to somebody else, as if she were watching a movie, that she wasn't really there. It was all happening in nightmarish slow motion, and she just wanted it to end before Chino hurt somebody.

Chino tried to open Kokojan's car, but his hand was trembling too much to find the keyhole. He beat on the door with his fist in frustration and anger.

Then the policewoman appeared a few yards away.
"Don't move," she said. "Don't move or I'll shoot."
The threat enraged Chino. Who was she to
threaten *him?* His lips curled in a snarl. He raised the
MAC-11 submachine gun and fired.

Chapter 1

On the morning of July 6, 2001, Paula woke up to find Chino shaking her. There was a wild look on his face and he already seemed to be in a manic state.

"Get up, I need you to fix breakfast."

Paula, twenty-one, was in a daze. She had been in a fog, off and on, for at least three years, but it had gotten worse in the past year. She didn't want to get out of bed, she was afraid all the time, and she felt that there was no hope of things ever getting better. She felt like she was in a pit and just sinking deeper and deeper. Much of the time she felt she was on the outside of her life watching somebody else go through the motions of living it.

The only thing Paula could find in the house to eat was oatmeal. There wasn't even any milk or sugar to have with it. She dutifully prepared the oatmeal and she sat with Chino and her two-year-old daughter, Ashley, to have breakfast.

"We're going to get some money," Chino said. "We've got less than a dollar between us. We're gonna get some."

Paula felt a chill of fear run through her. Four days

earlier, Chino had taken her with him while he robbed a flower shop in North Tampa. She didn't believe it was going to happen until Chino actually did it. They only got $45 from that robbery and Chino had been enraged with Paula.

"Why didn't you open the cash register and look in there?" he asked.

"You didn't tell me to."

"Stupid! Stupid! Stupid!" He pounded on the steering wheel.

Paula did what Chino told her to do, nothing more or less. She was like a zombie slave. A once beautiful girl with curly dark hair, soft brown eyes, and an ethereal look that made her appear angelic, she now wore a blank expression, kept her eyes downcast, and never smiled.

Back at the apartment, Chino shoved her around and told her she had no brains and was useless, that she couldn't do anything right. Paula was used to that; her arms were always black-and-blue and she believed him when he told her she was useless. She had been hearing it from him since she was fifteen years old.

Now they were broke again because Chino wouldn't work. They had no food, less than a dollar, and their Nissan Xterra SUV was about to be repossessed. On top of that, they had to move out of his mother's apartment today, where they lived rent free. There were a few boxes scattered around that held the few things they owned. They had no idea about where they would go and had no money to get there.

Chino was more hyper than usual. He couldn't sit still; he paced and ranted about their situation. Chino blamed the "system" for never giving him a break. "It's slavery," he said. "If you're not white, you don't get a break. They keep you down. The only way you can get anything is to take it."

This was typical of Chino. He blamed everyone and everything for his problems, but not himself. He accepted no responsibility. Frequently he took his frustration and rage out on Paula, using her as a punching bag, strangling her, threatening to kill her. Then he would become all weepy and apologetic, promising that he would change, that he would never do it again. But he always did.

Just before 10:00 A.M. he ordered her to get dressed. "We're going out to get some money. I'm going to call my mother to get Ashley."

Oh, my God, Paula thought. *It's going to be the flower shop all over again. He's going to rob somebody.*

She was terrified, but too afraid to say anything. Chino didn't like for her to contradict him, or question him in any way, and he might beat her. She didn't feel that she had a will of her own; she *had* to do anything Chino wanted her to do.

Chino found the blue bag they had used at the flower shop robbery and opened it. He gave Paula sweatpants, a bandanna, a fishing hat, a long jacket, and sunglasses. He told her to put them on. Something bad was going to happen, she thought. They were going to do something bad.

Paula was in the bedroom changing clothes when Lissette Santiago, Chino's mother, came to pick up Ashley. Until the past few months, Paula had not let Lissette take care of Ashley, because she didn't like the woman. But she had been feeling so listless and depressed that she couldn't even take care of the daughter she loved so much.

Paula didn't come out of the bedroom to see Lissette. The tension in the apartment was almost unbearable to her, and Chino had that enraged look on his face that terrified her. It meant he was on the brink of exploding in rage and would take it out on somebody, most likely her.

It's going to happen, Paula told herself. *It's the flower shop robbery all over again.*

Why didn't she just say, "No, I'm not going to do this?" she asked herself. The answer was simple: she was too afraid of Chino to disobey him. Most of the time, it didn't seem as if she even had a will of her own. Her insides were screaming, "No, no, no, I don't want to do this." She was filled with dread. She wanted nothing more than just to run, but all Chino had to do was snap his fingers and she did whatever he wanted.

They got in the bright yellow SUV and Chino drove around in what seemed to be an aimless way. He was tense, nervous, and silent. He kept driving around, not saying anything, but was in a heightened state of excitement. Paula didn't know where they were going.

"We need money," Chino said. "We're going to take it."

Chino's driving had not been without purpose, after all. He had been casing the Bank of America branch at Church and Neptune, in North Tampa. Chino told her to put on the bandanna and sunglasses. To Paula, things seemed to be happening in quick time and she didn't seem to be there. Her overriding emotion, she said, was fear of what was about to happen.

"We're going to rob the bank," he told her. "Are you ready?"

"No, I don't want to."

"We're going to rob the bank," he told her again.

I don't want to do this, she thought. *What will happen if Chino goes in and I don't?* The thought made her shudder. There was nothing that could happen inside the bank, she thought, that would be as bad as what would happen if she disobeyed him. Chino would kill her.

Chino stopped the car beside the bank, not far from the front door, and told Paula to put the bandanna over her face. In her haste she tied it too low on her face to suit him.

"No, like this," Chino said, doing it for her. "You have to cover your nose."

Chino handed her the gun.

"You have to do this," he said. "You have to hold the gun while I get the money. You didn't do a good job getting money the last time."

"I don't want to."

"We're going to do it."

Chino's words were commands. She was too afraid to say no.

Inside, she was screaming, "I don't want to do this. I just hope he drives away." But he didn't, and then everything started to happen really fast. Time was a blur to her and Chino was hyper with excitement and had a glazed look in his eyes.

He's rushing me, rushing me, Paula thought. *I'm not ready.*

"You're going to stand there with the gun," he said firmly. "Just do it."

He parked the SUV. "We're going into the bank," he said.

"No, I don't want to," Paula said. "I'm scared."

"We're going in."

Then he opened the car door. Paula stopped thinking about what would happen if she committed a crime. She thought, *If Chino finds out I'm not in there, I'm going to get it.* She told a detective later, "When we drove there, it happened real quick, and when he handed me everything, it was really quick. When he jumped out, it was quick, but when I sat there, it was . . . it was like long, like a movie, like a slow movie; when I was thinking about that, and then that's when I jumped out, and then everything else was fast. So that's when I jumped out of the car and I went into the bank."

Trembling with fear and excitement, the two robbers got out of the bright yellow Xterra. Chino had told Paula that with the baggy pants, hat, and bandanna, no one would be able to tell that she was a woman. It would make them harder to identify later. Chino didn't think about how suspicious they might look to people passing by. Few people with good intentions entered a bank wearing a bandanna over their faces and carrying a submachine gun.

Chino burst into the bank and Paula followed, holding the gun. "Everybody down!" he yelled. "Everybody down! Keep your heads down! Don't move!"

Chino kept shouting the same instructions and ran toward the tellers, where the cash was. There were about a dozen people in the bank. Paula, scared to death of what Chino might do if anyone moved, saw Chino leap over the tellers' counter. She yelled, "Keep your heads down. Don't move!"

She heard Chino screaming, "Keep your heads down."

Paula saw people raising their heads to see what was going on. She thought, *If Chino sees that, he's going to get real mad. He doesn't need the gun, he can kick them or something.* She continued to scream, "Keep your heads down!"

Chino and Paula didn't know it, but their escapade

had turned into a disaster before they even entered the bank.

Jim Cunningham was passing by the Bank of America outlet when he saw two suspicious characters go inside. He telephoned Emergency 911.

"Nine-one-one," the dispatcher answered.

"There's a bank robbery in progress," Cunningham told the operator.

"Can you calm down and tell me what you see?" the dispatcher asked.

"Well, two men ran into the store (bank) with masks and a blue bag."

"How many?"

"Two men," Cunningham repeated.

"Are they still there?" the operator queried.

"I have no idea, ma'am. I'm trying to hide because I'm a little scared."

Just earlier, Curt Jennings had passed by and saw an oddly dressed couple double-park and run into the bank. One had a gun. Jennings hid and dialed 911 and reported what he thought was a robbery in progress.

Sevtap Delarocha, a teller at the Bank of America branch bank, was sandwiched between "the two Joannes," Joanne McCullough and Joanne Coppola, when she saw Chino and Paula enter.

She ran into the back room, where there were windows that looked out over the street. She was hoping to see what kind of a vehicle they were driving. Then she saw that one of them had a gun. She pushed the panic button that set off a silent alarm to notify police that there was trouble at the bank.

Chino jumped over the counter and started pulling and shaking drawers, but he couldn't get them open. Delarocha noticed that he was wearing a fishing hat and a scarf, baggy pants and a loose top, and a bandanna covered the lower part of his face from just below his eyes. The eyes were concealed by dark sunglasses.

Chino managed to yank one of her money drawers open and grabbed several stacks of currency. Delarocha noticed that he grabbed one of the "bait" stacks, which contained a dye pack hidden inside.

Paula pointed her gun at the floor, instead of at the prostrate customers and employees. "Stay down!" she yelled. "Keep your heads down!"

The robbers left as quickly as they had arrived. Delarocha had seen what kind of car they were driving: it was a bright yellow Nissan Xterra SUV.

She picked up the telephone and dialed 911.

"What is your emergency?" the operator asked.

"This is 1501 South Church Avenue. We just got robbed. This is Bank of America."

"Okay. Are there any injuries?"

"No, but he had a gun. Please."

"Okay, ma'am," the operator shouted.

"Yes?"

"I need you to take a deep breath and calm down for me. Are the doors locked?"

"Yes. We just locked the doors."

"Okay. There's no injuries and the suspect is gone, right?" the dispatcher inquired.

"The suspect is gone."

Dr. Woody Leal York heard what he thought of as "commotion" outside the bank as he waited to be taken to a vault. At first he thought somebody had been hurt in the parking lot, and he wondered if he should go out and offer help. Then he saw two people running toward the bank.

As he wondered what had happened, the two people came hurrying inside. He could see how they were dressed and realized immediately what was happening. At least one of them was armed. They were no more than five yards from him.

There were nine or ten people in the bank, two customers with a bank employee behind Dr. York, a sweet-looking old lady sitting in a chair across from him, four or five people in line, and three tellers. He thought there might have been more.

Things happened quickly. Dr. York realized something was wrong when he got a better look and saw bandannas covering the lower parts of their faces. He couldn't tell whether they were men or women, but he believed one was a female and that she was armed. He thought the gun was a Beretta. Although he knew little about guns, he owned a 9mm Beretta and the gun was at least that big.

"It was very noticeable," he said. "And it wasn't a little bitty weapon."

The robbers started screaming orders. "Get down! Everybody put your face on the ground! Get down!" Everybody in the bank jumped to the floor at the first command, except for the white-haired old lady, who was sitting near the doctor.

Dr. York was frightened for her. She seemed to be close to ninety years of age. He thought he heard her say, "I can't get down." Dr. York was having trouble himself. Surgery on both his knees the preceding January had made it difficult for him to bend them. He was hoping he got down fast enough so he wouldn't be shot and killed.

"Keep your heads down and don't look!" Chino yelled. "This is a bank robbery. This is not make-believe. This is the real thing. Don't anyone pull any tricks on me."

Chino's voice was forceful and threatening enough to make everybody comply. His voice wasn't nervous or hysterical. Clearly, he meant business. "This is a damn bank robbery!" Chino said. "Get down and stay down!"

Paula kept the room covered with the MAC-11. She stood not more than two feet in front of Dr. York, her legs spread-eagled. He noticed that she wore tennis shoes. She stood facing Dr. York and she checked the room repeatedly and said forcefully, but not as loud as Chino, "Don't anyone look up. Don't anyone dare look up. Whatever you do, do not look up."

The one thing that made Dr. York feel somewhat secure was that the robbers seemed to be in control of themselves. Their voices were not nervous or quavering, but strong and forceful. He was not as calm. He felt hysterical as he worried that somebody might come in from the back. He was afraid of anything that might set off frayed nerves and cause a bloodbath. What frightened him the most was that a customer might become hysterical or start crying and upset the robbers and cause them to start shooting.

Dr. York felt confident the robbers would do them no harm so long as the victims did exactly as they were told. It seemed to take Chino a long time to get the money. All the while, Dr. York thought, *Don't anyone come in! Just take the money and get out!*

After what seemed like a long time, Chino jumped back over the counter and the robbers headed out the door. "You folks have a nice day," he said sarcastically. "Don't dare look up when we leave the bank. Don't look up!"

Naturally, Dr. York and the others looked up as soon as the robbers were out the door. He could give a good description of their heights and builds to the police. When he looked out to see what kind of a vehicle they had, he was surprised. "It was the brightest yellow SUV I've ever seen," he said. "It was parked right next to my car."

A teller yelled, "Lock the doors! Lock the doors!"

Dr. York looked at the time. The robbery had taken only eight minutes. The police arrived just three minutes after the robbers left.

Kelley Cruey and her fiancé, Tyler Welches, weren't regular customers at the Tampa bank. They lived in Ormond Beach, a small town near Daytona Beach, about three hours from Tampa on I-4. They were in the bank because Tyler's company had a job in Tampa working on a storage unit and he needed cash to pay his crew.

Ordinarily, Tyler left the banking to Kelley. But on July 6, 2001, he decided to go to the bank with her. They were the only customers at the counter when a man suddenly ran in and said, "This is a stickup!" Kelley went blank with fear when she saw a gun pointed right at her. She didn't know what kind of a gun, but it was big. She was paralyzed.

They were approaching a teller at the counter just as the gunman came screaming through the door, and said, "Everybody hit the floor!" as he waved the gun around. He jumped over the counter right next to Tyler, who was just finishing his transaction. He had withdrawn cash to pay his crew. The payroll amount varied weekly, but on that day, it was several thousand dollars; he wasn't sure of the exact figure.

The robber was within five feet of him. He knew it was a man because of the voice, the way he yelled and screamed, and the way he moved. He was also strong enough to jump over the counter.

When somebody's waving a gun, that's threatening enough, Tyler thought. When they ordered you to hit the floor, you hit the floor. After the intruder jumped over the counter, he was screaming at them, threatening, giving orders. Tyler grabbed his girlfriend and shoved her to the ground and got on top of her, using his body to shield her.

A smaller robber with a gun charged in. "Everyone just stay down and no one will get hurt!" she said. "Keep your heads down and this will be over in a minute." Both Kelley and Tyler believed the person giving orders was a woman. Tyler didn't think a man could imitate a woman's voice so accurately.

Tyler had several thousand in his hand and his fiancée was frozen. As soon as he saw the gun, Tyler folded the payroll cash and jammed it into his shorts. He hoped the robbers wouldn't find it. Kelley never looked up again. She heard a man say—in what she called a smart-aleck voice—"Have a nice day."

Kelley couldn't give police a description of the robbers. First, because Tyler had kept her head down so that she saw only the tile floor, and second, because she was so scared. "I was so shook up, I don't know," she said. "All I wanted to do was get the hell out of there. That's all I wanted."

Tyler thought the bigger man carried a gun with a strap on it. He seemed to have it wrapped around his right arm so that his right hand was free to hold the gun. What Tyler probably saw was the blue bag that Chino carried. There was only one gun used in the robbery—the MAC-11 that Paula wielded.

Although Tyler had been ordered to keep his head down, he couldn't resist looking around initially, to see if there was any way he could help. The female robber ordered him to put his head back down. She walked straight ahead, and then turned and said, "Keep your heads down, do not look up at us, and do not move, and we'll be out of here in a second."

Tyler couldn't tell what kind of a gun it was because things happened too fast. He thought he had a pretty good description of what they wore. "They had boots on, khaki clothes, lighter, tan clothes, and dark coats, a jacket or something like that, and they had handkerchiefs over their faces." That was all he had seen.

Tyler agreed with the other witnesses that the robbery was fast. He thought it took about two minutes. "It was really quick. He was in, over the counter, and out."

The robbers fled, after having robbed the bank of just under $10,000.

Senior Patrol Officer Lois Marrero was an exact opposite of Chino DeJesus in almost every way. He was brooding, morose, angry, and blamed the world for being an ugly place with the cards stacked against him. Lois was bright, cheerful, optimistic, loved people, and thought the world was a wonderful place, especially when there were opportunities to help others.

A pretty, petite brunette who looked younger than her forty-one years, Lois had been with the Tampa

Police Department (TPD) for a little more than eighteen years and was looking forward to retirement. Every day for her was a new, exciting adventure, to learn, grow, and help others.

Years before, she had met Mickie Mashburn, who was also an officer in the Tampa Police Department. Mickie was an attractive blonde who nicely complemented Lois. The two women got along fabulously. They fell in love in 1990 and became committed life partners in a 1991 ceremony at the Sovereign Evangelist Church, presided over by a duly ordained minister. They were married in the eyes of their church, even though same-sex marriages weren't recognized by the state of Florida.

This was never a problem in the police department. Superiors and coworkers considered them spouses. Mickie had less than two years to serve before she, too, would become eligible for retirement. Both were looking forward to having more time to travel, tend their garden, play with their dogs, and to work at part-time jobs.

Being a cop is a dangerous job, especially in Florida, where even grandmothers and grandfathers frequently have licenses to carry concealed weapons. A case of simple road rage can sometimes end in a shoot-out and death. A routine stop for a traffic violation can put a cop on edge because he never knows who he's stopping, whether or not the subject has a gun, and if he is ready to use it. Everyone has heard about normally congenial postal workers who go on murderous rampages, but those are few and far between. A cop's life is at risk every time he, or she, goes on duty. There is a saying among cops: "There is no such thing as a routine encounter."

No one understood this any better than Mickie

and Lois. They were veteran police officers and they sometimes talked about the dangers. They worried about one another. Mickie was especially concerned because Lois worked on the streets, a particularly dangerous aspect of police work, but it was what Lois loved. They made certain they told each other every morning how they felt about one another. Mickie would say: "I love you more today than yesterday." Lois would reply, "Me too."

Lois was in a particularly good mood on the morning of July 6, 2001. She and Mickie were looking forward to seeing a woman's basketball team, the Miracles, play in Orlando that night. Mickie, on the other hand, had an uneasy feeling, as if there were an inexplicable threat hanging in the air. The whole week had been strange, with a feeling that dark clouds were forming. Lois told Mickie that she had even talked with one of her supervisors about her own death.

That morning Lois was turned out to perfection, as always, not a wrinkle on her razor-sharp uniform, shoes and leatherwork all spit and polish. She liked to look sharp, and she did. She was really excited about going to the basketball game later. Mickie worried that Lois pushed herself too hard, even when it came to having fun.

"You've got to rest sometime," Mickie told her.

Lois just laughed. "When you die, you can sleep."

She looked out at the flower garden she loved and said good-bye to Kilo, her Rottweiler, and stepped into the bright sunny day to go to work. She believed, as did Mickie, that "when the Lord opens the book and says, 'Today is for you,' that's it." Once on the job, Lois didn't even think about such things.

Around 9:30 A.M., Lois and Mickie chatted again

on their cellular telephones just to see how things were going. At 10:30 A.M., Lois telephoned again, but Mickie wasn't available. Lois punched in a numerical message for Mickie's beeper, as she often did. The message was: 45683968. Those were the telephone keys that spelled "I love you." They were chatting again later when Mickie heard the buzzer on Lois's personal radio go off.

"Oops, I gotta go right now," Lois said.

"I had this feeling" Mickie said later. "It was like I got the chills."

To Lois, she said, "Please be careful. I love you. Be careful."

Chapter 2

When Chino and Paula fled the Bank of America, they were already in big trouble. The robbery had been reported twice before it even occurred, once while it was in progress, and again just after it was over.

Now they were going to have trouble with technology. Banks use dye packs to help them recover stolen money and to make it easier to catch robbers. The Bank of America and its branches routinely stash these "bait" dye packs inside stacks of money. The dye packs are simple and efficient.

Dye packs were invented to make bank robbery a profitless enterprise and, hopefully, extinct. Called a Security Pack, it is placed in the middle of a stack of bills. A few years ago, the pack was made with stiff plastic and could sometimes be detected by a bank robber; now the pack is so thin and pliable that only the most skilled robber would be able to feel it inside a stack of paper money.

Seventy-five percent of the dye packs used by banks in the United States are made by ICI Security Systems. Bank tellers have several packs near their windows at all times. The packs are kept in a "safe" mode by being attached to a magnetic plate. A small radio receiver inside the pack is activated by a transmitter mounted in the jamb of entry and exit doors of the bank. Once the pack passes through the door, its detonation device is activated and set to explode a few seconds later, after the robbers are a safe distance from people in the bank.

Chino and Paula didn't know there was a dye pack inside the money he had stuffed in his bag. After tossing the bag containing the cash in the backseat, Chino gunned the SUV to make a getaway. He hadn't gone more than a block when there was an explosion.

Red smoke, tear gas, and a dye called methyl-amino-anthraquinone filled the interior of the vehicle. Neither he nor Paula could see or breathe. Both went into fits of coughing and tears gushed from their burning eyes. Paula's lungs felt like they were on fire. Smoke and red dye were everywhere. Chino opened all of the windows, but he still couldn't get rid of the tear gas.

At the same time the dye pack detonated, a chemical reaction took place that caused the pack to reach a temperature of 400 degrees. The heat isn't enough to set the money on fire, but it can blister skin, making it too hot to handle. Robbers frequently throw the money away in an attempt to ease their suffering.

That's what Chino did. Desperate for relief, he found the bag containing the cash in the backseat and tossed it, money and all, out a window. Only a few of the stained bills remained in the vehicle.

Caesar Rodriguez pulled out of his driveway when a yellow SUV raced by. The driver seemed to be

throwing trash out of the window. He thought they
were emptying a garbage bag and it made him mad.

"Asshole!" he yelled at them.

Then he noticed that the people in the SUV
hadn't been getting rid of garbage, after all. They
were tossing money out of their car. Lots of it. Stacks
of bills hit the ground and a burst of money fluttered
up like a gathering of migrating butterflies. The
money scattered over a city block and was splotched
with red. Rodriguez could smell the tear gas.

One of his neighbors had come over to see what
was happening. Rodriguez said, "It's raining money.
I think it's money from a robbery. Go call the cops."

While they were waiting for the police to arrive,
Rodriguez took a snapshot of his neighbor standing
in the field of strewn money. Only a few minutes
passed before a police car arrived. Rodriguez told
the patrolman which way the SUV was heading and
the officer left in a hurry, speaking into his radio as
he sped away in hot pursuit. The police already
knew what type of vehicle the robbers were driving;
now they had narrowed down the area in which
they were located. It was just a matter of time before
they were caught.

In fact, police radios had been crackling with updates since the first "robbery in progress" was reported at 10:42 A.M. Officer Edward Durkin was
serving as dispatcher to route the calls. He han-
dled the first reports to and from the units that carried the code name "David" (for the letter *D*).

"David nine-one-one," Durkin said. "David nine-one-
one. Stand by a minute, David seven and David eight."

David 8: "Go ahead."

Durkin: "Both units copy a twenty-three (armed
robbery) to the Bank of America at Church and

Neptune, Church and Neptune, reference an eyewitness advising two men wearing blue masks and carrying a blue bag, entering the building."

David 8: "Ten-four (understood). This is in progress then?"

Durkin: "Ten-four. One of the customers or somebody was there and witnessed it. We still haven't received anything from the alarm company."

David eleven was now in the pursuit.

David 8 and 11: "Copy."

Durkin: "They advised that both men had sunglasses and bandannas and hats on. Break. Stand by for an update, I just got it. They advise that one of the subjects was a white male wearing a blue mask, a blue hat, a blue T-shirt, and khaki pants. Last seen driving a yellow SUV. An unknown make or tag. They were ten-oh (armed) with a gun. They got all the money and bait money, as well, with dye pack time lapse release. Last seen southbound on Church. Repeating southbound on Church in yellow SUV, ten-oh with a gun."

Davids 8 and 11 advised they were going into pursuit.

Durkin: "All units responding to the Bank of America, repeating, all units responding to the Bank of America, we just received a call from Estrella, Estrella. Someone came through and threw a bunch of money at that location. Break. The money's gonna be in front of that ten-twenty (location). Suspect was in a yellow Xterra. Repeating, yellow Xterra."

David 8: "Ten-four. David eight. I'll be there in a minute."

Durkin: "Ten-four. They said they were last seen going westbound on Estrella to Henderson. Time lapse within minutes. Complainant is there gathering the money."

David 11: "Have responding units slow down a little bit. Ah, they're gone. See if we have a chopper."

Durkin: "Ten-four. David eight, I'm getting some info that you have a group of people there, picking up the money. I do not know if they're gonna walk off with it."

David 8: "Everything's ten-four."

Unintelligible Chatter.

Unit 453: "I'm ten-fifty-one (en route) to the call."

Durkin: "Ten-four. We just had a signal twenty-three to the Nations Bank at 1501 South Church. Break. That's Bank of America, correction. The suspect was a white male, wearing a blue mask, a blue hat, ten-oh with a gun. They took some money, they dumped some out also. Break. They were last seen in the area of Estrella in a yellow Xterra SUV. It's gonna be a Nissan Xterra SUV, yellow color. Break. Last seen westbound on Estrella toward Henderson."

(By now, "Baker" units started to respond.)

Baker 13 (Lois Marrero): "Have one of the units that can give me a clothing description to go over to the sixteenth (precinct) because I'm close to the bank."

Unit 453: "I have another one. It's going to be the apartment complex just north of Hubert and Kennedy. It's parked far southeast, corner of the parking lot."

Durkin: "Baker thirteen, copy?"

Baker 13: "Yeah, I got the apartment complex. It's Regency here at Manhattan. It's on the east side of the parking lot."

Unit 453: "It's parked way down in the southeast corner. South end, against the fence, Baker thirteen. I saw it. It's up against a bunch of trees."

Baker 13: "Somebody at the bank can tell me if one of the suspects had a tattoo on his upper arm by chance."

Dispatcher repeated Baker 31's request for information about a tattoo.

Durkin: "Did you get the tag? If not, I've got it."

Baker 13: "Okay, have we got a unit that can go to the Crossings apartments at Cleveland and Church? There should be a white male named Chino. He's the one that drove this yellow Xterra over here and parked it at eleven twenty-two. He called somebody, then said it wouldn't start and to 'come give me a ride.' And he's got red tint to his hair from where it's been dyed or something."

Durkin: "That's Cleveland and Church, at the Crossings apartments?"

Baker 13: "Ten-four. Do we have a unit that can go by Cleveland and Church?"

Baker 41: "Already there."

Lois Marrero also headed toward the Crossings. She had responded to hundreds of calls in her career as a police officer. She loved the work, and every fitness report she had received testified that she was good at it. The reports from her supervisors usually spoke about her in glowing terms.

"A very professional officer with unlimited potential," one wrote in 1985. In 1988, she was called "an outstanding officer."

Lois had not always been a patrol officer. A few years ago she had held the rank of sergeant and was head of Tampa's community affairs bureau and gang suppression units. She was known as a "very energetic, very smart, dedicated cop." She was credited with reducing car thefts and destroying organized gangs by locating and undermining their ties with other crooks.

Lois was demoted to patrol officer when the police department charged that she charged six vacation days to personal leave. The department tried to fire her, but Lois sued for unlawful termination and the department settled with her. She kept her job on the force, but was demoted one pay grade.

Fighting for something she wanted was nothing new to the petite police officer. She was raised in Puerto Rico, where she graduated from Colégio Santa Rosa, in 1978. After that, it was on to Tampa to work her way through college. She joined the Tampa Police Department in 1982 and was widely known for her appearance, energy, and eagerness to learn.

The demotion to patrol officer wasn't that hard for Lois to take; she loved being on the streets because it gave her a chance for personal interaction and to have a direct influence on the lives of others. She enjoyed helping people. Nevertheless, after almost twenty years of being a cop, Lois was looking forward to retirement, a little over a year away.

She loved working in her rose garden with Mickey at their comfortable house in the Fawn Creek subdivision in northwest Hillsborough County. The plush landscaping and neat, well-tended lawn was a testament to their care. Mickie and Lois were not married under Florida law, but they had taken nuptial vows in a ceremony conducted by an ordained minister at the Sovereign Evangelist Church. They wore identical wedding bands.

The weather in July was sweltering and heat rising from the pavement distorted images, giving them a surreal look. In spite of the heat, Lois wore what is commonly referred to as a "bulletproof vest." But every cop knows nothing is 100 percent bulletproof. The heavy vest made it even hotter and more uncomfortable.

In just over a year, Lois planned to spend her time helping neighbors string Christmas lights, as she had in the past, prune her roses, and have good times with Mickey during her retirement. Right now, she had two bank robbers to apprehend.

Still coughing and splotched with red dye, Chino pulled the SUV into the Regency Apartments parking lot, close to the Crossings. His mother not only worked as a maintenance woman for the Crossings, but at the Regency, which was operated by the same owners.

Chino told Paula that they had to ditch the SUV. The bright yellow vehicle attracted a lot of attention. That was one of the things he loved about it, but now that characteristic had become a liability. The SUV seemed to pop out of any group of vehicles it was near. It would take the police no time to spot it, either from the air or ground.

Paula felt like she was in shock. She remembered little about the harrowing race from the bank. After Chino parked the SUV under some trees to help conceal it, he popped the trunk.

"You've got to change your clothes," he said. He was furious that things had gone wrong, and the money had contained a dye pack.

Paula's clothes were splotched with red dye and smelled funny because of the tear gas.

"Change into what? Change where?" she asked.

Chino pulled a swimsuit top and some other clothing from the back of the SUV.

"Wear this," he said, tossing her the swimsuit top.

Paula said okay, and looked through the remaining clothes for some pants or shorts.

"Nothing else in here belongs to me," she said.

Chino tossed her a pair of shorts. "Wear my shorts," he said.

The shorts were several sizes too big, and looked absurd, but Paula slipped into them in the parking lot. Chino changed, too.

"Hurry up!" he said, looking around nervously. "Hurry!"

They went into the Regency's Laundromat and Chino told her to wait there for him. He walked into an office that his mother sometimes used and picked up a phone. A short time later he returned.

"Come on," he ordered. Paula grabbed the bag and they stepped into the lobby of the Regency. In a few minutes, Lissette arrived with Ashley. Chino got in Lissette's car, followed by Paula.

"What's wrong with the truck, Chino?" Lissette asked.

"It broke down."

Lissette looked at him. "Chino, it's a brand-new truck."

Lissette noted that both Chino and Paula looked a little red, but she didn't mention it. Maybe they had been to the beach and gotten sunburned.

Chino and Lissette chatted on the short ride to the Crossings, but Paula was quiet. She felt "zoned out," as if she were in a dream and none of this were real. They pulled up at the Crossings, and Chino pushed her out of the car, then followed her.

"Ashley, come on. Let's go," Paula said to her daughter.

"No, I want to stay with Grandma," Ashley replied.

Lissette said she would bring Ashley back in a few hours.

After Lissette left, Paula and Chino showered and tried to wash away the red dye and tear gas that was still on their skin and in their hair. Chino was able

to wash most of the dye off himself without much
trouble. The shower helped calm Paula's nerves
and she started to cry with relief. She was emotionally exhausted now that the robbery was over. *Thank
God*, she thought, *it's finished now.*

After showering, Chino ordered her to get some
bleach and rubber gloves. Then they stood at the
bathroom sink and tried to wash the dye out of the
few dollars Chino hadn't thrown away. It wouldn't
come out. Chino cursed angrily and Paula sat down
to watch television. Before she could turn the set on,
Chino's phone rang and it was Lissette.

"The cops are looking for you," she said. "They say
you robbed a bank."

Chino became frantic. He appeared to be consumed by both fear and rage. Waves of fear washed
over Paula again.

Then Chino heard a helicopter.

Officer Earl Bingle was on patrol around 11:00 A.M.
when he spotted a yellow SUV parked under some
trees at the Regency Apartments. He stopped, walked
up to the vehicle, and put his hand on the hood. It
was still warm, as if it had been parked in the past
few minutes.

Patrolman David Shepler was across the street at
David's Bridal asking the proprietors if they had
seen anything unusual, when he received a radio
message from Bingle, informing him about the
SUV. He left and joined Bingle in the parking lot.

"What's the story on the vehicle?" Shepler asked.

"It's hot," Bingle said.

The apartment manager had seen the police and
joined them by the SUV.

"Do you know who owns the vehicle?" Bingle asked.

The apartment manager told them it belonged to the maintenance woman's son. "He might be in the laundry room," she said. "I saw him go in there. His name is Chino." She described him as a young Hispanic male between five-eight to five-ten. The woman had underestimated Chino's height. He was actually about six feet tall.

Three other police officers arrived. The five of them went to the Laundromat to look for Chino. He wasn't there. The manager approached them again and said that Chino often visited friends who lived in the building.

The police knocked on the door of the apartment and it was answered by an elderly woman. Bingle didn't get her name. A young man joined the woman and Bingle told them what they were doing there and asked if they could check the apartment.

"He's not here, but you can check anyway," the woman answered.

The police searched, but no one else was there. It was clean. As they walked back into the parking lot, the manager came back and told Bingle that Chino's mother lived at the Crossings. Bingle immediately got on the radio and told dispatch to have units go to the apartment and check.

Before he got in his car, he heard Officer Lois Marrero coming on the radio and saying she was in foot pursuit of the suspect. Bingle sped away to the Crossings apartments, which were only half-a-mile away. A police helicopter circled overhead, but Bingle was in too much of a hurry to notice. He sped to help Lois.

He went to Kennedy and then headed south on

Grady, because Lois was chasing the suspect through a veteran's cemetery. She was chasing him south-bound. Bingle figured Chino might turn down Cleveland, and he wanted to be there to apprehend him. The patrol officer pulled to a stop in front of the apartment complex on Church Street and got ready to confront the suspect.

Chapter 3

"We've got to go!" Chino yelled. "Hurry."

Paula was more worried than ever because the nightmare seemed to be starting all over. Chino was shouting and cursing. And where was Lissette? She was supposed to have been back with Ashley. Chino wanted to run from the police, who were closing in, but their truck was half-a-mile away.

First, Paula had to get dressed. She threw on a camouflage T-shirt and Chino's shorts. She was so rattled that she forgot to put on underwear.

"Pack a few things," Chino told her. "Hurry up."

Pack what? Hurry to go where? Paula wondered. Where was there to go?

Paula took the small canvas bag, which contained the MAC-11, and started to throw things inside haphazardly. She was so nervous, she couldn't think. When they ran outside the door, Paula put the bag down and started to lock the door. Chino, meanwhile, had run part of the way down the stairs leading to the courtyard and pool, and then he ran back. He retrieved the MAC-11 from the bag and ran down the stairs leading to the parking lot.

A few minutes earlier, Mark Kokojan left his apartment to take his broken cell phone to a repair shop. When he got to his car, which was an older silver Oldsmobile, he realized that he had forgotten the receipt. He went back to his apartment to get it.

On his way back to the car, Kokojan was surprised to find his neighbor Paula standing there, looking terrified. She asked if she could use his telephone. Kokojan was astounded because he had never heard Paula speak before, or even look directly at him. Paula ran off without waiting for an answer and went into the courtyard. Paula's boyfriend, Chino De-Jesus, ran up and snatched the keys out of his hand. Kokojan didn't know Chino, but he had seen him around the complex visiting his mother.

"Hey, what's going on, man?" he asked. "Just stop. I'll help you."

Chino kept running. In the courtyard Paula was in such panic that she couldn't control herself. She ran this way, then that, her brain not functioning. She had no idea how she had gotten where she was. Then she heard Chino screaming and screaming. Terrified, she ran after him. Kokojan ran after Chino to get his car keys.

"Paula! Paula!" Chino screamed.

"*Sí*, I'm here," she answered.

To Paula, everything seemed to be happening in quick time again. Events seemed to jump and skip about without logic or regard to the passing of time. She remembered being at the top of the stairs with Chino, but she didn't remember coming downstairs or how she got to the courtyard. And now she found herself running in the parking lot. She saw a policewoman running after them.

The three civilians reached Kokojan's car and

Chino tried to unlock it. He was shaking so much that he couldn't get the key in the lock. The door wasn't even locked, but Chino didn't think to try the handle to see. Paula stood by the right front bumper of Kokojan's car as Chino struggled with the car door. Sirens sounded, coming closer. A helicopter *thumped* loudly overhead, flying in wide circles. A policewoman had caught up with them and was just a few yards away, on the other side of the car.

Paula looked at the policewoman and their eyes locked.

Oh, my God, Paula thought.

Lois and Officers Cole Scudder, Gary Metzgar, and James Zipler were the first police to arrive on the scene. Lois updated the dispatcher on her police radio as she ran after the two bank robbers.

"I got him here," she said. "He's running. He's going eastward. Eastward through the cemetery with a gun."

The cemetery was a veteran's cemetery across the street from the Crossings. Chino tried to get away by cutting through it, but he was spotted by the police. He turned around and headed back to the Crossings.

Baker 13: "Okay, I lost him somewhere in the cemetery. Oh, he's headed back. He doubled back on me, back into the apartments."

A few minutes later, Lois reported: "He's gonna be with a female. Signal zero in the cemetery. He's got a gun on me! Get officers to come here; air service is going with him."

Seconds later, Lois said ". . . that gun!"

Gunfire exploded on police radios, and then Lois's radio was silent.

The radio came back to life a few seconds later and the words every cop dreads to hear came over the airwaves: "Officer down. Officer down. Need ten-thirty-two (ambulance), ten-eighteen (respond as soon as possible). We need them here. He's getting into a silver car . . . trying to get into a silver car. I'm going inside the apartment complex.

"There is an officer down. We need ten-thirty-two, ten-eighteen."

Mark Kokojan dived headfirst under the front bumper of his car when Chino fired a burst of gunfire from the MAC-11, almost point-blank, at the policewoman. Two bullets slammed into Lois's bulletproof vest and the third bullet ripped into her throat. Paula made eye contact with Lois as she fell. Lois reached out as if pleading for help, gasping for breath. To Paula, the woman's eyes seemed to be asking, "Why?" It was like being in a nightmare.

When she heard the woman tell Chino, "Put down your gun or I'll shoot," Paula prayed that he would. *Just put the gun down, Chino. Please. Put the gun down and it will all be over.*

But he had shot her instead. *Oh, my God,* she thought. *He's killed a cop.*

When the shooting stopped, Kokojan looked up and saw that Chino appeared confused and panicked. The seconds seemed to drag on for hours. It never occurred to Kokojan that Chino might shoot him, or that the police might think he was one of the suspects.

"Get her gun!" Chino yelled at Paula, while motioning toward Lois.

Paula grabbed Lois's 9mm Glock and raced after him as Chino fled back to the Crossings.

Kokojan saw Lois lying in the parking lot and realized that Chino had shot a police officer. He was wondering what to do when Officer Veronica "Ronnie" Hills arrived to help Lois. She ordered Kokojan to get into his car, close the windows, shut the doors, and stay there. Kokojan gladly obliged. He couldn't help thinking that if he hadn't forgotten the receipt for his cell phone and gone back to his apartment, the whole thing might not have happened.

Bingle didn't see Marrero chasing Chino. When he ran into the parking lot, he saw a policeman on the ground. He ran to help and saw that it was Lois. While he was checking her, he heard gunfire from inside the complex and bullets whizzed past him. Ronnie arrived and took up a position over her fallen comrade.

"Stay with her," Bingle said, and ran in a crouch to take up a position in one of the breezeways. He fired several shots back at Chino, who was still on the second-story landing. Dozens of police officers were on the scene now. Orders were being shouted, radios were crackling, and guns were at the ready as the police secured their positions. Bingle remained at his position, after the shooting stopped, and waited for the tactical response team (TRT) to arrive.

Scudder heard the first burst of gunfire that Chino fired at Lois. He was on the other side of the complex and ran to help when he saw her go down. Chino fired another volley, this time at him, and Scudder heard bullets flying past him and striking the pavement. One of the bullets grazed his right thigh. A few inches either way and he could have been killed.

The police officer hadn't seen Chino fire at him. "I didn't even see him before he started shooting," he said later. "He ambushed her and then he ambushed me." He scrambled to take up a position to contain the suspect and thought, *Hold still, so I can kill you, you son of a bitch.*

For a moment he had a clear view of both suspects and fired his revolver. He clearly saw the man grab the woman in a hammerlock and use her as a human shield. Then they disappeared.

John "J. T." Martin piloted the police helicopter that churned noisily overhead. He was flying solo, which was not the most efficient way to conduct a search by air. Martin and three other police officers were on duty in the aviation division when the call came to search for two suspects in a robbery that had taken place at the Bank of America. Martin was the only person available to fly; flight supervisor Jeff Fife and Officers Randy Miller and James Williams were with some other policemen at a steak house a block away, celebrating Fife's birthday.

Ideally, a search helicopter requires at least one spotter, who can devote undivided attention to looking at what's happening on the ground. The Tampa Police Department had no clear-cut policy to govern this situation. Martin debated the issue and decided that one pair of eyes from the air was better than none.

Once in the air, Martin had his hands full. He monitored the radio dispatches and communicated with air traffic controllers while flying at low altitudes.

He could see the activity on the ground when he circled above the Crossings apartments. He saw the confrontation between Officer Marrero and the fugitives. And he saw her pitch face-forward onto the hard pavement.

Laura Kent was in her apartment at the Crossings, waiting for a friend with whom she was going shopping. Laura, a pretty blonde in her twenties, had gone outside to her balcony because it was such a pretty day. She enjoyed the fresh air and sunshine, even though the scenery didn't exactly take her breath away. There were just a few cars in the parking lot. She could hear the distant whooping and hollering of people having fun at the community swimming pool.

The scene suddenly exploded into violence. A police helicopter circled low overhead and Laura knew that meant trouble; the police were looking for someone. She heard sirens wail. Then she saw a young man and woman in the parking lot. The man had a gun that looked like a military weapon. She recognized him as the maintenance woman's son. She saw a police officer chasing him. As if in a nightmare, she saw the man spin around and fire almost point-blank at the police officer. The woman dropped to the pavement and the young couple turned to sprint toward her apartment building. Laura telephoned 911.

When the operator answered, Laura was almost hysterical. She said, "There's an officer down right in front of my house."

"Hold on! Hold on," the operator responded.

"Somebody shot her right in front of me," Laura

said "She's laying on the floor. I think she was shot in the head or something."

"Are you sure?" the 911 dispatcher pressed.

Laura began to cry. "I'm sure. She's on the [pavement] at the Crossings apartments at Kennedy and Church. She's bleeding all over the place."

"Was she shot?" The dispatcher didn't understand yet that the police officer was female. *"Are you sure?"*

"Yes. I don't even think she's alive."

"We have ambulances on the way," the dispatcher told her. "Did you see the people that shot him?"

"They ran back into their house. I don't know which apartment."

"Are you sure?"

"Yes, I'm sure. There's cops everywhere and she's laying on the floor. I think she's dead. Oh, my God."

Laura could hardly hold the phone and it was hard to speak.

"Okay. Listen, honey, it's okay, okay? We have other police officers on the way and we have an ambulance coming," the operator consoled.

"I don't think she's alive. I think she's dead."

"She's fine, she's fine," the dispatcher said, trying to soothe Laura. "She's not gonna be dead, okay?"

"She's not even moving. Oh, my God . . . they ran next door to me . . . oh, my God!"

"It's okay. It's okay."

"Oh, my God."

"She's not gonna be dead, okay?"

Laura's hands shook. "She's dead."

"She's fine. Don't say that."

"Oh, my God. She's not moving . . . and all these cops are running around. I don't know. Yeah, I don't think she's alive because they're all crying. A couple of cops are crying . . . oh, my God."

Her son toddled up to her and asked, "Mommy, Mommy. What's wrong, Mommy?"

Laura comforted her child. "I was outside waiting for someone to come home and saw these cops chasing this guy," Laura said. "I never saw this guy do anything like that before. They're covering her."

"They're covering him?" the 911 dispatcher asked.

"Yes."

"Completely?"

"Yes."

"It's not your fault," the dispatcher said. "It's okay. I'm here. Even if I don't say anything, okay? Stay on the line."

"Oh, my God. I looked outside," Laura said. "I'm waiting for someone to come home."

"He's not going to be dead, okay?"

"She's not even moving."

"He's going to be fine, okay?"

"I think she's dead." Laura paused a moment. "She's stopped moving. She's just lying there."

"Oh! Is it a male or female officer?" the operator inquired.

"Female. I think she's dying. She's dead."

"No, she's fine, okay? Don't say that. I need you to stay inside your house," the dispatcher said. "Tell me what you see."

"She's not moving. I don't know."

The dispatcher told her to go inside and write down everything she saw.

"Okay," she said. "Today is just not a very good day."

Sherry Ann Williams, a student at Hillsborough Community College, heard a helicopter and went out on the patio to check. She saw the helicopter and then heard gunshots. She hurried back inside and hunkered down on the floor.

She heard her doorknob rattle as if someone were trying to get in. There were several heavy thumps against the door and wall. A window shattered. Sherry called 911 Emergency.

"Somebody's firing at my door," she said.

"Somebody's what?" the 911 dispatcher asked.

"Gunshots at my door."

"All right. Do you live on Cleveland?"

"Yes."

"Okay, ma'am, you need to stay in the house. They're chasing somebody from a bank robbery . . . wait . . . I'll talk to you in a minute, okay?"

"Okay."

"Are you in the apartment by yourself?" the operator questioned.

"Yes."

"Can you see anything?"

"No, I'm not looking. I'm on the floor, but there are shots still being fired."

"Are you sure?"

"Yes," Sherry said. "It hit the door I was leaning against."

"Don't lean against the door where they're shooting bullets, ma'am."

"Well, I'm in—"

"Go in your closet."

"Okay. All right. Bye."

Sherry hung up and the telephone rang almost immediately. It was the 911 dispatcher.

"Don't hang up on me, okay? I need you to tell me what you see."

"I don't see anything."

"Okay. Are they still firing?" the dispatcher asked.

"No. I hear some sirens, like an ambulance."

"Okay. Can you look out the window without getting hurt?"

"No," Sherry said. "My blinds are open. Let me . . . hold on . . . let me crawl over there and see if anybody's out front. I got to the bedroom. Let me look out the . . . see if I can see out the bottom of the blinds in the bedroom. Hold on." Sherry peeked outside. "I don't see anything but some joggers down Cleveland."

"Okay. You stay in your house, ma'am, and if you wanna know what's happening, just call me back, okay? Don't go outside."

"Okay, 'cause I know it hit my back kitchen door, 'cause I was leaning against it."

"Okay, but don't go outside," the operator urged.

"Okay, I won't."

Sherry hung up, but called back again a few minutes later.

"I'm at the Cleveland address where the bank robber was," she said. "Have they caught him yet?"

"Ma'am, I'm not sure. We haven't been informed of anything at this time."

"Oh, okay. They said they'd call me back if they—"

"What is your name? Hold on a second." A pause. "Is it Donna?"

"I'm the one they shot my door out," Sherry replied.

"Okay, ma'am. We don't have any information yet. . . ."

"Oh, my God."

"Still trying to find out. But we want you to stay inside and not come out, okay?"

"Oh yeah. I know that. Yeah, it was my door."

"Okay."

"I see the bullet hole, so . . ."

"We might have Detective Holland coming to see you."

Sherry hung up, not knowing whether or not a fugitive gunman was still on the loose.

Minutes earlier, Horst Gunther Albrecht was backing his car out of a driveway on the east side of Lindell Honda, where he worked, when he saw Officer Lois Marrero running on Church, near the Crossings apartments, with a gun in her hand. He braked to avoid hitting her as she ran directly behind his car. Albrecht heard Lois yelling, but he couldn't understand what she was saying.

She continued to yell at someone inside the apartment's parking lot, but Albrecht didn't see anyone there. He saw Lois take cover behind a van, and then he saw that she was shouting at two men and a woman on the west side of the parking lot. He heard her give what sounded like a command. Albrecht noted the positions of the people: the two men were on the driver's side of the car, facing west, and the female was on the passenger side. Lois was on the same side of the car as the other woman. They were within yards of one another. Albrecht heard Lois shout again, and after about thirty seconds, she walked toward the suspects with her gun in her hand.

Meanwhile, the men seemed to be trying to get the car door open. Albrecht saw the police officer run six feet or so from the right rear of the same car. One of the men raised a submachine gun, holding the gun with both hands, and fired at least four times. The bullets struck Lois and she dropped facedown on the asphalt. The other woman and one of the men ran back into the apartment complex, while the second man stayed under the car, where he had dived when the gunshots were fired.

When Lois approached Chino, Paula, and Kokojan, she held her gun, but she was not pointing it at them.

"Don't move!" she said. "Put down your weapon."

There was no response, so she spoke again. "Put down your weapon or I'll shoot."

Her eyes met those of the female suspect. Then she saw one of the male suspects raise the MAC-11 and fire. She gasped in pain, shock, and surprise, then fell forward.

Chapter 4

Paula tucked Lois's gun in the waistband of her shorts and ran with Chino toward the stairs leading to the second floor. He had a crazed look on his face, and she was scared. Gunfire seemed to sound from all around her. Chino turned and fired from the mezzanine, releasing a fusillade of bullets in two different directions. He fired more bursts from the second floor. Paula didn't remember climbing the stairs, only that they were on the second floor.

Officer Metzgar came under fire as soon as he pulled up to the Crossings apartments. At least one round slammed into the car door on the driver's side. Metzgar dived for cover and drew his gun. Scanning the area, he saw the shooter run into the breezeway, where the stairs were located. Then he saw Lois lying facedown on the pavement. He crouched and ran across the open parking lot, exposing himself to fire, to get to her. Metzgar leaped over Lois and ran toward Chino, but the gunman disappeared.

Metzgar hurried back to Lois and saw that she had bled extensively. He knew it was a massive wound, just by seeing the blood.

Officer Hill came to where Lois lay and Metzgar told her to stay with her; then he ran to take up a position. The police were intent on keeping the suspects contained in the apartment area. Hill knelt on one knee beside Lois, holding her gun in both hands, her eyes scanning the area. The danger of her situation was apparent: she was in the parking lot with no cover, an easy target for a shooter. She was scared to the marrow, but she held her ground.

She had heard heavy gunfire when she drove up to the apartment complex. There was a body on the pavement, but it seemed inconceivable to her that one of her comrades had fallen. As she worked her way closer, Hill recognized that the victim was Lois, who had once been her supervisor. During the chase Hill had passed Lois's cruiser twice, and she had been one of the officers who discovered the abandoned SUV. She had rushed to the Crossings when the radio informed her that there was a foot chase in progress.

As Hill knelt beside Lois, she heard more gunfire. She couldn't tell where the shooter was. She didn't know if he would come at her from the right or the left. Whatever direction the shooter might attack, she was out in the open. She was more frightened than she ever had been in her life.

Nevertheless, Hill, who had been on the force for ten years, was not about to abandon Lois. She started to pray, "Thy will be done, Lord. I can never leave her here alone."

It seemed ironic that Hill was standing guard over a woman who had previously protected and guided her through the rough patches she encountered when she was new to the force. She remembered Lois as a woman bursting with energy, who was vibrant, laughing, and full of goodwill. It was a heartbreaking contrast to the woman who lay crumpled on the hard pavement in a pool of her own blood.

She relied on her faith and her training to stay calm, to keep her vigil. She knew that if it was her lying there, Lois would not leave her side. Neither would any other officer on the force. They would be there until the end.

Fearful, in the open, and with bullets being fired, Hill continued to pray for the courage she needed. At last, the shooting stopped, and Officers Metzgar and Scudder came back to where Hill and Lois were. Scudder checked Lois for a pulse and couldn't find one.

The three officers knew that Lois was dead, but they didn't want to believe it. Maybe the paramedics would work a miracle and save her, but they believed she was gone. Hill continued to pray that God's will be done, and that all would be well.

An emergency ambulance with emergency medical technicians (EMTs) arrived on the scene within minutes of the shooting. The EMTs applied appropriate emergency measures, and speedily put Lois on a gurney, loaded it into the ambulance, and sped toward Tampa General Hospital's (TGH) emergency room (ER).

A skilled trauma unit was already being assembled at TGH. Lewis Flint, medical director for the TGH trauma center, was the first person who reported to the ER. He had left surgery just a few minutes earlier. Colleen Jaffrey, chief trauma resident, was in the cafeteria when the call came in. She immediately went to the ER. The trauma team included an anesthesiologist, radiologist, three trauma residents, five nurses, a physician's assistant, and David Oman, chief of emergency medicine.

TGH's trauma center had years of experience in treating gunshot wounds. As a regional trauma center, it treated shooting victims from a heavily populated geographic area. Police officers were regular visitors because they often accompanied shooting victims or people who suffered other traumatic injuries. The staff was on a friendly basis with the police, and some families were so close that they attended social functions together. Waiting for a police officer with a serious shooting injury had a jarring emotional effect.

Paramedics had tried furiously to save Lois; now the trauma team would try to work its magic. But this time, there was no rabbit to pull out of the hat. Doctors pronounced Lois dead at 11:55 A.M., but said she was most likely dead on arrival (DOA). She was the first Tampa policewoman to be killed in the line of duty.

Mickie Mashburn was at her station, but she listened to the radio reports about the robbery and shooting. She knew that Lois was in the thick of it, especially when she heard transmissions from Baker 13, Lois's designation. The bad feeling she had experienced early that morning had gradually intensified.

She was filled with dread when the radio broadcast, "Officer down, officer down." Mickie was sick to hear that a comrade had fallen. *Please don't let it be Lois,* she thought. She thought of the ominous feeling she had experienced that morning. She thought of the short time she and Lois had before retiring and having time to do all of the things they wanted.

But when she saw a lieutenant coming toward her, and from the expression on her face, Mickie's heart sank. Even before the lieutenant told her, Mickie knew that Lois had been shot and killed. Mickie felt as if she had been kicked in the stomach. Her knees turned to rubber and she couldn't breathe as tears streamed from her eyes.

Isaac Davis, a sophomore at the University of South Florida, lay on a futon in his living room watching television. He had taken the day off from school to recuperate from the flu. He thought he heard firecrackers going off in the parking lot from kids celebrating Independence Day a couple of days late. There was a lot of yelling outside, too, and it occurred to him that a mother was chastising a child for playing with fireworks.

Suddenly there were three loud thuds against his door. Someone jiggled the doorknob, as if trying to break in. On the fourth blow, the door splintered off its hinges and came crashing into his apartment. A woman carrying a gun stumbled in. Following her was a man who had a gun that appeared to be a military weapon.

Davis quickly considered his options for escape. The only door leading outside, besides the one that had been kicked in, would have left him trapped on the mezzanine. The only thing he could think to do was to hide in the bedroom closet.

Davis turned and ran.

"He's in here," Paula said.

"Get him," Chino ordered.

Paula caught him in the bedroom before he could get inside the closet.

"Come on," she said.

"Don't hurt me," he begged.

"We're not going to hurt you."

Paula marched him into the living room.

"Come here for a second," Chino said.

"Please don't hurt me," Davis said. "Please don't kill me."

Davis thought the man and woman looked familiar, but he couldn't place them. He didn't know whether this should make him more, or less, afraid. They were two strangers who had broken into his apartment with guns.

Chino grabbed Davis and marched him to the smashed door.

"C'mon," he said.

At the door Chino looked around Davis's shoulder and yelled, "I have a hostage!"

Then he unleashed several volleys of gunfire before moving away from the door. He ordered Davis to wait in the dining room with Paula while he forced the broken door upright, and then he braced it closed with two dining-room chairs.

Davis noticed that the home invaders seemed confused and in a state of panic. Chino paced and kept saying, "Oh boy. I've done something really bad. I think I killed a cop." Paula sat with her head in her hands, mumbling. They both seemed to be at the end of their ropes.

In just seconds Davis recognized them. He had caught glimpses of Chino when their vehicles passed in the parking lot. And he had seen both Chino and Paula in the swimming pool. Davis and his roommate couldn't remember names, so they had nicknames for everyone. Chino was "nasty belly man," but was also known as "the monkey guy," because they thought he looked like a monkey. Once Davis made that association, he connected Paula with Chino and a beautiful little girl that he and his roommate called "Star-Kist." They had no nickname for Paula, who seemed to be a nonentity who never spoke or lifted her eyes from looking downward.

He had not had a conversation with Chino, either.

Both Chino and Paula were extremely tense and frightened, but Chino was also snide. "She thought she could kill me," he said in a mocking tone. Davis thought he was disparaging the police officer he had shot. Chino couldn't stop pacing and talking to himself. Paula sat in the dining room, burying her head in her hands and shaking her head. They were frightened, and so was Davis. But so far, they hadn't threatened him. Maybe they wouldn't kill him, after all, he thought.

As minutes passed, the situation became more intense. Paula and Chino made Davis think of dogs that had been chased, trapped, and had nowhere else to go. He thought they were afraid to surrender and afraid to fight. Like stricken deer caught in headlights, he thought.

"Come on," Chino said. "Come with me."

Chino left Paula sitting in the dining room while he marched Davis around the apartment to look out the windows. If anyone was going to be shot at a window, it wasn't going to be Chino. Davis peeked out the windows. He had never seen so many policemen, some of whom were wearing what looked like combat gear.

Chino took Davis back into the apartment. He looked just as scared as Paula. But mostly he seemed angry. Davis had never seen anyone so angry. Davis went to the dining room and sat down, which Chino had ordered him to do. They all stayed in the dining room because the only furniture in the living room was the futon on which Davis had been resting when the intruders burst in.

Chino paced and mumbled continually. "We did something really, really bad! Do you think I killed a cop?"

When Davis had heard the popping sounds in the parking lot earlier, he had thought of firecrackers going off. Now he realized that it had been gunfire. Chino made Davis lower all the blinds and periodically made him look outside to see what the police were doing. When Davis was sitting, Chino lowered the gun, but he kept it pointed at him when he made Davis move around to check outside the windows.

Only minutes had passed since the home invasion occurred, but it seemed longer to Davis. Paula took the bullets out of Lois's gun and placed the gun on the table. Chino fiddled with the magazine of his gun, taking it out and counting the bullets before he put it back in.

"Do you have a roommate?" Chino asked.

"He's not here."

Chino, staying clear of the windows, checked each room to see for himself.

Paula sat fidgeting with her hands most of the time. She touched her hair, hugged herself, and rocked; she knit her fingers together and buried her face in her hands. The longer they were there, the more nervous and unpredictable they became. Chino made Davis continually look out the blinds to see what was happening, and he followed him around with the gun trained on him.

Paula clicked on the television set and the robbery and shooting were being broadcast on every channel. The television screen showed the apartment complex, a circling helicopter, police cars with flashing lights and howling sirens, and scores of policemen with an assortment of guns.

That's when Chino started talking about them committing suicide.

Chapter 5

Melba and Luis Gutierrez left Medellín, Colombia, in 1983, the same year that forty people were murdered in that city during a weekend of drug-related killings. The Colombian city, home of the world's most powerful and ruthless drug syndicate, had the highest murder rate in the world. Cocaine dealers, such as Pablo Escobar and Carlos Lehder Rivas, even recruited children to act as bodyguards, lookouts, mules and *sicarios* (assassins), who murdered their victims from speeding motorcycles. Children were not immune from murder, either. The Colombian Department of Criminal Studies and Identification estimated that twelve hundred children were murdered in 1983.

"Grandpas bury their grandchildren here," one Colombian said.

To protect their infant daughter, and to make a better life for themselves, Luis and Melba Gutierrez immigrated to New York, where they found a one-room apartment in the Bronx. They lived there with their daughter, Paula, and Louisa, who was born a year later.

None of them spoke English, and both parents had to work hard to support the family. The Bronx was a tough area of New York, but Luis and Melba found it to be an improvement over Medellín. The cold winters and hot summers, however, made them yearn for the more temperate climate in Colombia.

Paula enrolled in Public School 122 and attended bilingual classes. She was an average student, who got along with her classmates, even though she was terribly shy. Eventually the Gutierrez family moved into a larger apartment in the Bronx, where they could have more privacy. Stephanie, Paula's youngest sister, was born when Paula was six, just a few months after the family immigrated to America.

At the age of twelve, Paula was restless and bored with school. There was a much bigger world outside of the classroom and she wanted to explore it. She started skipping school, wandering around the city, or hanging out at shopping malls with other kids. Paula had more than a passing interest in boys and they liked her. Both parents worked and had trouble finding the time they needed to control their adventuresome daughter.

Soroya Benitez was one of Paula's best friends during their preteen and early teenage years. Soroya practically lived at Paula's apartment. They smoked pot together, even before they were teenagers, but managed to avoid harder drugs, such as LSD and crack cocaine.

Luis and Melba worried about their daughter. Devout Roman Catholics, they took their daughters to church and encouraged them to follow the church's teachings on morality. They worried about Paula's falling grades, skipping classes, and going to malls with kids they didn't find desirable. They saw their daughter headed for trouble.

"You need to have more discipline," Luis told her.

"This isn't Colombia," Paula said. "Things are different here."

As Catholics, and South Americans, they believed that Paula should be a virgin when she got married. They suspected that Paula was sexually active even before she was a teenager. Paula denied it, but became pregnant when she was thirteen.

The pregnancy caused a major upheaval in the family. Paula wanted to keep the baby. She didn't want to give it up for adoption or, even worse, have an abortion. Luis and Melba were torn between what the Catholic Church taught them, and what they believed was common sense.

Paula, they thought, was much too young to have a baby. How could she take responsibility for a child when she couldn't even take care of herself? She had no discipline, so how could she raise a child? Although Paula wanted to have the baby, she was secretly frightened. Emotionally, the situation overwhelmed her, and she yelled at her parents. Paula and her parents talked with priests, counselors at school, and family services.

They learned that teenage pregnancies were not that unusual. Nearly 822,000 unmarried teenagers became pregnant in the United States the same year that Paula did. A third ended up being aborted. Luis and Melba were told that those who were born were more likely to end up being abused and going to prison. After stormy and unresolved differences of opinion, Paula's parents decided that the pregnancy had to be terminated. Paula was angry and resentful; she felt ashamed and guilty. The seeds had been planted that would grow into a lifetime of feeling inadequate and unworthy.

Luis and Melba were ashamed. In their eyes and those of the Catholic Church, the abortion was a mortal sin. Melba wept inconsolably and felt like a hole had been torn in her heart. They prayed for all of their souls, including the baby that would not be born, and asked for forgiveness.

Worried about their inability to control Paula, they concluded that New York offered too many temptations for young girls, especially when no one could watch them twenty-four hours a day. Louisa and Stephanie were well-behaved, but who knew what might lie ahead in this sin-filled city?

They thought of the more tranquil life in Colombia. Even with all of the drug-related crime, there weren't as many opportunities to get in trouble as there were in New York. Especially where sex was concerned. Luis and Melba decided to send all three girls back to Colombia to live with their grandparents; they would have closer supervision there. Luis made arrangements for a private tutor so the girls wouldn't be exposed to outside temptation at school.

Paula hated living in Colombia. She missed the excitement of the big city, her friends, and the freedom she had to move around. She had tasted forbidden fruit and liked it. She felt like a prisoner in her grandparents' house. Colombia frightened her, too. The violence associated with the drug trade made the streets of Medellín dangerous. Paula begged her parents to let her return to New York. She promised she would behave. She wouldn't run away from home, skip school, and would be the kind of daughter they wanted her to be.

When her parents didn't relent after nine months, Paula raised the stakes. "If you don't let me come back, I'm going to kill myself," she told her parents.

Luis and Melba took the threat seriously. Paula and her sisters returned to New York where her parents had moved into a nicer, larger apartment in Queens. Paula's stay in Colombia had done little to curb her appetite for sex and a life more adventurous than attending school.

"You must remember that school is very important," they told her. "We cannot tell you how important it is. We want you to understand that."

Paula had been "grounded" too long, and she could hardly wait to get back to having fun. Cutting classes, smoking marijuana, and having sex were too much fun to give up. But many of her old friends had moved on to other things, and Paula had to find new ones. She wandered the malls and the streets looking for adventure. Luis and Melba tried their best to steer her to a different path, but it didn't lead anywhere Paula wanted to go.

Her parents loved Paula and tried to convince themselves that she was just going through the normal throes of adolescence. Maybe her behavior was normal for a girl her age. And then Paula met Chino.

Lissette Santiago was twelve years old, and living with an abusive man, when she gave birth to Chino. Not long after her son was born, Lissette's fiery temper gave her the courage to walk away from the beatings and threats received from her boyfriend. She left Luis DeJesus when Chino was a toddler. She was a child raising a child in the Bronx, one of the toughest boroughs in New York.

Lissette believed that children deserved two parents. Because of that, she allowed Chino to have regular visits with his father, even though Luis was a heroin addict and had AIDS. Once, when Chino was seven years old, he came back from a visit with a bizarre story.

"Daddy's friend was taking blood out of him," he told his mother. "Daddy says it's pain medicine for his back."

Lissette knew that someone had been helping Luis mainline heroin, but she didn't say anything. She didn't want to destroy Chino's delusions about his father. Luis DeJesus died in prison of AIDS when Chino was twelve years old. Following Luis's death, Lissette told Chino about his father's drug abuse and AIDS. It marked a turning point in his life.

Chino at age thirteen was a swaggering tough guy that Lissette couldn't control. He was aggressive, violent, and always spoiling for a fight. Lissette couldn't discipline him because Chino would yell at her and become so violent that Lissette was afraid of getting hurt. She looked at the son she adored and saw that he was mean, morose, and violent.

Chino's contemporaries were afraid of him. He picked fights, stole lunch money, and he shoplifted. He beat up other kids on a regular basis. She was accustomed to seeing him coming home covered with blood.

"I don't know if it's his blood or someone else's," Lissette said. "I never clean him up or look for cuts."

Lissette knew Chino was out of control, but she felt helpless.

By this time Chino had two sisters, and Lissette was thankful that his violent outbursts didn't include them. She attributed that to the closeness of the family.

"Chino has had a temper," she said. "He came out just like me. But you don't hit a woman. Never."

Chino reacted to his mother's attempts at discipline by calling her names and cursing her. She yelled right back. *God, he's just like me,* she thought. *He got his rage from me.* Like thunder and lightning, mother and son created a scary storm when they got into arguments.

At some point in the argument, the veins in Chino's face would swell, his eyes would bulge, and he would get a blank look on his face. That meant danger for anyone who happened to be near him. It even frightened Lissette. She was terrified that her son, who was bigger and stronger than she was, would beat her up.

"Everybody's out to get me!" Chino screamed at her. "Everything that happens to me is your fault because you brought me into this world."

Chino screamed in frustration and stormed downstairs to Lissette's car. He pounded on the hood and roof with his fists. He kicked the fenders and the side doors while he screamed obscenities. He stood on the hood and stomped on it, and then he kicked in the windshield before smashing the other windows with a club.

Chino fought on the streets almost daily. His rage at everything consumed him. He was paranoid about people and he hated society. He believed that non-whites were nothing more than slaves, and that, if you wanted something, you had to take it. Lissette didn't even ask what happened when Chino came home with bloody clothes. Something as innocent as that could cause him to explode.

Chino had not been diagnosed, but he exhibited all the characteristics of a "rageaholic," someone who is addicted to anger. Anger is a primitive emotion that causes adrenaline to rush through our bodies and brains. It makes us stronger and more alert. In primitive times it gave us extra strength to fight for our lives or to run for our lives. Anger creates a "rush" that rageaholics find addictive. A rageaholic usually bottles up his real feelings, such as sadness, fear, shame, or unworthiness. When he reaches a saturation point, he snaps and goes into a fit of rage that endangers everyone around him.

Chino was a boy who didn't get many breaks in life. He was born to a child and raised by one parent, had little supervision, no feeling of belonging. His role models were drug dealers.

"Ma, I'm going to be a drug dealer," he told Lissette. "They're the only ones who have money, cars, nice clothes, and girls."

Lissette listened and shook her head. What was going to become of him?

When she was fifteen, Paula skipped school and went to Manhattan to look for something to do. She spotted a boy about her age watching when she got off the subway train. Paula felt a rush of excitement. The boy was about six feet tall, muscular, Hispanic, and he had close-cropped hair that fit him like a helmet. He made every part of her tingle.

Paula was giddy when he approached her. He introduced himself as Nestor DeJesus, but people called him Chino. Paula's heart skipped a beat. Chino made her feel wonderful. He was charming, attentive, affectionate, and made her laugh. He seemed mature for his age. As long as they were just killing time, he suggested that they do it together. When he asked to see her later for a movie, Paula eagerly agreed.

Paula didn't tell her parents, who were still at work, that she was going out. Instead of seeing a movie, she went to Chino's apartment, where the two teenagers smoked pot and had sex. Chino continued to be charming, and he told Paula how beautiful and special she was. She was so enthralled by him that she didn't think about going home, or telling her parents where she was, until three days later. By then, Paula and Chino were madly in love.

"You're my one true love," Chino told her, gazing into her eyes. "You're my first true love."

When Paula returned home, her parents were beside themselves with worry. Where had she been? What had she been doing? Why didn't she get in touch with them?

"You're grounded," Luis told her. "You can be at school or you can be at home. You can't go anywhere else unless one of us is with you."

Paula said they couldn't make her.

"You can go to boarding school or back to Colombia," Luis said.

"You're trying to raise me like we're still in Colombia," Paula said. "You can't ground me."

"Yes, we can," Luis said.

She told them about the boy she had met, and they wanted to meet him. Paula had him come over the next night.

Paula's parents looked at Chino and saw nothing but trouble. He was rough, as only life on the streets can make you. He was also rude and showed them little respect. All of Luis's instincts told him that Chino was a young man with a lot of problems. So far as Luis could tell, Chino and Paula had nothing in common.

"We don't want you to see him anymore," Luis said when Chino left. "That boy has nothing in common with you. He's going to be trouble."

Paula refused to listen and continued to cut class and see Chino. She liked it that he always had money and pot, and he treated her so well. He made Paula feel special. Over the next few weeks, Luis and Melba tried to break up the relationship, but finally they gave up. Paula spent more time with Chino, not less. Having failed to break them up, Melba and Luis decided on another plan. They invited Chino to spend more time at their apartment. Maybe he would change if he saw what a normal family was like. Melba wanted to take him to church and hoped that Chino would find Christ. Just as important, they could act as chaperones.

Melba was a devout Catholic, and that played a major part in their decision to try and help Chino. "There is some good in everyone," she told Luis. "Everybody can be saved."

Chino shoved Paula so hard that she almost fell over. "Don't do that, Chino," she told him.

He glared at her. "I'm the man. I can do anything I want to."

A month into their relationship, Paula had seen Chino change. He wasn't kind, gentle, and loving anymore. Instead, he shoved her around. They weren't gentle pushes, but hard shoves where his palms stung and sent her reeling. The shoves were becoming more frequent and more forceful. Chino also gave her orders on how to act in public.

"Keep your eyes on the ground and don't look at anyone," he told her. "Don't make eye contact and never speak to anyone. Walk a step behind me. That's how a woman shows respect for a man."

Even though she loved Chino, Paula began to feel that he was overbearing. It seemed that he wanted to own her, body and soul, and didn't want her to see anyone but him. Paula attended John Brown High School and Chino started popping up there to check on her.

"What are you doing, Chino?" Paula asked.

"I'm checking to make sure you're the one."

"The one what?"

"My one true love who will never betray me."

On the plus side, he picked her up from school and always had marijuana and money. The sex was great, but it was changing. Chino started being rough. "I know that's the way you like it," he said.

Sometimes he forced himself on her when she didn't want it. Their social life consisted mostly of smoking pot and having sex. Once or twice, they tried some LSD, but marijuana was what they liked. She wondered where Chino got his money, since he didn't seem to work.

"I shoplift designer clothes and sell them," he told her. "That's how I live."

Paula didn't object to the shoplifting, but she worried about Chino being caught. She liked having the money and the drugs, plus the clothing he gave her that bore designer labels, such as Tommy Hilfiger.

On one surprise visit at school to check on Paula, Chino found her flirting with another boy. He flew into a rage. He attacked the boy and knocked him to the ground. Chino screamed and cursed and said he would kill him if he ever flirted with Paula.

Then he turned his rage on Paula. He grabbed her by the throat and almost lifted her off the ground while he choked her. Paula's eyes bulged and she could hardly breathe.

"You can never leave me!" he said, his snarling face just inches from her own. "You hear me? You'll never leave me."

Chino turned and ran away, leaving Paula gasping. She was confused. What had gotten into him? The charming boy she met in the subway station had turned into a raging monster. He wanted to control every part of her life. She made up her mind to break up with him.

Paula was at home only a few minutes when Chino telephoned. He begged her to forgive him and told her how much he loved her. "I'll change," he told her. "Everything will be okay if we can just be together. I love you. I'll change."

"I don't want to see you anymore, Chino," she told him. "I don't want you coming around and I don't want to go places with you."

"No," Chino said. "We're not going to break up."

"Good-bye, Chino," Paula said, and hung up. But a short time later she was back on the telephone talking to him, and then they started to communicate on their computers. He wrote sweet, tender things, and Paula felt herself being drawn back into his orbit.

After hours, Paula agreed to meet with him. She would tell Chino to his face, once again, that they were breaking up. He obviously wanted a more exclusive arrangement than she did.

Chino was at the station when Paula got off the train. He walked quickly to her, grabbed her wrist, and pulled her after him as he headed toward a group of stores.

"Stop it, Chino," Paula said. "You're hurting me."

"I'm just holding your hand," he said, not looking at her.

When they arrived at the stores, Chino whirled around to face her. His face was almost purple and his eyes looked funny as he grabbed her by the throat and shoved her against the building, almost lifting her off her feet. He pushed his face inches from her own.

"We're not breaking up," he said. "I'll kill you if you leave me." He recited her mother's Social Security number. "I have it memorized," he snarled. "There's no place she can hide. With that number, I can always find her. The only way you'll leave me is in a body bag, and I'll kill your mother, your father, and your two sisters."

Paula, terrified, struggled to breathe. "You're bad, Paula. You're just like me; you're no good. Do you want me to tell your mother about the things you do with me? About the dope and the sex? I will, if you ever threaten to leave me."

Chino eased his grip and Paula gasped for air. "Remember what I said," he told her, and then he shoved her against the wall so hard that it knocked the breath out of her. Things started to go black, but not before Paula saw Chino punch his fist through a display window, then release a flurry of punches against the building. He ran away with his hands bleeding profusely. Paula slid down the wall and settled into a crumpled ball on the sidewalk. A few minutes later she gathered her wits about her and looked around for Chino, but he was gone.

My God, she thought as she struggled to her feet, what was she going to do?

* * *

On Thanksgiving, Melba prepared a feast. The apartment was filled with the smell of cooking food. In addition to her daughters, Paula, Stephanie, and Louisa, Melba had invited Paula's old friend, Soroya Benitez, and Chino to dinner, even though Paula was still trying to dump him. Chino had won Paula back through his usual flood of apologies and promises, his vows to change and professions of true love. Paula wanted to believe him, but she was afraid. He hadn't kept his promises to change in the past, and his violence toward her increased. She was so stressed and frightened that she didn't know what she was doing half the time. She felt like she was sinking into a pit from which she couldn't escape.

If she wasn't so terrified of what Chino might do to her and her family, Paula believed she could find the strength to break away from him. She intended to tell him at the Thanksgiving dinner that they were through.

Chino yelled a lot at dinner, as he usually did. He railed against society because it was prejudiced against Hispanics and was holding him back. You had to be white to get anywhere. Whites were the masters and everybody else was a slave. If a nonwhite wanted anything, he had to take it. Cops were lower than snakes.

Chino especially loved to bait Melba about her religion. Knowing how devout she was, he tried to tear her religion apart. The Catholic Church, he told her, was nothing more than an organization created to control people. It would be stupid to think that there was any more to it than that. Chino said he hated the Church, just as he hated people.

Soroya was nervous because this was the first time she had met Chino. He struck her as a wild, raving maniac. Paula wasn't anything like she was when he wasn't around. She smiled and chatted when Chino wasn't there, but in his presence she was like a shrinking violet, always looking down, saying little.

"She got so quiet when he was around," Soroya said. "It wasn't even like she was like herself. She was like totally reserved, quiet, kept to herself. When she wasn't with him, she was a totally different Paula."

Chino struck her as being weird. "I was young and really didn't pay much attention to it, but yelling, he did a lot of," Soroya said. "The most vivid picture I have of him is he just went on and on about how he hated cops, and how religion was just an institution made to manipulate people and their minds," she said. "It was, pardon my French, all bullshit. He was quite adamant."

When the Thanksgiving dinner was finished, Paula dropped her bombshell.

"Chino, I want to break up. I don't want to be with you."

Chino immediately flew into a rage. His jaw clenched and he pounded on the table with his fists. Then, to everyone's horror, he took a razor blade from his pocket and put it in his mouth. He moved the razor around with his cheeks and tongue. Blood poured from his mouth.

"You don't want to be with me?" he yelled. "Then I'll kill myself."

He took the razor blade from his mouth and slashed at his throat. Blood appeared where he cut himself, but it wasn't a life-threatening wound.

"If you leave me, then I'm going to kill myself!" he yelled. He knocked his chair over when he got up, ran from the table, and closed the bathroom door. Paula, Melba, Soroya, and Louisa were petrified. They frantically talked about what they should do.

In a few moments they went to the bathroom door and tried to open it. It was locked. Melba pounded on the door.

"What are you doing in there?" she shouted.

"Killing myself!"

"Maybe he's had too much to drink," Louisa said.

The three women forced the door open and found Chino standing over the sink with a razor. He was covered with blood from cuts in his mouth, on his throat, his hands, his forearms, and his wrists. Instead of being shocked, Melba was furious. She exploded at this wild teenage boy who mocked her religion and showed her no respect. She grabbed his forearm and pulled him roughly from the bathroom.

"You want to kill yourself, leave my house," she told him. "You've got a right to kill yourself, but not in my house. Have some respect!"

"Melba is a pretty tough cookie," Soroya said. "She basically told him, you want to do it, it's your freedom to kill yourself. You are not doing it in my house."

Chino charged out the door, but first he grabbed Paula by the hair and dragged her out with him. She screamed in pain. Chino dragged her for about a block. Melba had hoped that Paula would break free, but when she couldn't, Louisa, her boyfriend, and a boy named Joey went after her. They got into a free-for-all with Chino.

Chino was already out of control and the attempt to take Paula away fed his rage. He fought like a devil and was giving Joey a severe beating. The others couldn't pull him off. Melba called on a neighbor, a brawny man, and asked for help. He ran over, picked Chino up, and slammed him to the ground.

While Chino was momentarily stunned, the others helped Paula get back to her mother's apartment.

Chino raged like a maniac—he cursed, threatened, and beat his fists on anything that was handy.

Paula was inside, but still she didn't feel safe. There was no telling what Chino would do. When she heard scuffling and scraping sounds outside, her worst fear came true. She looked up and screamed. Chino's bloody face glared in at her while he tried to open the second-story window. He had shinnied up a water pipe to get there.

Melba already had called the police, and before Chino could break the window and get inside, a patrol car arrived and two police officers took Chino into custody. No one wanted to press charges against him. They knew he would only be held for a few hours, and would be even angrier when he was released. There was no telling what he might do. They were all scared to death.

The police officers put Chino in the patrol car and hauled him away to give him a chance to settle down. They released him on Main Street in Flushing, Queens, to make his own way home.

Chapter 6

On April 9, 1999, Paula gave birth to Chino's daughter, a beautiful baby they named Ashley. The event caused Paula to experience a jumble of emotions and tied her even closer to Chino. She intended to keep the baby, but worried about how she could take care of her. Paula didn't feel ready to have responsibility for a child, and she didn't think Chino was prepared, either. Paula had antagonized her parents to the point that she didn't know whether or not she could rely on them to help.

She reconciled with Chino after he performed his ritual performance of apology, promises to change, and pledges of undying love. Paula couldn't understand why she couldn't break up with him. Why did she put up with being shoved, choked, punched, and threatened? Paula didn't have the slightest doubt that he could kill her and her whole family in one of his rages.

Chino was proud of himself for fathering a child. "You have to marry me now," he told Paula. "We're going to be parents."

Paula refused to marry him, but she agreed to live

with Chino if he got a regular job because she didn't want to worry about him going to jail. Chino agreed and attended a class to learn how to fix air conditioners. He finished the class and found a job in College Point. Cathy Donnelly, who hired Chino, liked him. She thought he was a "nice young man and he worked hard."

Chino didn't like the commute to work, but he didn't have enough money to move. Donnelly loaned it to him. She considered Chino a "beautiful young man," but she had seen him blow up and she warned people, "Don't pull his trigger."

Six weeks after Chino moved to College Point, Donnelly received a telephone call from Paula.

"Chino won't be in today," she said. "He was arrested for shoplifting."

"Has this happened before?" Donnelly asked.

"Yeah."

"I hope you understand that we can't have him working here."

"Yeah," Paula said again.

Chino was convicted of shoplifting and served six months in a juvenile detention facility. He had a long string of petty crimes for fighting in public, skipping subway fares, writing graffiti, and—his favorite—shoplifting. None of this would follow him into adulthood because juvenile criminal records are expunged when an offender becomes an adult. It's a chance for them to start over with a clean slate.

Paula and Chino argued about his shoplifting. Chino became angry and telephoned Luis.

"Come and get your daughter!" he shouted. "I don't want her anymore."

Luis arrived at the apartment to find Paula and Ashley standing outside. Paula was crying.

"What's wrong?" he asked. "What happened?"

"We had an argument." She refused to say anything more about it.

She was back with Chino the next day. She didn't understand what was happening to her. Nothing she did ever pleased Chino. Maybe she really was no good, as he often told her. She wanted to leave, but she *didn't* want to leave. She felt herself sinking into a dark pit and was unable to stop herself. A lot of times, her life seemed like a bad dream.

One thing everybody agreed on was that Paula and Chino were good parents. There was no doubt that they loved their daughter. Ashley was a beautiful child, with dark curly hair, brown eyes, and a bright smile. Both Paula and Chino doted on her. Chino even shoplifted designer clothing for his daughter.

Soroya Benitez, Paula's old friend, was struck by how attentive Paula was as a mother. "I was almost in shock to see how much she adored this girl," Benetiz said. "My cousin had a child around the same time. She was a very wonderful human being, but Paula was unbelievably attached, an unbelievably wonderful mother. It was all talk of Ashley, Ashley. 'Ashley is doing this.' We were at her mom's house, and she had brought all of her toys with her. It was like Ashley, Ashley. She didn't take her eyes off of her for two seconds."

But even Paula's talk about Ashley stopped when Chino was around. She immediately became quiet, submissive, and withdrawn. Benitez thought she was like two different people.

Those who thought Chino was a good father might have changed their minds if they had seen him on a Sunday trip to church with the Gutierrez family. They were in Luis's car, with Chino and Paula in the front seat with Luis. The others were in back, with Ashley securely fastened in a child's safety seat.

On an expressway Ashley cried to be fed. Paula reached back, lifted the baby from the safety seat, and started to breast-feed her. Chino hit the ceiling. He cursed and slammed the dashboard. He accused Paula of endangering Ashley's life by taking her out of the safety seat.

"Put her back right now!" he demanded.

Paula put the baby back, then climbed into the back and crouched down so that Ashley could nurse from her seat. Chino continued his rampage.

"It was terrible," Luis said. "She was feeding the baby standing up. When I saw that, I seek to pull out, get out of the expressway."

Luis had never seen Chino like that. Chino's face changed: it twisted into a mask of anger and hatred. He shook his fists, clenched his teeth, and punched the dashboard. Everyone was terrified.

Luis finally got off the expressway and pulled into a fast-food restaurant. Suddenly everything changed. Chino laughed and joked as if nothing had happened. The others were shaken up still.

Chino went through the motions of straightening out his life. He went back to Cathy Donnelly and asked her to give him his old job back. Donnelly turned him down.

"I understand," Chino said. "Thanks for being so nice to me. I'm sorry I disappointed you."

This reaction from Chino was not at all what Donnelly expected from her explosive former employee. She was touched by it.

"He didn't have to do that," she said. "It was a very sweet gesture."

Meanwhile, Lissette Santiago, Chino's mother,

decided to give up on New York, where she had
such a difficult time making enough money to live
on. She moved to Tampa, Florida, where at least the
weather would be more to her liking. Chino joined
her in December 1999, and for a few months, Paula
was free.

April Hildreth's bad luck was about to become
worse. A pretty fifteen-year-old blonde, Hildreth
was living with her brother in Temple Terrace on the
northern side of Tampa. She had run away from an
abusive home. Hildreth had very low self-esteem, like
most abused children, and was a prime target for a
controlling man.

The air conditioner for her brother's apartment
needed repairs and he had telephoned a service for
a technician. Chino showed up with the company
truck and tools. April thought he was cute. He joked
with her, complimented her, and told her she was
pretty. Hildreth was flattered by the attentions of a
man who was five years older, and who had his own
money, car, and apartment.

Chino asked for a date on their first meeting, but
Hildreth turned him down. He kept calling, flatter-
ing her more and more, until she gave in. In a short
time she left her brother and moved into Chino's
apartment.

"I thought I was so in love with him," she said. "But,
you know, a fifteen-year-old girl doesn't know what
love is."

The pattern of the relationship was familiar. Chino
treated Hildreth well for the first three months, and
"then he started to show his true colors." He exploded into fits of rage for no reason that Hildreth

could see. He punched, shoved, and scratched her. Several times he knocked her down, straddled her, grabbed her by the ears, and beat her head against the floor.

"He did it on a regular basis," April said. "He would beat me for no reason—maybe just because he was having a bad day."

April didn't think she had anywhere to turn. She didn't want to go to the police because they would discover that she was a runaway and take her home. She couldn't contact her parents because she was afraid of being abused again. April simply took the beatings.

Chino's mother noticed the cuts and bruises all over Hildreth's body and asked about them. Hildreth always made up a story to cover for Chino. Lissette seemed to accept the stories as the truth.

Beating Hildreth was not enough for Chino. He told her constantly about Paula, his girlfriend in New York. "She's my one love, the one who is always true to me," he said. Chino made Hildreth wear the same perfume, lip gloss, and lotions that Paula did, so Hildreth would be more like her.

Hildreth left Chino once, but she went back to him after he begged her, promised that he would change, and told her that he loved her. It was the same routine he had used so successfully with Paula. Once Hildreth was back, Chino would keep her in the apartment for days and the cycle repeated itself. Chino saw her talking to a man on Florida Avenue and gave her a severe beating. Later that night, April told him she was leaving.

"I'll kill you if you try to leave!" he told her. "The only way you're leaving is in a body bag."

When Chino went to sleep, Hildreth slipped out of the house and fled to her parents' home. They were shocked when they saw their battered daughter. She was covered with scratches and bruises, and there was an abscess the size of a golf ball on her breast, where Chino had punched her. Hildreth's parents reported it and Chino was arrested by the Hillsborough County Sheriff's Office on a charge of assault and battery. Contrary to all logic, Chino talked April Hildreth into seeing him one last time. This contact occurred before Chino was indicted and the authorities had no choice but to drop the charges against him.

Hildreth stayed with her parents, but she said she wished she could see Chino one more time. "I want to spit in his face," she said.

In 2000, Lissette began living in other quarters and told Chino he could live in her apartment at the Crossings without paying rent. He immediately drove to New York and brought Paula and Ashley back with him. It was a pretty two-bedroom apartment on the second floor of a two-story group of apartments called the Crossings Apartment Complex.

Located in North Tampa, the Crossings was not far from Busch Gardens, one of Florida's most popular tourist attractions. There were four apartment buildings situated to make a large square that enclosed a big courtyard with a pool, dining tables, and grilling areas.

Things seemed tranquil, but, in fact, were getting worse. Chino was fired from one job after another. His temper was worse and he took each rejection as proof that society was never going to let him get ahead.

"This is a caste system," he told his neighbor, David Honeycutt, while lounging at the pool. "I'm poor and I'm always going to be poor unless I take what I want."

Chino was making plans to start taking things by force. Some of his ideas were far-fetched. He tried to convince Julio Palau, one of his few friends, to loan him a gun. Palau refused, but Chino persisted.

"We could make sixty thousand dollars by robbing a Lamborghini dealership," he told Palau.

"Man, you have to be crazy to try anything like that," Palau said. "You're better off robbing a bank."

Then Chino approached Edelmiro Alvarez, a friend he partied with sometimes. "Man, you want in on a robbery? It would net one hundred fifty thousand."

"I don't do robbery," Alvarez said. He also refused to loan Chino a gun.

Melba and Luis were concerned because Paula got in touch with them rarely. In the winter of 2001, they took their other two daughters to Tampa. They found Paula very withdrawn and almost like a zombie. She kept her eyes downcast, and she was so tired and disinterested that she could hardly take care of Ashley. Paula had even enlisted Chino's mother, Lissette, whom Paula didn't like, to help with Ashley. Lissette usually picked Ashley up in the mornings and brought her home at the end of the day. Paula never left the apartment without Chino and never spoke to anyone. One of her neighbors thought she was unable to speak.

"Why don't you go out or have friends come to visit, Paula?" Melba asked.

"Chino won't let me. He says friends are no good. He doesn't want me to have friends."

"You don't have to do this," Melba said. "You can come back home."

"I miss my friends and family in New York,"

Paula replied, "but my home is with Chino and Ashley."

Paula was hiding a secret. Chino was more violent and unpredictable than ever and talked about committing a robbery to get money. They lived rent free in Lissette's apartment and she also made payments on Chino's Xterra SUV, but they were still desperate for money. Chino was increasingly disinclined to work for a living.

A few days before Paula's family went back to New York, Chino invited everyone to the beach. It was a clear, sunny day, with a gentle sea breeze that made the palm trees do a hula dance. The turquoise water on the way to the beach was dotted with expensive motor yachts and colorful sailboats.

The beaches on Florida's Gulf Coast are so white and fine that they appear to be made of confectioner's sugar, and the ocean moves gently, with small waves breaking on the beach in a shower of white foam. Melba and Luis basked under the sun while Paula and Chino took Ashley into the water on a plastic raft.

Chino suddenly splashed water on Ashley and she started to cry. This made Chino so angry that he shouted profanities and threw as much water on her as fast as he could.

"Stop!" Paula shouted. "She doesn't like it."

But Chino kept at it while Paula tried to protect their daughter. Chino circled and splashed. Finally Paula grabbed Ashley from the raft and ran up on the beach. Chino was so enraged that he took the plastic raft Ashley was floating on and tore it to pieces. He roared for more than fifteen minutes while Ashley cried and the others cringed in fear. Chino, face gorged with blood, kicked the sand and snorted in disgust.

"Pack up," he ordered. "We're leaving."

None of them wanted to get into the car with Chino driving, but they were afraid he might hurt one of them if they refused. They had previous experience with his episodes of road rage. They were right to be worried.

Once everyone was in the car, Chino burned rubber as the car screeched out of the beach parking lot. He drove the SUV as fast as it would go, weaving in and out of traffic, tailgating other drivers, pounding on the horn, and cursing. They all were scared to death, and were glad when they arrived at the Crossings.

Chino was still in a rage. He dragged Paula, who was carrying Ashley, into their bedroom and slammed the door. Luis and Stephanie heard things being thrown and smashing against the walls and floor. Paula screamed, Ashley cried, and over it all, Chino roared.

Luis was afraid of Chino's rages, but he had never seen one like this. He opened the door to the bedroom and stepped inside. Chino had Paula against the wall and was strangling her while Ashley watched from the bed. Luis knew that if Chino had one soft spot in his barnacle-encrusted personality, it was Ashley.

"Chino! Stop it!" he yelled. "You're scaring the baby! Don't let Ashley see this. Stop it! Think of Ashley!"

Luis continued yelling as he and Stephanie tried in vain to pull Chino away from his daughter, wondering when one of them would feel a fist smash into them. He looked for a telephone to call the police, but Chino had torn it from the wall. Suddenly Chino threw Paula across the room, smashed the bedroom door, and ran from the apartment.

* * *

Luis remembered another one of Chino's road rages about six months prior, on a previous visit from New York.

Chino invited them to go to Busch Gardens. They spent several hours wandering through the lush gardens, watching zebras, giraffes, and other jungle animals in an exotic setting. They had a good time until the trip home. On the expressway a car swerved in front of Chino, missed a turn, then pulled onto the shoulder and stopped. The driver seemed to be lost.

Chino screeched to a halt, leaped out of his car, and ran to the other vehicle. He jerked the driver's-side door open, grabbed the driver by the front of his shirt, shook him, and tried to drag the man out of his car. All the while Chino screamed in the man's face and called him names. Paula's family screamed at Chino to stop. They didn't know how far he would push this. He was a madman. Fortunately, the other driver didn't fight back.

"Stop it, Chino!" Paula screamed. "You're scaring the girls. You're scaring Ashley."

"Get out!" Chino shouted. "If you're a man, get out!"

The light changed and the car shot forward. Chino ran back to his SUV and raced after it, pushing close to the bumper, or moving into another lane, then trying to sideswipe the other driver. Chino jumped out again at the next red light and ran to the other car. He tried to jerk the door open, but it was locked. Chino pounded on the roof and kicked the door before going back to his own car, cursing. He tried to run the other car off the road until it pulled off the expressway.

That burst of angry behavior, plus the brawl Luis had

broken up just before Chino burst down the door and left, made Luis worry about Paula's safety.

About a half hour later, Chino came home. He had gone to the grocery store and bought some ground beef. Acting as if nothing out of the ordinary had occurred, he went about picking up the things he had thrown.

"Okay," he said when he was finished. "Let's have a barbecue."

Luis took Paula aside and gave her the telephone number for a women's shelter that he had looked up.

"You don't have to be here," he told Paula. "You and Ashley can come and stay with us in New York. But if you won't come, keep this number. You can take Ashley and go there if you need to. What happened here today will happen again. Many times."

"I can't, Daddy," she said.

"Why not?"

Paula shrugged. "I can't say."

Chapter 7

In April 2001, Lissette stopped by her son's apartment. He wasn't there, but the apartment was a mess. Paula sat on the couch. She was crying and looked frightened. One side of her face was an angry red.

"What happened?" Lissette asked.

"Chino slapped me," she said.

Lissette wasn't shocked or surprised. She knew Chino's violent temper better than anyone.

"What else did he do?"

Paula shook her head and said nothing.

Lissette knew there was a lot more trouble in the relationship than the beatings. Chino had been fired several weeks ago from his most recent job. Chino had come home in a rage and started throwing things.

"They accused me of stealing a check," he said. "How could I do that when the check was made out to somebody else?"

Actually, Chino had kept several hundred dollars that one of the customers had paid in cash. After he was fired, Chino was so angry that he didn't bother to turn in the company truck. He drove it home, loaded with thousands of dollars' worth of tools. The owner was too afraid of Chino to pick it up, and finally negotiated a deal with Lissette to get it back.

Chino was broke and didn't bother looking for a job. He was increasingly volatile and flew into rages every day. Their electricity was disconnected for nonpayment and Lissette paid that. Chino missed several payments on the SUV, which Lissette tried to make up. But the payments were still in arrears and the finance company threatened to repossess it.

Paula and Chino frequently didn't have enough food to feed themselves, and Lissette loaned him money. Lissette had a low-paying job and couldn't afford to support Chino and Paula, although she rarely turned him down when he needed financial help.

Now she had learned that she would have to move back into the apartment that Chino and Paula lived in without paying rent.

Chino was desperate, and the more desperate he became, the angrier, moodier, and crazier he became. He threatened to kill himself, and Lissette took him seriously. "If Chino says he's going to kill himself," she said, "he's going to kill himself. I know my son."

Chino blamed Lissette. "It's all your fault, Ma," he said. "You never should have given birth to me. If you hadn't, I wouldn't have all of this trouble."

Looking at Paula now, Lissette was afraid for her. "You can't stay here," she told Paula. "Chino's too unpredictable. You have to think of the baby."

Lissette, convinced that Chino could seriously hurt them, bought an airplane ticket for Paula and Ashley to fly to New York and stay with her parents for a while. Chino started to telephone Paula's parents even before she got there. He demanded that she call him the moment she arrived.

After saying hello to her parents, Paula, looking wan and subdued, went into a bedroom to call Chino. Luis and Melba couldn't make out the words, but Paula sounded anguished. She wept and seemed to plead with Chino. This went on for an hour.

Paula refused to say what was wrong. But later that evening, Luis received an e-mail from Chino with an attachment. The attachment was chilling. Chino had become proficient at using magazines, photos, and computer enhancements to make composite pictures. In this attachment he had depicted himself as the Devil, with red eyes, horns, and a barbed tail, standing in a pit of fire. There was a photograph of Ashley in the fire, and the day and year of her birth was turned upside down to read "666," the mark of the Antichrist.

The threat was clear to Paula. Chino had told her that if she tried to leave, he would kill her and the entire family. This threat even included his daughter, Ashley. Paula realized that she had to go back, rather than put her family at risk. Better that Chino kill her, she thought, than anybody else.

The situation hadn't improved for Paula and Chino in June 2001. They were strapped for money, he wouldn't work, and she was in a deep depression. Once, she had gone to the ER at St. Joseph's Hospital and told nurses that her throat hurt because she had swallowed glass.

The ER personnel who first looked at her didn't find anything wrong with her throat, except that it was inflamed. On her medical chart they noted that "the patient seems agitated." Further examinations revealed no evidence of glass in Paula's throat. The second chart also noted her agitation and anxiety.

Paula didn't know it, but people who suffer from battered spouse syndrome (BSS) or post-traumatic stress disorder (PTSD) frequently "invent" physical problems to mask the real one. Psychologically, they aren't able to recognize what is actually causing problems for them and will create something that might have similar symptoms. Paula's complaint of feeling like she had swallowed glass is consistent with how a person with either disorder might describe being consistently choked.

While they were struggling to find enough money, Chino decided that he wanted a gun. He didn't allow Paula to have visitors, and when she mentioned that someone Chino knew had dropped by the apartment, he was angry, even though Paula hadn't let him in.

"When he doesn't see my truck in the parking lot, he knows I'm not home," Chino said. "We should get a gun so you can protect yourself."

"It's not a big deal," Paula said. "He didn't try to force himself into the house or anything."

Chino was adamant. "No. You're going to get a gun."

Chino liked to buy things in Paula's name whenever possible. That way, nothing could be traced to him. He liked flying under the radar. His juvenile record of petty crimes had been expunged when he became an adult, and Chino could have purchased the gun himself. In Florida it's so easy to get guns that even hard-core career criminals have no problem buying military assault rifles, such as AK-47s.

Chino parked outside the University Gun and Pawn, on East Fletcher Avenue. He told Paula to buy the gun, but he would pick it out. Paula wasn't worried about Chino having a gun because he seemed excited by the idea and he was less likely to hit her when he felt good.

Paula thought he would get a "little gun," like some handguns she had seen, but Chino had different ideas. He rejected those guns immediately and asked for something with more firepower.

"It's dangerous out there," Chino told the salesman. "There are a lot of bad guys."

The salesman agreed and brought out a MAC-11, a submachine gun that wasn't made for hunting or sport. The gun was developed by Military Armament Corporation for military forces waging urban warfare. The MAC-11 is a sinister-looking weapon, similar in appearance to the Israeli Uzi submachine pistol that is often seen on television shows and in the movies. It is only 460 millimeters in length when the stock is open and 258 millimeters with the stock folded. The gun can be hidden under a jacket. The gun has the capacity to fire an astonishing sixteen hundred rounds a minute, making it a deadly killing machine. It uses 9-millimeter ammunition and the magazine holds thirty-two rounds.

Chino's eyes lit up. "That's a nice gun," Chino told Paula. "It's a good price. Get it."

"Okay."

Paula gave the salesman a $100 deposit to hold the gun. No license permits or certificate of training is needed to buy a gun in the United States. Florida and a few other states require that three days pass from the purchase of a gun until the new owner can pick it up. The waiting period is sometimes called a "cooling-off" period to help prevent crimes of passion. A background check is supposed to be conducted during this time to see if the buyer has a criminal record, but the check is lax and sometimes even ignored. Gun dealers find ways around it.

From September 13, 1994, until September 1, 2004, the MAC-11 that Chino and Paula bought could not have been obtained legally in the United States. President Clinton signed the Violent Crime Control and Law Enforcement Act banning the sale of such weapons—except for police or military use. President Bush allowed the act to lapse in 2004. Now these guns are available to anyone who can pay for them. The MAC-11 was one type of gun found in the armory of the Branch Davidians after the Waco, Texas, standoff on February 28, 1993, which resulted in the deaths of four ATF agents and the wounding of sixteen others by gunfire. Every major police organization in the nation supports a ban on the sale of such weapons.

On June 2, 2001—the third day after Paula made the deposit on the gun—Chino left money for her to pay the balance. He telephoned later to see if she had it.

"Not yet," she said.

"Go pick it up."

Then he gave her specific directions on how to do it. For some reason, he even wanted her to drive a certain route. She was to take an expressway and get off at Fletcher to get to the pawnshop. Paula didn't ask questions. She took the money from a kitchen drawer, paid for the gun, signed the papers, and went home with the MAC-11.

Chino called a little later. "Have you got it?" he asked.

"Yeah, I got it."

"Did you get bullets?"

Paula was surprised. "Don't they come already in there?"

Chino told her to check the magazine. She did and the magazine was empty.

"Go back and buy some bullets."

The gun got Chino so excited that he wanted to take pictures. Paula took a picture of him with Ashley on his lap with her hand touching the gun and his finger on the trigger. Paula put on lip gloss, pulled her hair back, and gave a big smile as Chino took a snapshot of her with the gun.

Now that he had a submachine gun, Chino was happier. He had the means to "take what he wanted" from the society he hated so much.

Chapter 8

Detective Roberto Batista had Friday off and was taking his time about starting the day until his radio beeper went off and he heard that there had been a bank robbery and that an officer was down. It was one of the worst scenarios he could imagine. He knew that the suspects were holed up at the Crossings apartments, not far from his South Tampa home, and that there might be a hostage. He got dressed and was at the crime scene in about fifteen minutes.

A twenty-three-year veteran of the Tampa Police Department, Batista was a top hostage negotiator on the tactical response team, which also included a special weapons and tactics (SWAT) team. Batista would try to resolve the situation without further bloodshed. He would try to establish rapport with the suspect so they could have a conversation. During this time he would try to convince him that there was a better way to end this than with a gunfight. He wanted to save the lives of the hostages, but his primary focus was the safety of the hostage and police officers who had contained the suspects.

Batista always went into a negotiation feeling optimistic. You had to, if you wanted to be effective. He entered a negotiation with the belief that he could get everybody out alive. He didn't care what a suspect had done, that would all be sorted out later by the criminal justice system. Batista was there to help, not to judge or condemn.

Batista had negotiated with a cop killer on one other occasion. In 1998, a thirty-year-old ex-convict named Hank Earl Carr and his girlfriend took their four-year-old son to a fire station emergency room. The child's face was blown off. Carr initially explained that his son was dragging the gun around and that it accidentally discharged when he yelled at his son to put it down. That started the wildest, bloodiest day in the history of Florida law enforcement.

Carr, who lived in Brookville, a small town not far from Tampa, had a record stretching from 1986, which included burglary, domestic violence, assault, grand larceny, possession of cocaine, and resisting an officer with violence. Two detectives questioned him about his son's shooting and decided they should take him to headquarters. Once Carr was sitting in the backseat, he managed to slip out of his handcuffs and stripped a gun away from one of the detectives. He shot both of them to death, then highjacked a truck at gunpoint, and fled. A rookie state trooper tried to stop him and Carr shot and killed him.

With more than two hundred police officers in pursuit, Carr tried to escape, reaching speeds of more than ninety miles per hour in the stolen truck. He told a radio talk show later, "Blew my tires out ninety miles an hour. I finally got the car on the road. I was hit in the ass, a bullet through the truck. I'm bleeding bad."

He pulled into a gas station and took the young

female attendant hostage. In an odd twist, a local radio station telephoned him, and a radio personality conducted most of the negotiations. Batista was in Tampa when the police officer negotiating with Carr called. Batista talked with Carr, who demanded to see his wife. The Tampa detective found her and they flew to the hostage scene in a helicopter. After talking with his wife, Carr released the hostage, then blew his head off while the SWAT team fired tear gas into the building and charged inside.

The police didn't get to take Carr alive, but the negotiation was a success because no other lives were lost. Saving as many lives as possible and getting Chino and Paula to surrender were Batista's goals.

When he pulled up to the Crossings, he saw total chaos. Cops were everywhere. They were taking up positions to contain the subjects and patrol cars blocked off streets to and from the apartments. Batista drove to the east side of the apartments and asked some cops where the command post was. None had been set up yet, but they told him it would be in another area. Batista drove around and pulled up to another patrol car barricade, got out, and walked over in the sweltering Florida heat.

Officer Terry Mims walked up to him, carrying a cell phone. He handed the phone to Batista.

"What's going on?" Batista asked. He didn't know anything except that there had been a bank robbery and that an officer had been shot. He had few facts, and didn't know the condition of the officer who was shot.

"I have the suspect right here," Mims said. "Here you go."

Batista took the phone. "What's his name?"

"His name is Chino."

Batista took the phone, thinking, *Well, I'm a nego-tiator, so even though I don't know anything, I'm gonna talk.* He got on the phone and immediately started speaking.

"Chino, this is Detective Batista. I'm here to talk and resolve the situation. See what's going on."

As Batista tried to get Chino to talk, he realized that he was standing in the middle of the street, almost directly in front of the apartment complex, where he could be shot. He knew the first thing he had to do was find cover. Chino had shot one cop—what was another one to him?

Batista walked over to a pickup truck, which happened to belong to Chino's mother, and crouched behind it. "Let's get down on our knees," he said to Mims. "At least we'll have some cover."

Talking with Chino, Batista was surprised at how calm he was. He was a lot calmer than the detective thought he should have been, considering the circumstances. Chino didn't seem to be the least bit agitated. He knew he had shot a police officer, and he didn't know whether the officer was dead or alive. Neither did Batista.

"She's still alive, Chino." So far as Batista knew, Lois *was* still alive. He hadn't received much official information about anything, including Chino and Paula. At that point he wasn't even sure if a third man, said to be a hostage, was being held against his will or not. There was some doubt in Detective Gene Black's mind. Black and Batista had been looking for a robbery team, consisting of a black male and a Hispanic male, who had been working the area.

"You shot the officer," Batista told Chino. "She's in critical condition, but she's still alive. We can get past this, Chino. She's going to be okay."

Chino said he wanted to think about it.

"You take your time, and talk it over with Paula, think about it," Batista said. "Then we'll talk some more and get this resolved. I'll call you back in five minutes."

The negotiator broke the connection and thought he better find a more ideal command center. He looked around and saw a single-story house almost directly across the street from where Chino and Paula had barricaded themselves. That would do just fine. Batista knocked on the door and asked for permission to use the house for the police command headquarters. The owners gave him permission, and in a short time he was back on the line with Chino.

While Batista talked with Chino, the police were getting organized. A SWAT team had deployed and established a field headquarters. The massive police force surrounding the building had lost its feeling of chaos and had taken on a sense of order and control. Batista still had the cell phone and discovered that it belonged to Chino's mother. She had called Chino to tell him he was wanted by the police. When Mims discovered what was going on, he confiscated the telephone and gave it to Batista.

Batista used what time he could to find out as much as he could. He had gone in cold, not knowing much of anything. He was still pretty much in the dark when he called Chino back. What he wanted to do was keep Chino calm and get as much information from him as he could, have the hostage released, and get Chino and Paula out alive.

The negotiator fished for ways to establish rapport with Chino. They were both Hispanic, but they had totally different perspectives on how the world worked. He discovered that Chino had a chip the size of a two-by-four on his shoulder, and he blamed everyone but himself for his problems. That was something Batista was seeing more often; no one wanted to take responsibility for what they did. It was always somebody else's fault, not theirs.

Lissette Santiago had just arrived at the Ashford apartments when she received a telephone call from her boss, Karen Whitney.

"Where's Chino?" Whitney asked.

"I dropped him off at the apartment."

"Well, the cops are looking for him."

Lissette was confused after the short conversation. Why would the cops be looking for Chino? She was pondering this when, just a few seconds later, the telephone rang again. Whitney was back on the line.

"Chino robbed a bank," Whitney said. "He used your car (the SUV). He parked it at the Regency and it's steaming hot."

Lissette grabbed Ashley and raced to her truck and headed toward the Crossings to see Chino. She was almost there when she spotted a cop car and a police officer, who waved her to pull over.

"You can't go in there," he told her. "You have to leave now."

"What's going on?"

He didn't tell her. "You just have to leave, ma'am. Now."

Frustrated and worried, Lissette left and drove to a coworker's house and dropped Ashley off. Then she got in her pickup and drove back to the Crossings. On the first trip there hadn't been many police on the scene. Now there was pandemonium with cops everywhere. She felt like everything was going crazy. She had never seen so many cops. She didn't know that an officer had been shot.

Once again, the police stopped her at the entrance and wouldn't let her go in. One of the cops was getting angry because she refused to leave. When they learned she was Chino's mother, they kept her from leaving because they thought she might be the driver of the "getaway" car. Then her cell phone rang and it was Chino.

"We robbed a bank and shot a cop," he told her. "Paula and I are going to kill each other."

"No, Chino! What about Ashley?"

They talked about Ashley for a little while, and Chino asked Lissette to bring his daughter over so he could see her.

"I'm not going to bring the baby here," she said. "Not until this thing is over."

Paula came on the line. "I'm going to kill myself!" she screamed. "I'm going to kill myself!"

"Think about Ashley."

"I want to see Ashley. Bring Ashley here."

Lissette repeated what she told Chino, that she wouldn't bring Ashley until "this thing is over."

Paula said, "We robbed a bank and we killed a cop."

Lissette knew in the depths of her soul that if Chino wanted to kill himself, he would do it. He wouldn't be bluffing. Her son had been suicidal for years. But not Paula.

At this point Mims realized who Lissette was talking to and asked for the telephone. Lissette protested, saying she needed to talk with him, that he was going to kill himself.

"We're going to convince him not to kill himself," Mims told her.

"He's going to kill himself," Lissette said firmly. "I know him."

Chino and Paula were riveted by the breaking news being broadcast over Bay 9 News. They saw a massive police effort under way to keep them contained, and perhaps even storm the apartment. Davis noticed that Chino, in addition to being "very, very angry," was also scared. So was Paula. She sat with her face buried in her hands, while Chino ranted and paced.

The television mentioned that a cop had been shot. Chino stopped pacing and listened carefully, straining toward the TV set. The announcer didn't say whether the cop was alive or dead, or even mention her condition.

"What about the officer?" he yelled at the TV. "What about the officer, what if she's dead?" He looked at Paula. "Oh God, do you understand what this means?"

"I don't know, Chino. What do you want me to do?"

Davis thought she was trying to calm Chino, even though she was frightened herself. Davis wished her luck. The more agitated and frightened Chino became, the greater the chances that he would turn his anger and frustration on Davis. The man had shot a cop, after all, and still had the gun.

"I don't know if the cop is alive or dead," he said, pacing and holding his head. "What are we gonna do? Oh, my God. Do you understand how much trouble we're in?"

He stopped and looked accusingly at Paula. "You

never said that this was gonna happen," he said. "It was all for you. All I was trying to do was to keep you happy." Chino glanced at Davis. "I was trying to keep my women happy."

Paula remained silent. She just sat at the table with her face buried in her hands. Then Chino noticed Davis's cell phone on the table and started to dial someone. He made several calls. Davis thought he was incredibly rude, just using the phone without even asking for permission. Chino might have a gun, but would it have hurt him to ask?

Chino and Paula started making telephone calls from the land phone and the cell phone. Davis couldn't tell whom the calls were to, but he thought one was to Chino's mother, and that Paula made several long-distance calls. He couldn't understand Paula because she spoke in Spanish. He heard her say something to Chino, but only got bits and pieces of it. She said, "We've got to call (inaudible) before whatever's gonna happen, happens."

The TV news started showing a lot of movement by the SWAT team, making Chino and Paula increasingly frightened. They were afraid the apartment was going to be stormed.

"Go lay down in the bathtub," Chino ordered Davis. "You'll be safer from stray bullets when they storm the place." Then he spoke to Paula, "Well, Paula, you know we talked about this already. You know what we have to do."

"I can't do it!" Paula said. "I can do time. I was in the bank, but I didn't shoot anybody. I can handle time. I can do it."

"Do you know what you're saying, Paula?" Chino asked. "We talked about this before. Do you understand what's happened? I shot a cop. A cop may be dead. Either way it goes, we're gonna die. Either they're gonna kill me or I'm gonna kill myself. But either way, it's leaving in a body bag."

More than an hour had passed since the stand-off began and there was no end in sight. "Maybe we don't have to. Maybe we'll just do some time."

Chino lit a cigarette, inhaled deeply, then squatted in the hallway. The MAC-11 at the ready, he kept an eye on the door.

Detective Batista had Chino on the line again. In the few minutes that he was off the phone with Chino, he found out as much as he could. The apartment the suspects were in belonged to Isaac Davis. He had discovered that the woman's name was Paula. He didn't believe, as Detective Black did, that Isaac Davis was part of the robbery gang. Instead, he believed that Chino had taken him hostage at the point of a gun.

Chino wanted to know how the officer he shot was doing.

"She's in critical condition, but she's still alive," Batista said.

"I want you to be nice to my mother," Chino said. "Don't be mean to her. She didn't have nothin' to do with this. Neither did Paula. Paula wasn't even in the bank. I don't want you to step on their necks."

At this point Batista didn't have much official information. Perhaps Paula wasn't involved in the robbery and shooting, as the police thought. Of course, Batista realized, Chino could be shading this for his own purposes.

Batista started to chat about various things, trying to steer the conversation away from the shooting. He asked about Chino's family and learned that he had a little girl named Ashley. Batista noticed that he spoke lovingly of his baby daughter, and whenever Chino started to get agitated, Batista steered the talk to Ashley. It brought Chino right down. That was the key to calming him; he adored his daughter.

"C'mon, Chino, what's it gonna take to resolve this?" Batista said. "You didn't wake up this morning and say, 'Hey, I'm going to kill a police officer.' You didn't plan for it to happen. We can resolve this."

"My father died in prison," Chino said. "I'm not going to prison. A day in prison is like a week in prison."

Obviously, Chino had strong feelings about staying out of prison, but that didn't necessarily mean he wouldn't eventually give up. *Nobody* wanted to go to prison, and everyone Batista had negotiated with said the same thing. Sometimes they were bad guys who lacked the courage to kill themselves and would start a gunfight so that the cops would kill them. The police call it "suicide by cop." There was always that possibility that Chino, having nothing to lose, could decide to go down in a blaze of glory with his gun firing.

From time to time, Chino became very agitated, as if he were losing control. Every time it happened, there was greater danger for further bloodshed. Batista was able to soothe Chino by bringing Ashley back into the conversation. "You know, she's gonna need her dad, Chino. You come out, you have a chance to do time, you get to see Ashley."

Chino went all over the place in his conversation. He told Batista one of his pet peeves, one of the many things he blamed, instead of himself, for his misfortunes. "White people are to blame for all my problems," he said. "They have everything, we have nothing. I blame them."

This didn't wash with Batista, who is Hispanic. This had not stopped him from making a good life for himself and his family.

"Oh, Chino, you have what you work for," he said. "I've worked hard for everything I have. I've worked hard all my life. If you want something, you have to work hard for it. You do that, you'll get it."

Chino muttered something about stacked laws, slavery, the way the blacks and Latinos are kept down like slaves, the whites being the slave masters.

"It's not slavery," Batista said. "It's a civilized world. We have to abide by the laws. People make the laws and we have to live by them. If you violate the laws, you have to live with the consequences."

Batista knew better than to try and bullshit Chino. He tried to be as truthful as he could; otherwise, Chino would catch him in a lie and he would lose his trust. Chino was too intelligent to think he might get out of this mess without paying some kind of price.

"I tried to be completely honest with him," Batista said. "Here he is, he just shot a police officer. I didn't want to tell him, 'Oh, you're not going to jail.' Oh yeah, you *are* going to jail, to prison. There's no doubt about that. He didn't want to hear that, because he didn't want to go to prison."

Civilians in the area saw how tough it was for the cops and started to bring them cold sports drinks and water.

More than an hour had passed and the end was nowhere in sight.

Chapter 9

Paula dialed her mother's number in New York and the answering machine picked up to take a message.

"Chino and I messed up," she said in Spanish. "We robbed a bank and killed a cop. We're going to kill ourselves. I'm sorry. Please take care of Ashley."

Davis didn't understand Paula's message. Chino was also making and receiving telephone calls. Both Chino and Paula were nervous and scared. The more frightened they became, the more Davis worried about his own safety.

Chino hung up and started to pace. He left the MAC-11 on the table without the magazine. Paula had Lois's gun on the table in front of her.

"Is she alive or dead?" Chino screamed at the television. He held his head with both hands while he paced. "Oh man. What are we gonna do?"

The television news showed more movement by the SWAT team. "Come here," Chino said to Davis. He grabbed Davis around the neck and marched him from window to window. "Tell me what you see."

Davis saw twenty or thirty police cars, and police

officers, who had taken cover and had their guns out. He reported it to Chino.

"They're gonna rush the place," Chino said to Paula. "You know what we gotta do."

"No, man, you don't want to do that," Davis said, knowing Chino was talking about suicide again. "You—"

Chino's lips curled into a smirk. "At least I got to take one cop with me."

Paula said, "Maybe we'll just get some time."

"I think the cops are gonna rush us," he said again to Davis, who hadn't moved.

A note that Paula had scribbled lay on the table. It read, "Mamacita, I love you so much! Please forgive us for messing up! Mami, I will miss you!"

Davis couldn't understand much of the conversation from the bathroom, but he heard telephone calls being made. He heard Paula say "Ashley," and then she started to weep.

Detective Batista established a command post in a house on Cleveland Street, almost directly across the street from where Chino and Paula held Davis hostage. He could see the window of the apartment and noticed that the blinds occasionally lifted up an inch or two, as if Chino and Paula were keeping track of what the police were doing.

Batista was back on the telephone with Chino, still trying to establish a rapport and to convince Chino to release the hostage and give himself up. Batista still didn't know that Lois had been killed, although he knew a police officer had been shot.

"I know you want to do the right thing, Chino," Batista said. "We don't want to hurt you. We don't want

to hurt your girlfriend. We don't want to hurt anybody.
We don't want anybody else to get hurt. And I know
you want to do the right thing, and I know you want
to see your daughter. When is your daughter's birthday coming, is it coming up, or is it past?"

"It's past."

"Just past? She just turned two?"

"Yeah."

"You know, it's not easy what you're going
through," Batista said. "And I know . . . you are
trying to decide the rest of your life here. You are
going to live through this . . . and you are going to
live many, many more years. That's what you want,
Chino."

"Of course. Yeah, I want to live a couple of more
years, but not in prison."

"It's better to live in prison, man . . . knowing
that you have a daughter. . . . You have somebody out
there, somebody that is part of you, Chino. That's
never going to change, man. You may be in prison
for a while . . . but it's still up to you to keep her close
to you. I mean letters and calls and visits. You're
going to be able to do that."

"Yeah, but do you know . . . what kind of torture
that is?" Chino asked.

"What about her . . . knowing what happened
today?" Batista asked. "Because she is going to find out.
She is two years old. She doesn't understand. . . . It
may take you five, six, seven years . . . and she's going
to ask, 'Hey, what happened to my dad? What did my
dad do?' And then she's going to go to the public library and read the newspapers and she is going to find
out. Do you want your daughter to find out about this
from the newspapers? Or do you want to have her
here? You want to be able to tell her, 'Hey, look, I

made a mistake. I'm paying for my mistake. I'm going to be out. You're my daughter.' But you want her to find . . . 'My father, the quitter . . . he gave it all up. He gave me up. And then it ended on July sixth.' Come on, do you want her to find that out about you? I know, man. You're Hispanic like I am. I know the way you think. I think the same way. We are a very proud people."

"Okay. So you know about pride, then you know, basically, surrender is slavery. You know, I would never allow anyone to enslave me."

"Chino, you make a mistake, you pay the price. That's not slavery."

"But who owns the price? The price you made up? Fuck the society."

". . . We both live in society."

"Yeah, but that's the thing," Chino said. "If I walk out, I'll probably kill you and . . . all your shit. . . . White people did it. They took over control of everything. And then what the fuck do we got?"

"We got everything we want to have," Batista told him. "We work hard for it, man. We make mistakes, we have to pay for them. Once we pay the price, it's over, you're done. I know that you want to go on with life. I know you do, because ending it, that's the easy way out, man. Come on."

"Yeah, come on. Easy for who?"

"It's the easy way for you."

"No, that's the hardest way. It ain't easy to take your own life."

Chino's voice broke. He was getting emotional and that meant he would be more dangerous. Batista had found out that talking about Ashley was the only thing that would calm Chino.

"It's over with them, man," Batista said. "But you

don't want to do that. You got to think of Ashley. That's who you got to think of. And what about Paula? What about Paula? What about her future? How old is Paula?"

"Twenty-three, twenty-four."

"You got Paula, too. You love Paula. She loves you. You're together. How long have you known Paula?"

"Since '93."

"That's a long time, man. That's a long time. Is Paula Ashley's mother?"

Chino started to cry. Batista waited for a few seconds, and said, "It's okay, man."

"I'll call you back." Chino sobbed and then hung up the telephone.

"Are you recording this?" Batista asked Detective Black, who had joined him in the new command center.

"Okay. We'll stop for now."

Batista thought over his conversations with Chino. He had heard absolutely no remorse from Chino, except for himself, Ashley, and Paula. Chino was worried about whether the police officer he shot was dead or alive, but only because of how it affected him. He had expressed no regret for shooting her. Batisa was once more struck by how calm Chino seemed, except for the few times he broke down and wept. Chino had expressed concern for Paula, Ashley, Davis, and his mother.

"You know," Batista said to Black, "he seems to be worried more about everybody else than he is about himself."

Davis lay in the bathtub and peeked from behind the shower curtain that Paula had closed. By looking at some shiny tiles, he could see a blur of motion as Paula and Chino moved about, but he couldn't tell what was going on. Paula seemed to be making a lot of telephone calls and saying good-bye to people.

Chino walked into the bathroom and pulled the shower curtain back. He had the MAC-11 and looked scared. That scared Davis.

"Do you need any medicine, man?" Chino asked. "Do you want some water?"

"I'm okay," Davis croaked.

"Relax, man. We ain't gonna hurt you." Chino made a motion with the gun, indicating he wanted Davis to come with him. "Come on. We need to check the windows."

When they walked to the different windows, Chino kept the gun trained on Davis and gripped his neck, not hard enough to hurt, but to signal that he was in control. The police were still swarming outside. When the window check was finished, they went to the dining area. Chino placed the MAC-11 on the table beside Lois's Glock and brought some crackers and juice from the kitchen. He offered some to Davis, who accepted.

The television was broadcasting constant updates on the standoff, but the condition of the officer Chino shot wasn't known. Paula and Chino were described as "armed and extremely dangerous."

"Tell me about the cop! Is she dead or what?" Chino said in frustration. He started to pace, faster and faster. The more Chino paced and the angrier he became, the more frightened Davis became. Davis hadn't been threatened, but he still worried about being killed.

"Let's give ourselves up," Paula said. "Maybe doing time won't be so bad."

"You don't know what you're talking about," Chino responded. "You should kill yourself rather than give up. We talked about this before."

They continued to argue until the telephone rang just a few minutes later. Paula picked up the phone. It was Detective Batista.

"Paula. How are you doing? This is Detective Batista. How are you doing?"

"Okay," Paula said meekly.

"Okay. How is Chino doing? I know that he was a little upset there a minute ago. Is he okay?"

"Yeah, we're all right."

"Is anybody in there with you, besides you and Chino?"

"Excuse me?"

"Is there anybody else, besides you and Chino, in there?"

"Yes."

"Who else is there?"

"Who else is in here, I can't tell you that. Somebody else is in here. Didn't you see him out the window? Are you close?"

"No, I'm not," Batista said. "I'm not near a window here. I'm inside of a house. Does somebody live there?"

"Yes."

"More than one person or—"

"Do you want to know his name?"

"Yeah, can you tell me his name?"

"Hold on." Paula turned to Davis. "What's your name?"

"Isaac Davis."

Paula repeated it into the phone.

"Can I talk to him, Paula?" Batista asked.

"Hold on."

Paula held the phone to Davis's ear. "Hello," he said.

"Davis, are you okay?"

"Yes, I'm okay."

"Are you in there against your will? Or are you—"

Paula interrupted. "He's all right."

"Did Davis leave?" Batista asked.

"Yeah, he left. He's all right. He's standing here."

If Batista could convince them to let Davis go, the SWAT team would have one less person to worry about if they had to rush the apartment. It was a long shot, but Batista had to try it.

"Could you let him go?" Batista asked. "I mean, does he want to go? Does he want to stay, or what?"

"Well, we're not going to let him go," Paula said firmly.

"Okay. Who else is in there besides you and Isaac and Chino?"

Chino spoke up. "Is everything okay?" he asked Paula.

"They want to know how many people are in here."

"We don't want him to know that," Chino said.

"We can't tell you that," Paula said.

Batista switched tactics. "Okay. Listen, we want to resolve this, Paula. . . . What is it going to take? We don't want anybody else getting hurt. We really don't want to hurt anybody. Paula, you're not going to jail. You weren't involved in this robbery. I already talked to Chino. I explained that to him. Why should you go to jail? You weren't involved. I know you're afraid that you're going to go to jail, is that it?"

"Of course."

"You're not going to jail."

Paula didn't buy it. "Yeah. You have to prosecute when we go to court."

"Why would you be arrested if you weren't involved in the robbery?"

"Yeah, but I was with him. I was in the car."

"No, no, you weren't involved in this robbery," Batista said. "He was in there, you were outside. He (Chino) has his own reactions. He does what he wants to do. I mean, if you had walked in there with him, it would have been different, but you were outside. You need to talk, to settle him down. We need to resolve this because Ashley . . . is Ashley your daughter?"

"Yes, she's my daughter."

"How about Ashley?" Batista asked. "Who's going to take care of Ashley? She needs her mother. She needs her father, too. It's better to have a father, even if he may be in prison for a while, than no father at all."

"You know, I will go to jail?"

"I'm sorry?" Batista asked.

"I will go to jail."

"Why do you say that?"

"Well, you people haven't looked at the bank tapes," Paula said. "I was there."

Batista was surprised. Up until this point, he had been under the impression that Paula was little more than a bystander. Now it appeared that she had been actively involved in the armed robbery, and if so, that made her an accessory in the murder of Lois Marrero.

"Well, we haven't looked at the bank tapes," he said. "I really don't know much about what's going on here."

"Okay. I was there."

"Okay, you might have walked in there. Were you in there with a gun?"

"Yes."

Batista fumbled around as he tried to regain control over the conversation. Above all, he didn't want to lose Paula's and Chino's trust because they thought he was lying to them.

"You may . . . What kind of a record do you have?" he asked. "Do you have a long criminal history? Probably not. Have you ever been arrested before?"

"No, nothing."

"Okay. You see, the first time people are arrested, they are very lenient with you," Batista said. "People can make one mistake, you know."

". . . lenient."

"Very lenient. They go very easy on first offenders. They have first-offender programs where people have never committed any crime. People that got in with the wrong person or the wrong crowd and committed a crime. This is the first time, they are not going to throw the book at you. You have to think about that. But the longer this goes on, the tougher it is going to get for you, for him, for everybody. I mean, we don't want this to drag on for hours. We need to resolve this. You want to resolve this, too, don't you?"

"Of course."

"You don't want anybody else to get hurt, do you?"

"No, of course not."

"I promised Chino that I would let him see Ashley. And I would let him talk to his mother if he wants to."

"No, I think, we won't even see her," Paula said. "Because you guys will come in here and beat us."

"No, we're not."

"And step on our necks."

"No, wait a minute. We're not going to do that."

"Yeah. One of your officers is dead. You guys should be angry."

"She's not dead," Batista said. "She's in the hospital."

So far as Batista new, Lois was still alive. The updates he received from Detective Gene Black had not mentioned that she had been killed. Batista tried not to think about Lois because they were good friends and had been on patrols together in their early days on the force. Batista feared that his emotions might cloud his judgment during negotiations, and a mistake could have murderous consequences.

The negotiations were going fairly well, he thought, because he had managed to establish a tenuous bond with both Paula and Chino. Batista was optimistic that he could resolve the situation without anyone else getting hurt. Of course, there was the possibility of a shoot-out at any moment with bloody consequences. If Chino found out that Lois was dead, things could change drastically; he would know that he had nothing left to lose and he might want to go out in a blaze of glory.

And then, in a move that defied credulity, the Tampa chief of police made the situation even more volatile and dangerous.

Chapter 10

The news media swarmed like bees around the Crossings. The robbery, hostage standoff, and murder of a female police officer was major news in the Tampa Bay area. So many news helicopters circled overhead that police officers, including the SWAT team, couldn't hear their radios. Sergeant John Bennett, who was in command of the SWAT team, had to order the helicopters out of the area. Reporters badgered police relentlessly for additional information to put into their news updates. They were particularly keen on the condition of the wounded police officer.

Under this badgering, and the emotional pressure cooker that engulfed him, Police Chief Bennie Holder spoke at a press conference and reported that the wounded police officer, Lois Marrero, had died. The negotiators were dumbfounded. The revelation could change how Paula and Chino felt about giving up or shooting it out with the police.

"Once they know someone is dead," said Sergeant Bennett, "it's easier to kill again." He defended Holder, stating that a hostage situation after the murder of a police officer was "a very chaotic, emotional scene."

The news media's coverage of the standoff was not always conducted with good sense or with the safety of the police officers in mind. Some of the harshest critics of the media's coverage came from other journalists, notably Bob Steele, director of the ethics program at the Poynter Institute for Media Studies, an organization that owns the nearby *St. Petersburg Times*.

"My goal is to urge journalists to think about these situations before they're in the minefield," Steele said. "Just as a SWAT team prepares, so should journalists."

Reporters, Steele said, should assume that a suspect has access to the news. Because of this, they should never report on police movements or mention situations that could change the status quo. One television station circled the apartment complex where the standoff was being staged and showed a SWAT tank moving onto the scene. The media was broadcasting information that could allow the suspects to spot and kill police officers.

"You could see the sniper in the tank," Bennett said. "That infuriated me."

Paula and Chino were watching the news when a television journalist reported that the wounded police officer was dead. They lost what little composure they had, shouting, cursing, and wondering how they could get out of the situation. Chino had nothing left to lose, and Paula wasn't sure how the law would view her involvement with Lois's murder.

"I just robbed a fucking bank and killed a cop!" Chino yelled over and over. He seemed ready to jump out of his own skin. "How many times did I shoot her?"

Paula was too tied up in knots to answer. She held

her face in her hands and shook. "I'm not going to jail," she said. "I'm not going to jail."

"God! I just killed a cop!" Chino repeated.

Davis was scared at the heightened tension in the room. What would stop Paula and Chino from killing him, since they already had committed murder? He was almost certain he was going to be killed, and he was sure that Chino would commit suicide. He trembled.

"It was all fucked up," Chino said to Paula. "It's all your fault."

Paula said, "I don't want to do it (commit suicide)."

"Are you crazy? Don't you know what we've done?"

"Yeah, okay."

"I'll probably get like ten or fifteen years and then I can come out of prison," Paula said. "My mother can take care of Ashley while I'm away."

"Why did the cop have to do that?" Chino asked. "We were running and she jumped out behind us and said, 'Stop or I'll kill you.' Kill me? Kill me? That's what she said to me. Can you believe that?"

Nobody said anything.

"How could she say that to me?" he asked angrily. "Can you believe that?"

"I was only involved with the bank robbery," Paula said.

"Yeah, you're an accessory to bank robbery."

"I can't really be charged with anything but the bank robbery."

"No, you're gonna be charged with conspiring and being an accessory to all of this," Chino explained.

"No, I don't think so."

"We should have stolen a car."

Bay News 9 continued to update events at the standoff. Paula telephoned her mother again and told her to take care of Ashley and apologized for "messing up." Davis didn't think that Paula was considering suicide now, although he thought Chino would probably kill himself.

The telephone rang and Paula picked it up to find Batista on the other end.

"She's dead!" Paula screamed at him. "Why are you lying to us?"

"I wasn't lying," Batista said honestly. "This is the first I've heard about it."

In fact, Batista felt sick to his stomach. He had tried not to think of Lois and now he had found out that his friend was dead from one of these suspected killers.

"Yeah, one of your officers is dead. You guys should be angry. When are you guys going to beat us?"

"We're not going to do that, Paula. You know, we have all the news media out here. We got cameras everywhere. We got helicopters."

"Okay, you've got helicopters—"

"We're not going to beat you."

"You're going to beat us and step on our necks," Paula said. "When you don't have the helicopters and media."

"This is 2001," Batista said. "This is a new century. We're not talking about—"

"[It's] 2001, yes, but it still happens. I've seen it."

Batista thought fast to stay on top of the negotiations. The news about Lois had made things much more difficult. Chino was now a man who had committed one of the worst possible capital offenses: killing a police officer. Batista felt that the negotiating process was sliding downhill fast.

"It's not going to happen here," he said. "There is media everywhere, there are witnesses. I promise nothing is going to happen to you guys. You know, all you have to do is surrender. You put your hands behind your back, you're going to be handcuffed and taken away from here. We'll give you a chance to see Ashley. You both want to see Ashley, right?"

"Of course."

"What's going to happen to Ashley, you know?" Batista asked.

"I don't know. I don't know."

"What's going to happen to her? Think about Ashley. A week, two weeks, a year from now. Ashley is two years old. What is going to happen to Ashley when she is three, five?"

"Three, five. I'll . . . I'll be in jail. I . . . I was in the bank. I'll . . . I'll be in jail."

"Chino will probably be in jail for a while, but you won't be," Batista said. He knew he was fighting an uphill battle now. Suicide, at the very least, seemed probable. Talking about Ashley was the only thing that calmed either Paula or Chino. "You're a first-time offender. I don't know what happened in the bank. It has to come out in court. You know, it's a lot. We're talking about—"

"One of you guys is dead. Are you going to come in here and shoot?"

"No, we're not going to come up and shoot. We have the SWAT teams all over the place. We're not going to leave. We're not leaving. We're not going anywhere. We're going to talk as long as it takes. We want to resolve this."

"Don't come in here," Paula warned, "because there will be a shoot-out."

Batista instantly picked up the threat. He had expected that from Chino, but he thought Paula might surrender. Batista's first impression was that Paula had little to do with the robbery or shooting; now he believed she was an equal partner with Chino. He no longer viewed her as even a partial victim of domination by Chino. He felt that negotiations were falling apart once again.

"Well, we don't want that," Batista said. "We don't want anybody to get hurt. If you give up . . . that's different than if we have to go in there and get you."

"Yeah. I'm scared, though."

"What? If you surrender, it's a lot easier for everybody. The judge looks at that, the jury looks at that. You're a mother. You have a two-year-old child. Her father made a mistake. Her father is going to go to prison. We're not going to destroy his entire family. We've got the father going to prison and the mother may have to do some jail time, but not much. Somebody has got to bring up that little girl."

"I'm not going to go to jail and get raped by all those bitches," Paula said.

"Come on, Paula. You've been watching too many movies."

"No, I don't think so. I know it happens in there."

"Paula, you want to resolve this," Batista pleaded. "You want to be with Ashley. Think about her. What's going to happen with Ashley? If you both aren't around, what's going to happen to her?"

Paula said something that was inaudible.

"Like I told Chino, she's going to grow up to be a young lady," Batista said. "A couple of years from now, she is going to go to the public library and she is going to see what happened to Mom and Dad. And it's going to be all over the papers, Mom and Dad."

"If I leave, will the newspapers all catch my face? I don't want nobody to see my face."

"Nobody's going to see your face," Batista said.

"What we are going to do is bring you into a house, let you spend some time with Ashley. And then we are going to put you in a police car and take you to the police station. They will close off the camera. You'll be surrounded by police officers. Keep your head down. We'll put something over your head. They won't have to see your face." Batista heard Chino talking nervously in the background.

"Is that Chino?" he asked.

"Yes. He won't shut up."

"He's scared about what's going on. This is very tough. It's not easy for you. It is not easy for you. We could resolve this. We could end this. That way, nobody else gets hurt. You get to see Ashley."

"Okay . . . I want to talk to him (Chino)," Paula responded.

"Could I talk to Isaac?"

"Isaac, no."

"Is Isaac okay?"

"Yes, he is fine."

"We don't want anybody to get hurt, okay?"

"We won't hurt him."

"You know, if you let Isaac go, that's one less problem you have to worry about," Batista said. "You will talk to Chino?"

"Okay, I will talk to him," Paula said, and then added a warning: "Don't come up here, please. Just let me talk to him. Give me five minutes."

In his previous conversation with Chino, Batista had convinced him that they should converse on a police telephone to avoid outside interference. This telephone also contained a hidden television camera that broadcast to a police receiver. The camera was fixed and offered a limited view, but it helped police determine the layout of an area that might have to be raided. Police can get a better idea of how an area was defended and the subject's state of mind.

"Isaac doesn't need to be there," Batista said when Paula gave the phone to Chino. "What do you need Isaac for?"

"If Isaac wasn't here, you would have been up here already."

"Come on, man, come on."

"*Come on,*" Chino mocked.

"Chino, we don't want to do that. We don't want anybody else to get hurt. We don't want Paula to get hurt and we don't want you to get hurt. I promise you, we want to take you into custody without a scratch. You come out, you put your hands on top of your head, you're going to be handcuffed. We're going to get Ashley over here, you know. If you want to talk to your mom, you can talk to your mom."

"Yeah, but I did," Chino said. "You interrupted it."

"You want to talk to your mom face-to-face or on the cell phone?"

"I'd have to go downstairs, face-to-face."

"Face-to-face. Down here in a room."

"No. No."

"Chino, we can't stay here doing this forever," Batista said. "We'll wait it out, whatever it takes. But we have a lot of people out here. All of these SWAT guys are out here in the hot sun. That's what they get paid for. But you know human nature. People get out there in the sun, they get irritable. I know it is a big decision you got to make. But think about Ashley. Think about your future. Paula doesn't have a criminal record. They are very lenient with people who have never been in any type of trouble."

"She is an accessory."

"Chino, she has a clean record, as far as she told me."

"Yeah, she has never been arrested, never."

"She doesn't even got a parking ticket," Batista said. "She may do some jail time, but she will get out to take care of your daughter . . . Ashley."

"Do you have a point system?"

"I don't know the point system," Batista replied. "I'm a burglary detective. I worry about doing my job and if I arrest people . . . the court system . . . What's the point system have to do with it?"

"The higher the points, the higher the minimum. And I think we are high up there. At least I am."

"You have to go before a judge. You have to be convicted. We are talking about months, maybe years. . . . A lot goes into play here, you surrender."

"Listen, I've been in jail . . . like a week. I got twenty days."

"What's the other [choice]? Death. Dying? What about your kid? What about Ashley?"

"What I did is a capital crime, correct?" Chino asked.

"It's a crime. It's not—"

"It's a capital crime."

"It's a serious crime."

"A cop died."

"Yeah, it is a capital crime."

It didn't get any worse for a suspect than this, Batista thought. His mind raced to find something that might convince Chino that he wouldn't spend his life in prison if he surrendered.

"I'll get the death penalty now," Chino said.

"You won't."

"I'll get the death penalty. I'm thinking, 'What am I doing? Should I let you come here and kill me?'"

"You didn't wake up this morning and say, 'I think I'm going to out and kill a cop,'" Batista said. "It was not a premeditated action. It happened in the heat of passion."

"It wasn't premeditated."

"So what are you saying here, Chino? What are you telling me?"

"I feel like I'm going to get the death penalty anyway."

"How do you know that, Chino?" Batista had thought of something he could use to help calm Chino. "Jackie Simpson was involved in a shooting of a police officer in 1988 in the city of Tampa, and he got life. Life doesn't mean life anymore. You do twenty years, you are a model prisoner, and you educate yourself. Fifteen years go by. You go before the parole boards and say, 'Look, this guy made a mistake in 2001. But in the last fifteen years, he has been a model prisoner.'"

The case of Jackie Simpson, who murdered rookie police officer Porfirio Soto, was bizarre in more ways than one. Soto's partner was Charlotte Rowse Johnston, whose twin sister, Jennifer Rowse, was also a Tampa policewoman. Johnston was in a gun battle with Simpson as he struggled with Soto, who was attempting to deliver a warrant.

Simpson received life in prison for Soto's murder and thirty-five years for the attempted murder of Johnston. The sentences were to run concurrently and Simpson could have been free in twenty-five years. Unfortunately for him, Simpson hanged himself in prison with a pair of trousers.

The twin police officers were never the same. They resigned from the police department and were routinely arrested on drug charges over the next several years. They committed suicide together in 2005. The tragedy was an example of how a murder can reach out to change the lives of family members and acquaintances.

"Hold on for one second," Chino said. "Do you have people in the attic? On the roof?"

"I don't know. I'm not in a room. I'm in a house."

"Do you have a SWAT team on the roof right now, because I hear walking?" Chino's voice was pitched with anxiety.

"I don't know. There may be a SWAT team. There are SWAT people all over the place. But they're not coming in there."

"No? What are they doing?"

"They take different positions," Batista said. "I don't know. I'm a negotiator. I've just been told there is nobody up on the roof. So you may be hearing something else from next door. There's nobody there, but we have SWAT people all around us. The building is surrounded. . . . There are police cars everywhere. There are media people everywhere. You're probably watching on TV. Television shows you everything that is going on. I'm sure you're watching TV right now. Is Paula okay?"

"What happened?"

"Is Paula okay?"

"I think so."

"How about you, man? Are you settled down a little bit?"

"Yeah, I'm settled down." Chino had asked earlier for a pack of cigarettes. "What happened with the pack of cigarettes?" Chino asked. "I'm fucking, like, shaking like a fucking leaf."

"Nobody is smoking. We're trying to find somebody with a—"

"My mother."

"Your mother smokes? She's not here. Let me see if I can get you at least a couple of cigarettes out there until we get a pack or something."

"I need a new pack. You people can be snakes."

Batista knew that Chino wanted an unopened package of cigarettes because he was afraid the police would lace the cigarettes with poison or a drug to knock him unconscious.

"We want to get the cigarettes to you," he said. "But we don't want you to hurt anybody else trying to deliver them. What do you do for us if we give you a pack of cigarettes? Let Isaac go?"

"Yeah, I'm going to let him go *for a pack of cigarettes*?" Chino mocked. "And you rushing right out there, so I have to give up or you'll shoot me right down there."

"No, we're not going to rush anything. We got all the time in the world. We want to resolve this. I told you that from the very beginning. We don't want you to get hurt, we don't want Paula to get hurt."

"I'll call you back in a little bit."

"I'll call you back. You want to come out of this alive, and you want everyone to come out of this," Batista said. "I don't think you want to hurt anybody else. I don't think you want to hurt yourself or Paula or Isaac or anybody else in there. Do you?"

"This is not all about hurting people," Chino said. "This is all about profiting."

"You don't sound like a bad person at all. I talk to a lot of people on these things. You sound like a person who is down on his luck. You made a mistake and you got caught."

"Yeah, that sucks."

"You've got to surrender and move on," Batista

told him. "What's done is done. You can't change the past, man, but you can change the future. Think about your daughter and your girlfriend, and your girlfriend raising your daughter, not some stranger or state agency. Ashley's father needs to talk to her, too, and you will be able to as long as you are on this earth. I could talk all night, whatever it takes. The bottom line is you are in control here. It's up to you."

"If I was in control, I would be seeing my daughter right now."

"You could see your daughter very quickly. All you got to do is tell me you want to come out. I'll tell the SWAT guys. They'll take you into custody, bring you downstairs, and you can spend some time with your daughter. We can make that happen like that. It's up to you. You could show me some good faith by letting Isaac leave. That will show everybody, 'Hey, look, this guy really doesn't want to hurt anybody. This guy wants to work things out.'"

"Let me talk to Paula."

"I'll stay on the line. Go ahead."

"No, like I want it to be private."

"You want me to call you back then?"

Batista asked Chino if there was a solid door by the kitchen, where a police officer could place the telephone that they would use for further communications. This was the telephone with the miniature camera that would telecast what was happening inside the apartment to the police. Chino told Batista there was a door that faced the stairs. Batista rejected that.

"It's not safe for our guys, man. We want a solid door. Is the kitchen a solid door?"

"There is going to be no solid doors," Chino said flatly.

"Does the kitchen door have a window? Let me talk

to these SWAT. Let me see what's going on. Let me call you right back."

Batista watched as a member of a SWAT team crouched low and went upstairs to place the telephone by the kitchen door. It was a risky maneuver by the police officer to expose himself to fire. Fortunately, Chino didn't see him.

"All right, we've put the phone there," Batista said when he called Chino. "We wanted to put it there safely and back away. That's what we did. You want to go get—"

"How's my mother?"

"Your mother is okay. I haven't seen her in a while, but she is okay."

"I don't want anyone treating her like shit, you know."

"Nobody's going to," Batista said. "She is a very nice lady. She is very upset, of course. She wants this thing resolved. She wants to see you. She wants you to come out alive. You think that we are going to hurt you and we're not going to. We want everybody to come out alive. So, when you—"

"Okay, I'm going to get the phone now."

"When you get the phone, there is a button you have to press to talk. If you don't press the button, I'm not going to be able to hear you."

"It's like a two-way radio?"

"More or less, but it's a secure line because the media is listening," Batista said. "It's nobody's business, just us."

"Isn't that against the law?"

Batista agreed that it was and Chino said he would get the telephone and call him back.

* * *

The clock was ticking and almost 2½ hours had passed since the standoff began. The July sun glared white-hot and turned the asphalt, where police were stationed, into a griddle. Police officers baked beneath their bulletproof vests and inside an armored tank that was at the staging area. The police were prepared to do whatever it took to defuse the situation, and an assault was becoming more probable with each passing minute.

State Attorney Mark Ober looked out at the scene and worried out loud: "This could turn out to be a real bloodbath."

Everyone hoped it wouldn't.

Chapter 11

Chino looked nervous and scared. The television had just broadcast a news update showing police swarming around the apartment grounds, including SWAT teams with their military-type uniforms, rifles, and shotguns. Davis thought that Chino believed that time was running out and that the apartment would soon be assaulted.

Paula said, "We need to call people in New York before whatever's gonna happen, happens."

"You know what we have to do," Chino said. His voice was persuasive, but he wasn't giving a command, so far as Davis could tell.

"Come on," Chino said, motioning toward Davis with the MAC-11. "You've got to stick your hand out the door and get a telephone."

Chino marched him to the kitchen door at gunpoint, Chino's hand grasping Davis by the neck. A knot twisted inside Davis's stomach as he thought about the SWAT teams outside and the guns that were probably being aimed at the kitchen door. At Chino's direction he got on his knees, opened the door a crack, then reached out, grabbed the telephone, and brought it inside.

"Maybe we should turn ourselves in, Chino," Paula said, sounding hysterical.

Paula started talking in Spanish on a cell phone and Davis thought she was saying good-bye. She wept and her voice cracked.

Chino pointed the muzzle of the MAC-11 toward the ceiling and pulled the lever back. It made a clicking sound. Davis saw him remove the magazine and take two bullets out, look at them, put them back, and reinsert the magazine. He did the same thing a second time and placed the gun on the table next to the Glock.

Chino picked up the MAC-11 again and counted the bullets in the magazine. He looked at Davis.

"It looks like a toy," Davis said.

"You pull the trigger and it fires many times," Chino said.

"It goes *brrrrrtt!* Like an automatic?"

"Yes. You pull the trigger and it keeps on firing." Chino looked at him. "Don't worry. We aren't going to hurt you."

Chino lit one of the cigarettes from the package the police had left with the telephone. He inhaled deeply, held it, then exhaled. The television newscast showed a panoramic scan of the apartment building, which teemed with police officers.

"They're everywhere," Paula said. "They're everywhere."

The feeling of imminent danger grew inside the apartment. Although they were both scared, neither Paula nor Chino showed much affection toward the other, nor did they try to comfort one another. Davis was frightened: Chino and Paula could kill him or he might get killed in the cross fire of a shoot-out with the police. He felt his heart beat.

"I'm going to do it," Chino said.

"Yeah, okay," Paula said.

"We talked about it before."

"There are alternatives," Paula said. "I'll probably get ten or fifteen years and then come out of prison. Then I can take care of Ashley."

"I want to go home with my father," Chino said. "I don't want to go to prison. I just want to put a bullet in my head."

Paula, on an emotional roller coaster, changed her mind again and decided that she should commit suicide. Chino wanted her to do it and she always did what Chino wanted. She made a last telephone call to her mother in New York and left a message in Spanish on the answering machine:

"We went to rob a bank and the police came up from everywhere. Please take care, very much. I love you with all my heart, and please, you can be with the mother of Chino. Call me if you can do that . . . mistake. What am I going to pay for this, I know. Good-bye, Mommy. Bye, Daddy. Ciao, Lisa [Paula's sister Louisa]. Ciao, Helen. Bye to everyone. Say hello to the entire family. I love you very much. Bye."

The cell phone rang while Chino talked to Batista. It was Paula's mother, Melba. "Don't do it," she said. "Please, please, do not do it. I am going to send angels to come and get you."

Lisa, Paula's sister, came on the line. "He's brain-washing you," she said. "You've got to snap out of it."

"I know, I know."

"Please do not do this," Lisa pleaded again. "Think of Ashley."

On the police phone Batista yelled, "Chino! Can you hear me?"

Chino slumped in a corner facing the front door, where he expected the SWAT team to attack. He held the MAC-11 and smoked a cigarette as he cradled the telephone between his shoulder and ear.

Paula got off the phone with her mother. She stepped across Chino's legs. Both Paula and Chino appeared to be calm.

"You can come out first," Batista said. "It's up to you. Nothing's going to happen to you."

Chino lit another cigarette and inhaled deeply. "Man, I'm shaking like a fucking leaf."

"What do you say, man?" Batista asked.

"I think I'll send Isaac out first."

Chino called Davis out of the bathroom, where he had been hunkered down in the tub to avoid gunfire if the police staged an assault. Davis took the telephone from Chino and listened as Batista told him to strip down to his shorts and come out with his hands up. Davis did as instructed.

"Go stand by the front door," Chino told him. "Stand facing inside."

Davis did so, his knees trembling.

Chino put the telephone down and looked at Paula. "I'm killing myself," he said.

He demonstrated how they would kill themselves together by putting the muzzle of the MAC-11 under his chin. Paula was to use the Glock.

"Like this," Chino said. "On the count of three. One, two, *pow.*"

Paula leaned over and kissed Chino on the lips. Davis's stomach couldn't take the tension anymore and he threw up.

"Are you ready?" Chino asked, putting the gun back under his chin.

"I can't do it!" Paula screamed hysterically. "You do it for me."

"What's going on, man?" Batista yelled over the telephone.

"I'm gonna put a bullet in my head," Chino said.

"No! Don't do that, man."

"Yeah. I'm leaving on three. Ready?" he asked Paula.

Paula wasn't ready, she was scared. "Yeah," she said.

"On the count of three," he said.

Chino pushed the muzzle of the MAC-11 into his chin. "One, two . . ."

The MAC-11 fired and sent a bullet through Chino's brain. He slumped to his right side and slid down the wall. Davis's knees gave way and he fell to the floor. He not only saw blood gushing from Chino's head, he heard it. Paula didn't pull the trigger because she kept thinking that Ashley needed her. She stepped over to Chino and touched his shoulder.

"Good-bye, sweetie," she said. She picked up the telephone. "Hello?"

"What happened?" Batista asked.

"He's dead."

"It's over, Paula. Come on out. Your daughter needs you."

"They're gonna charge me with the killing of the officer."

"That's not going to happen," Batista said. "Go to the front door and close your eyes. A SWAT team is coming."

A SWAT team took Davis into custody, placing handcuffs on him. He was taken to police head-quarters and held until police were satisfied that he was a victim and not part of the robbery and murder. Paula was also taken downtown, where she would be interviewed. She felt relieved that it was all over, but everything had a dreamlike quality to it, as if not really happening.

At police headquarters Paula was given a bottle of springwater. She had not eaten since breakfast, but she wasn't hungry. More than anything, she wanted to see Ashley. The police would allow that, but first they wanted to take her statement while everything was fresh in her mind.

Batista was emotionally drained. He had tried for three hours to defuse the standoff and have everyone come out alive. No other police officers had been killed and the hostage was released unharmed. Throughout the negotiation he had not allowed himself to think of Lois because of the emotional impact it would have on him. Now he remembered their friendship over the past eighteen years, her bright smile, perky attitude, and her generous spirit. He wept.

Chapter 12

Detective Aubrey "Gene" Black, of the homicide division, began interviewing Paula at 4:39 P.M., shortly after she was taken into custody. He had been the second point man with Batista during negotiations with Chino and Paula, keeping Batista informed of police activities. Black was an experienced police officer, having served twenty-five years with the Tampa Police Department. Seventeen of those years were as a detective and he had conducted hundreds of interviews with suspected lawbreakers and knew how to get them to talk. Paula wore a camouflage T-shirt and denim shorts; she looked small, fragile, and vulnerable. She was meek and spoke in a soft voice with a Spanish accent.

The interview was held in the conference room at the downtown police station. It was a large, comfortable room, with carpeted floors. Joining Black were Detectives Jeanette Hevel and George Lease, both of the robbery division. Black read Paula her rights and she initialed a form acknowledging that she understood. At the top of the form was a blank line the detectives used to write in the crime with which a suspect was charged. That space was left blank on the sheet Paula signed. Black began asking questions that Paula answered mostly in monosyllables or with the fewest number of words possible. Black established that Chino was her boyfriend, that they lived together, and had a daughter named Ashley.

"What I'm gonna ask you is, would you like to talk to us and tell us about what happened today?" Black asked. "And if you would, what I'd like to have you do is just sign your signature across the bottom line."

"Okay," Paula said. "I have a question."

"Yes."

"I don't know. I've never been in this situation. I don't know if I should talk to a lawyer first. I wanna cooperate," Paula said, "but I really don't want to go to jail."

"You go to jail on the basis of evidence," Black said. "You have to make that decision; I can't make it for you. I'm not gonna lie to you, there's a possibility you will go to jail. But you would go to jail even if you didn't talk to us right now."

"Do you have a lawyer here?"

"No, we don't have one here. That's the only problem."

At this point of the interview, there was a long pause. No one said anything for twenty seconds. This would be a major point that Paula's lawyers would use in her defense.

"Okay," Paula finally said. "I'll go with it."

Paula signed to acknowledge that she had been informed of her rights and that she had agreed to talk. Black quickly established that Paula had not been under the influence of alcohol, medicine, or drugs at the time of the robbery.

"Nothing that would distort your remembrance.

Have you been hit in the head in the last few days, which would cause you not to remember something."

Paula said no. But she did note that she has had problems with depression, but she had never seen a doctor about it. She answered no when Black asked if she had ever been classified as a schizophrenic or a neurotic by a trained psychiatrist or psychologist.

When Black asked Paula what precipitated the bank robbery, she told him about Chino being fired, that they only had a dollar, no food, and a baby to take care of. They had a hard time paying the bills.

"So you were hurting for money?" Black asked. "Was this a split-second decision to go and rob the bank today or had you thought about it for a while?"

She said that when Chino woke up, he was "really stressed" and told her that they needed money.

"Why a bank?" Black asked. "Why not a convenience store? You just needed a lot of money right then and there?"

"We were down to a dollar. . . . We have a truck. . . . We need to pay bills."

"Right, right."

"No food in the fridge."

"Did he set up a plan about how you were going to do this?"

"No. We woke up and, you know, he was really pissed off, and he said we have a dollar and we had no cash, no food, no milk, or anything; he said, 'Let's go, we gotta do it.'"

Paula told the detectives that she didn't want to go into the bank because she was scared. She had followed Chino with the MAC-11 after he jumped out and ran to the bank.

"I didn't wanna go in," Paula said. "He was already in there."

"But were you trying to protect him?"

"I don't know. I was scared then."

"He didn't force you to go in though, right?" Black asked.

Paula said no.

"He just asked you and you wanted to please him, so you did it, right?"

"I didn't wanna do it. I never did anything like that. . . . I was scared and he told me that we needed to do it in order to get food and . . . pay the bills, catch up."

"So you were thinking of your baby, you wanted to feed her?"

"Yeah."

Paula described her version of the bank robbery. According to her, Chino went into the bank first and she followed. Paula said she went just inside the door and no farther. After the dye pack went off in the car, Paula said, she couldn't see, and she had no idea what route they took to get away from the bank.

"You weren't expecting that, were you?" Black asked about the dye pack.

"No, of course not," Paula said. "I don't even know what happened."

Paula related going to the Regency, changing clothes in the parking lot, and then calling Chino's mother. She said they were at the Regency for five to ten minutes.

"Did you change your clothes?" Black asked.

"Yeah, I put my shorts on, yes."

"Okay. And the reason for that was because you didn't wanna be caught wearing the clothing you—"

"Well, that and . . ."

"And the dye . . ."

"It stunk."

Paula told how they had gone back to the Crossings with Chino's mother.

"Did she know anything about what had happened, what you guys had done?"

"Uh-uh."

"Did you tell her what had happened?"

"She was just wondering why our faces were so red and irritated."

"Did you tell her?"

"Chino told her."

"He told her that you had robbed a bank?"

"Yeah, and she was mad."

"What did Chino ask her to do?"

"She was mad, she dropped us off. She was pissed off."

(Paula was lying here. Chino's mother already knew about the robbery, although the police didn't know this yet. Most likely, Paula was trying to protect Lissette, who may have been considered the getaway driver.)

Black touched lightly on the time Paula and Chino spent in the apartment at the Crossings. This would be another area that the defense would pounce on during Paula's trial. He questioned her in detail about Officer Lois Marrero being killed.

Lois was in the courtyard beside the pool when Paula said she first saw her. The police officer had a gun in her hand and told Chino to stop or she would shoot. Chino, she said, ran a short distance and grabbed a blue bag that the MAC-11 was in, then ran across Church Street.

"You just saw him grab the gun . . . ?" Black asked.

"No, no, no. He ran when the lady was yelling. I don't know where he went. And then I started going upstairs. I didn't want to get between that. And then he came back. He started screaming, 'Paula, Paula.' And I came down and then the gun was down in the bag. He grabbed the gun and then the guy from upstairs was coming down."

Paula didn't know the neighbor's name. (It was Mike Kokojan.) Chino snatched the neighbor's keys, and then Paula saw the police officer coming again.

"He was opening the door for the car," Paula said. "And she said, 'Stop or I'm gonna shoot you, I'm gonna shoot you.' She was grabbing her gun. And then he shot her."

"How many times? Do you remember?"

"Three times."

"Okay. What happens then?"

"And then he's squeezing me; he tells me, turn it . . . open the car, and then he tells me, 'Grab the gun, grab her gun.'"

"We're gonna go back to the point to where you mentioned that Chino had gone up to the car, he was trying to get into the car, he has his gun, and the officer comes up to him, and the officer tells him to stop or she'll shoot. What do you see happen then?"

"I'm just frozen. I didn't know what was gonna happen."

"What did you see?"

"I saw him shoot her."

"Did she go down immediately?"

"Yeah."

"Did she ever fire her gun?"

"Uh-uh. I don't think so."

"Did the officer say anything after she was shot? Did you go up and look at her?"

"She was right in front of me."

"Okay, so you saw her?"

"I saw her."

"Did she appear to be dead then?"

"I don't know."

"All right. You could see blood coming from her, though?"

"I saw blood."

Paula said she didn't remember hearing sirens or other police officers arriving. She remembered following Chino toward the apartment building. Paula started to sob, and Black asked if she needed a moment to compose herself. No, Paula told him, she just wanted to get the interview over.

Paula remembered seeing Chino shoot the gun right after he kicked an apartment door in, but she didn't see who he was shooting at. She said she believed it was at other police officers. Chino, Paula said, told Isaac Davis that they had robbed a bank, but didn't remember him saying anything about shooting a police officer.

"And what did the man say? Did he ask you guys to leave?"

"No, he just . . . He was kind of sick. . . . He said he had been sick for two weeks."

They told Davis they weren't going to hurt him, she said.

"Did you hold him there against his will?" Black asked.

"Well, yeah. He was just . . . calm."

But Davis was throwing up in the bathroom, too. She said Chino turned on the news and they saw cops everywhere, and that the apartment was surrounded. Paula and Chino looked out the window, she said, and saw Lissette talking with the police.

"He calls her and she's telling him to give himself up," Paula said, "and they're arguing, saying, 'Now you gotta go to jail. You killed a cop.' That he (Chino) was gonna shoot himself."

"Because he didn't want to go to jail?"

"He said he ain't gonna stop and . . . I know he really regretted everything, but he said . . . he wasn't gonna go to jail for the rest of his life or get, you know, the electric chair."

"Uh-huh."

"And he just wanted to take his life. And he wanted me to do the same."

"He wanted you to kill yourself?"

"Yeah."

"Why didn't you?"

"My daughter."

"Right, right."

"I spoke to my mother. . . . I called her up in New York. She was begging me not to do it. So I didn't do it."

"Where is the officer's gun?"

"It's under the bed. . . . We were sitting on the floor and he wanted to count to three and just shoot ourselves."

"He wanted you to shoot yourself with the police officer's gun and then he would shoot himself with the gun that he had?"

"Yes."

Paula said Chino couldn't buy the MAC-11 because he had a criminal record, and even though the gun was in her name, she had never touched it until that day. Black, noting that Chino couldn't be hurt anymore, asked if he had committed any other robberies. Paula said no, but he was a shoplifter.

"Let me ask you this," Black said. "Have you done any other robberies in the city, other than this one?"

"No . . . that's it."

Black asked her again if she had ever been involved in a robbery with Chino. Paula again said that she hadn't.

"Has Chino talked about doing these types of things with you?" Black asked.

"No . . . we were doing fine, and then he got fired and then we started getting late on the car payment. They kept calling me, they were gonna repo. And we couldn't pay the bills and today . . . woke up and he just couldn't take it. Said he couldn't live like that."

Hevel asked, "So other than that bank, when y'all carried that bag with the gun, I mean, did he take it anywhere else for protection or anything like that?"

"He always carried it," Paula said. "He always says, 'Oh, we need to take it.'"

Black noted that Paula looked emotionally drained and stopped taping so she could have some time to rest. The police concluded the first portion of the interview with Paula at 5:34 P.M. The second part of the interview began with Black and Detective Hevel questioning Paula about the robbery at Flowers By Patricia. Paula had told Hevel during the break that she and Chino had committed that robbery.

"Can you just explain to me in your own words what happened that day?" Hevel asked.

"We needed money, Chino and I. We didn't know where to go. We went to the flower shop."

She told Hevel how they had parked in back of the flower shop, told the clerk that they wanted a bouquet, and then robbed her.

"We pulled out the gun," Paula said. "He told her to sit on the floor, and [asked] where is the money?"

She said she had retrieved the woman's purse, dumped it, and that it contained $45. Then they restrained the woman's arms and legs with duct tape and "just went home."

"What happened to the lady?" Hevel asked.

"Nothing. We just tied her up."

"When you left, where was she?"

"By the door to the fridge, where the flowers are at."

"Was she inside the freezer?"

"She didn't want to be inside," Paula said. "She freaked out a little. She shifted so that she could hold the door open with her feet from the inside."

Hevel had the confession that she wanted and concluded the interview at 6:12 P.M. After a short break, Black questioned Paula to learn more details in the shooting of Officer Lois Marrero.

"She came up to the back (of the car) and you said she had her gun drawn?" he asked.

"Yes."

"Had Chino pulled his gun out yet . . . ?"

"Yeah . . . he had it in his hand."

"Tell us what you remember the officer saying."

"Well, to put . . . that she . . . she didn't want to shoot him."

"And she had . . . enough opportunity to shoot him . . . if she wanted to?"

"Yeah . . . she could have shot him when he was running from her."

"And then Chino . . . shot her because she hesitated, right?"

"Yeah."

"Because she didn't want to kill him?"

"No . . . no, she didn't," Paula replied.

"By her act of not firing first, that gave Chino more than enough time to fire at her?" Black asked.

"Yeah."

Paula said again that she didn't remember running to the apartment or see whom Chino was shooting at. She said she was in shock from having seen the police officer killed. Paula wasn't sure that Lois was dead.

"I saw blood," she said.

"A lot of blood?" Black asked. "Were her eyes open?"

"Yeah, they were open. . . . I think she was awake."

"Could you hear her saying anything?"

"No. She didn't say anything."

"She was just lying there?"

"Uh-huh."

Black then took another break so that Paula could visit with Lissette and Ashley. She ate some pizza, went to the bathroom, and drank some bottled water. The interview started again at 8:30 P.M. Black read Paula her rights again and she acknowledged that she understood what these were and that she wanted the interview to continue.

"Did Chino ever mention to you any planning if you committed a robbery and . . . the police happened to locate you?" Black asked. "Did he have a set plan for how you would deal with such a situation?"

"No."

"There had to be previous planning about how you would deal with the possibility if the police—"

"We thought about it," Paula said. "He said that he'd rather die."

"So you took that to mean that if . . . he was cornered or caught or something like that, he would probably kill himself then?"

"You're right, but I didn't think that he was going to do it."

Black asked Paula how long she and Chino were in the apartment at the Crossings. She said it was about fifteen minutes or even less. Paula agreed that they had changed clothes so that they wouldn't be seen in the clothing they wore to rob the bank.

"Why did you leave your apartment?" he asked. "Why didn't you stay there? You went to the apartment and changed clothes. Why didn't you just stay inside the apartment? What were you worried about? Why did you leave? Was there a reason for leaving?"

"He was nervous," Paula said. "Helicopters flying above."

"So you could hear the police helicopters flying? And he thought the police might be on their way there?"

"Yeah."

"So he was still thinking about trying to get away from . . . the police."

"Yeah. He didn't want to get caught."

"Uh-huh."

"And neither did you?"

"Of course."

"Of course not, right? So what was the plan? Obviously, just before Officer Marrero came up, he was starting to walk away and you were getting ready to walk with him, right?"

"I was closing the door, and he was already around, you know, by the pool."

Paula said that Lois started chasing Chino when he was at the pool. As Chino and Lois ran toward the cemetery across the street, Paula saw Kokojan come out of his apartment and ran to him. Paula told Black that although she had never spoken with Kokojan before, she asked him to let her inside his apartment.

"Because you wanted to hide?" Black asked.

"Yeah, I was scared. I saw the cops and everything. And Chino came, calling my name and stuff. Asking me about the gun. And the officer came, like, not too long after he came, that's when it happened."

Paula said that she was on the passenger side of Kokojan's car when Chino shot Lois.

"And your plan was to get in the car, too?" Black asked.

"Yeah."

"Just to get away, right?"

Paula said that was correct, but that Lois appeared before they could get inside.

"Did he never tell you that if he was cornered by the police, he was going to shoot an officer?" Black asked. "He would rather shoot an officer than give up?"

"He never said that. . . . He said that he would take his life."

Black asked Paula if Chino had been arrested for anything in the past, and she told him that he had been to jail for shoplifting.

"He never told you about doing any robberies before, or anything like that?"

Paula said no, and then Black asked if she wanted to say anything that would help with the investigation.

"I didn't want that . . . the cops to get shot."

"Okay."

"He did it."

"Okay."

"But he did it. I don't know why he did it. I don't want to be in this position. I want to be with my daughter."

Black concluded the interview and Paula swore that everything she said was the truth and nothing but the truth.

During the four-hour interview, Paula had confessed to the Bank of America robbery, buying the MAC-11, invading Isaac Davis's home, and being present when Lois was shot and killed. She lied when she said that the Bank of America armed robbery was the first, omitting the one at Flowers By Patricia just four days earlier.

Although Paula appeared meek, the detectives were convinced that she was more than an unwilling participant. Black believed that Paula may have been the driving force behind both armed robberies, and that she tried to look like a victim to avoid culpability.

Chapter 13

The sky wept on the day funeral services were held for Lois Marrero at the Sacred Heart Catholic Church in Tampa. Warm rain fell from a gray sky and drenched more than two thousand mourners who stood outside to pay their final respects to the first Tampa policewoman to be killed in the line of duty.

Police officers from all around Florida gathered to say good-bye to one of their own. Lois's casket sat near the altar draped with more than three hundred roses that had been donated by Catharine Hadaad, who had been robbed at gunpoint at Flowers By Patricia by the same man who had killed Lois. Lois's sister, Brenda, and Lois's domestic partner, Mickie Mashburn, walked into the church, hand in hand, in what was the last show of solidarity before their relationship ended in anger, hurt, accusations, and additional grief.

Lois was eulogized by friends and family. Edmond Anctil, a deputy sheriff and deacon in the Catholic Church, prayed, "Hasten to meet her, angels of the Lord." The Reverend Joseph H. Diaz, who gave the sermon, told the assembly that "Lois isn't dead. She's just walking a new beat."

Lois's body was carried from the church by a police honor guard while bagpipes intoned a dirge of deep sorrow while thousands of ordinary citizens, some who had created monuments to Lois, kept a silent vigil. A procession of eight hundred police vehicles accompanied Lois to Myrtle Hill Cemetery, where she was laid to rest.

In a final symbolic act, dispatchers issued a call to Lois M. Marrero, Badge 327: "Do I have Officer Lois Marrero on frequency?" There was only silence in response.

Representative Jim Davis, of Tampa, entered a tribute to Lois into the Congressional Record as he spoke on the floor of the U.S. House of Representatives. Davis said he joined thousands of mourners who were saying good-bye to Lois, "one of Tampa's finest, who was struck down when a bank robber opened fire." Lois was the first policewoman to be killed in the line of duty in Tampa, Davis said, but he added that her legacy included her dedication, courage, and an instrumental role in cracking the gangs in Ybor City.

"It is our duty to remember Lois for the ultimate sacrifice that she made to keep our community safe," Davis said, and "show our gratitude to the entire law enforcement community."

Chapter 14

Deeann Athan was having lunch at a lawyer's office in Tampa when she heard helicopters. She knew something big was happening. Athan, an experienced trial attorney with the Hillsborough County Public Defender's Office, knew that her services might soon be needed.

The television was on when she reached her office and she watched it off and on as the hostage drama unfolded. When it was over and Paula came out, Athan joked with Julianne Holt, a mitigation specialist: "We should send somebody to the police station so they don't coerce a confession out of her."

But a public defender can't do that: they have to be asked to provide counsel for a defendant who can't afford a lawyer. Athan decided almost immediately that she wanted to represent Paula. As she explained, "A couple of years before, I represented another young woman, a teenager who was accused of killing her mother with her boyfriend and another friend. It was a high-profile case. In a lot of high-profile cases, your client is not well liked by the public, so you're not well liked. It's tough from the very beginning."

Athan believed that defendants went into court as underdogs, even though the burden of proof lay with the state. Furthermore, she thought that "presumption of innocence" was a matter of law, not reality; she thought people automatically believed the person charged with a crime was guilty.

"We talk about presumption of innocence, but it's a very foreign notion to human beings," Athan said. "You see somebody stopped by the police on the side of the road. You look over and say, 'Oh, they must have been speeding.' We assume they're guilty of something. Human nature fights against presumption of innocence. It takes a special, open-minded person to do that, and, I'm sorry to say, the vast majority of people who sit on juries just aren't that way."

Public defenders weren't lining up to rush to Paula's defense. It would be a difficult case, uphill all the way. Athan was assigned to the case as soon as she asked to be Paula's attorney.

Athan met Paula at the Hillsborough County Jail, a forbidding compound surrounded by a high fence topped with razor wire. Inside, the jail is loud with the clanging of metal and the shouts of guards and prisoners. Until they're completely processed, detainees are kept in spartan quarters with no amenities before being sent to the general population, where there are two persons to a cell and a dayroom with a television set.

Paula was in the jail's most restrictive program. Paula was also under a suicide watch and a twenty-three-hour a day lockdown, which meant she was only allowed out of her cell for an hour a day. Athan was surprised at how young and innocent Paula looked. The defense attorney shuddered to think of this frail-looking girl, who had been through such a horrible day, being in a room with three experienced detectives without a lawyer to advise her. She thought it was worse than unfair.

Athan believed that Paula's confession was illegally obtained. When Paula asked Black if she needed a lawyer, Athan maintained that he should have stopped the interview. Instead, she believed that Black steered her away by telling her that it would be a problem to get a lawyer.

There was no problem so far as Athan was concerned; the public defender's office was only fifteen minutes away from where Paula was interviewed. The police also had a hotline to reach a public defender at any hour—a lawyer to represent Paula could have been at the interview in less than a half hour.

After she introduced herself, Athan explained her job to Paula. She told Paula that a psychiatrist would be interviewing her. Paula appeared to be under so much duress that Athan didn't think she understood half of what was going on. Paula told her that she couldn't sleep and that she was still afraid of Chino.

Athan spent several hours with Paula, partly to allow her to have time outside of the small cell. Then she went back to her office, thinking how meek Paula was. Violence of any kind appeared absolutely impossible. "It's just not in her nature," she told a colleague.

Paula's eyes snapped wide open: *"One, two, pow!"* The voice was Chino's and it seemed to be coming from everywhere. It repeated, *"One, two, pow!"* Paula shuddered as Chino's voice continued to taunt her.

"You were supposed to do it. We agreed."

Along with the accusing voice, Paula heard unearthly chanting and music that seemed to fill the cell and accompany Chino's voice. She would not have been surprised if he had appeared in the cell and killed her. Dimly, Paula realized that Chino was dead, but she was so terrorized she thought he could still hurt her.

She curled into a fetal position on the bed and held her hands over her ears to block the voice, chanting, and eerie music. *"One, two, pow!"* She felt the bed shake violently.

Dr. Michael Maher, a Tampa forensic psychiatrist, glanced at Paula's medical record at the jail on July 9. The records showed that the jail's doctor found Paula "depressed (immediately following arrest) and possibly suffering from hallucinations." Concerned about her having a psychotic condition, an antidepressant medication called Trilafon, which is used to treat schizophrenia, was prescribed for several days. On July 10, Maher met with Paula for the first time at the Orient Road Jail, where Paula had been transferred. Lolly Fulgueira, Deeann Athan's co-counsel, was present. She told Paula to be as open with Maher as she could.

The psychiatrist wanted to conduct a psychiatric interview and obtain her history to see if there was anything that was relevant to her legal problems. He explained that he was a confidential defense expert and everything they discussed would be confidential, unless he was called as a witness, or if her attorneys asked him to write a report.

Paula appeared to be confused and frightened.

She sobbed constantly and gave Maher the impression that she still didn't understand his role, and she was surprised that she could help prepare her defense.

Paula told him about her past experience, and for the past year or so "she was very confused and upset, and thought she was having a nervous breakdown. She didn't really know what to call it. And that nothing like this had ever happened to her before."

"I don't understand what happened," Paula sobbed. "When I think about the shooting, it doesn't seem real. It seems like a movie."

Paula looked terrified as she described her memory of the shooting. Frequently she switched topics, as if unable to focus. Paula alternated between talking rapidly and sitting mute and unresponsive. Maher noted that Paula "appeared to be extremely frightened" that Chino wanted her to kill herself. She still was afraid that he was going to kill her or make her kill herself.

"I know that's crazy," she said. "I'm pretty sure he's dead. But I keep hearing, 'One, two, three,' and then he tells me, 'We're going to kill ourselves. I'm gonna count to three and then we're gonna fire.'"

Sobbing almost hysterically, Paula said that Chino counted to three over and over and she didn't kill herself. Chino kept counting and she couldn't sleep. If she did go to sleep, the counting continued. "Chino yells at me. I don't understand what he's saying, but he's yelling at me."

"Well, do you hear him yelling at you now?" Maher asked.

"No, no, it's not that I hear him yelling at me now, but if I'm trying to sleep, or if I'm falling asleep, I hear that 'one, two, three' and then it seems like he's yelling at me. And I hear the shot sometimes."

Paula couldn't remember the shooting clearly, but it was still shocking to her. She told Maher that on the day of the robbery, she didn't believe Chino would hurt anyone.

"Do you understand why you're here in jail?" Maher asked.

"Yes, Chino killed that cop and because of the bank."

"Were you at the bank?"

"Yes."

Paula didn't remember what she did specifically at the bank. "That's going to be important for us to talk about," Maher told her. "We'll talk about it when I come to see you the next time."

Paula said she had been trying to get away from Chino, that he wanted her to kill herself, and she fully expected to do it. When she couldn't do it, Paula said, Chino offered to do it for her. She said there were a lot of problems between them.

"Problems between the two of you before this?" Maher asked.

"Oh yeah, it goes back a long way."

She told Maher that Chino made her do things she didn't want to do and threatened her if she didn't. "Well, he tried to get you to kill yourself before?" Maher asked.

"No, this is the first time that had happened. Sexually, he tried to force me to do things I didn't want to do."

Maher didn't pursue this area at the time because he hadn't heard about it before. There would be plenty of time to explore it later. The psychiatrist didn't delve into anything with great detail, since this was an orientation visit. Paula spilled out information as if it had been bottled up inside her, or she sat weeping, dazed, and unresponsive.

Maher found Paula "in a pretty erratic state" and was concerned about her ability to make sense. The primary purpose of the visit was evaluation, to meet her and the defense team, and to have the public defender say, "This is the doctor. We want you to talk to him."

"I was afraid of him before this," Paula said. "He hadn't tried to kill me before, but I was afraid of him. I thought I was going to die before he was shot. I'm afraid he's still gonna be able to get me to kill myself." Paula believed that Chino exercised power over her, even though she knew he was dead.

Maher believed that Paula was terrified of Chino on July 6, when he killed himself, and that she had been terrified for several months. Although Paula couldn't follow a train of thought in a logical manner, Maher believed that was temporary because of her emotional stress.

Paula was worried Chino could still hurt Ashley. She was afraid Chino would kill both Ashley and herself. Maher noted that Paula believed "there was some malevolent force" connected to Chino that could hurt her.

"You understand he died there?" Maher asked. "Do you understand that he's dead?"

"I know that," Paula answered. "They've told me that."

Even so, Maher left the interview with the feeling that Paula was in intense emotional and psychological denial. She was able to acknowledge partially that Chino was dead, but on an emotional level, she believed that he could still influence what happened. Her understanding that Chino was dead was impaired.

* * *

Officer John E. Romak took statements and gathered evidence immediately after the crime scene had been secured. Sherry Ann Williams told Romak that she had stepped onto her patio after hearing a helicopter directly overhead. Williams then heard six or eight gunshots nearby.

Williams ran back inside her apartment and leaned against the door. Someone shook the door violently from outside. Then she heard more gunshots and a bullet crashed through the door, just missing her. Terrified, she dropped to the floor, crawled to the telephone, and called 911 Emergency.

Just before she went into the closet for safety, Williams heard somebody outside yell, "Call an ambulance." She didn't see any police officers fire their weapons.

Next on Romak's list was Mark Kokojan, who related the events as he saw them. He told Romak that he had known Chino, Paula, and Ashley for about a year, but that they rarely spoke. Although they had been neighbors all that time, Kokojan didn't know Paula's name. However, he said, he could identify her.

The first time Kokojan saw Paula on the day of the shooting was when "she appeared very nervous and scared and was in a hurry" to use his telephone. He identified Chino as the man who ran up, snatched his keys, tried to steal his car, and then shot Officer Marrero.

* * *

Romak's report noted that Chino started to fire at Lois when he saw her approaching. He wrote that Chino fired at least three shots and Lois fell toward her right. Kokojan didn't know whether Lois was hit or not, but he dived under his car for cover. Kokojan didn't know whether or not there were any more shots.

When the shooting stopped, Romak wrote, Kokojan crawled from beneath his car and was sitting on the ground when he noticed that Chino was still there. For a chilling moment their eyes locked. Chino seemed to be scared before he turned and ran toward the apartment building. Romak wrote that Kokojan saw the gunman run after Paula, who was already headed toward the apartment building. When Kokojan stood, Romak said, he saw Lois's body on the ground, with blood all around her.

Shortly afterward, Romak's report stated, a second woman police officer arrived. Kokojan, who had gotten inside his car, opened the window and asked if he could help. The officer told him to stay inside his car and to lock the door. Romak reported that Kokojan said he could identify Paula and Chino.

Police obtained a search warrant to search and seize property found on Chino's body. This was a list of everything he had:

- MAC-11 machine pistol Cobray SWD Corp brand
- One 30-round magazine for the above-described machine pistol
- 13 live 9mm caliber bullets
- One black nylon strap that was attached (to the gun)

- One clear drinking glass
- One black Panasonic cordless telephone
- One clear plastic Ziploc bag
- One blue Bic lighter
- One torn note written by the deceased
- One Glock 9mm pistol (previously the issued property of Officer Lois Marrero)
- One magazine for the above-described Glock pistol and 18 live 9mm bullets
- Two pieces of bone fragments
- Ninety-five dollars in United States currency, with varying quantities of red dye upon them
- One pair of gray pajama bottoms

Officer Luis R. Adan, of the forensic unit, took Horst Gunther Albrecht's statement. Albrecht had seen part of the foot chase, and he had witnessed the shooting. He said he could positively identify Paula and Chino.

Adan talked to Jessica Alfaro and her daughter, Jessica De Nobrega, at their apartment. They told him they heard shooting, and that bullets flew by them as they huddled on the floor for safety.

During his investigation Adan found that a window screen, glass, and blinds had been shot. There were several pieces of lead near a dresser, where the bullet apparently had disintegrated on impact. Adan noted that the bullets probably came from Chino's gun when he fired in the parking lot. Had anyone been standing by the dresser, they could have been hit easily.

Adan marked all of the evidence as exhibits and then went outside into the courtyard. He saw "numerous" shell casings littering the breezeway by the stairs leading to Chino and Paula's apartment. Adan found a large number of bullet fragments and casings on the second-floor landing. He started to mark them with crime scene tape, but switched to numbered evidence markers.

The number of bullet fragments and empty shell casings found made it almost miraculous that more people hadn't been shot. Bullets and shrapnel from large-caliber weapons were everywhere—in apartment doors, doorjambs, inside apartments, in the inside and outside walls, and embedded in the floors beneath carpeting.

A blue-and-gray sports slipper belonging to Isaac Davis was found on the landing.

Adan, armed with a search warrant, entered Isaac Davis's apartment, where Paula and Chino had held Davis hostage and kept police at bay. Adan found a handwritten note that had been torn up and tossed into a kitchen garbage can with miscellaneous trash. Athan pieced the note together on the floor and read it: "Mamacita, I love you so much! Please forgive us for messing up! Mami, I will miss you."

This was the note that Paula had written for her mother when she thought she was going to commit suicide or be killed by Chino.

There was a black Panasonic telephone in the apartment with four messages asking Chino to call back. At least two of them were from his mother. The other callers weren't identified. Athan entered the bedroom and found the Glock lying on the bed. He noted the serial number. "I unloaded this firearm at approximately 2015 hours and observed that a round was inside of the chamber," Adan wrote in his report. "The magazine was fully loaded with seventeen Winchester 9mm Luger rounds with silver shells and jacketed hollow point projectiles."

A fragment of a human skull was found a few feet from Chino's body, which was slumped to the right against a wall outside the bedroom. The MAC-11 was removed from Chino's body. There was a live round in the chamber and twelve rounds in the magazine. Adan's team bagged and marked everything for evidence.

Detective J. D. Tindall, of homicide, took a statement from Laura Kent, who had made a 911 call reporting Lois's shooting. The detective wanted to gather information while everything was still fresh in Kent's memory. They reviewed the information she had reported to 911 and Tindall probed for additional details.

Kent told how she had seen them run into the cemetery, then head back. She added details that she had not given to the emergency operator. Chino ran underneath her second-floor balcony, Kent said, followed by Lois. Lois stopped and looked up at Kent.

"Which way did he go?" Lois asked.

"'That way,'" Kent had said, pointing to the building next to her. "It seemed to happen so fast. Before I knew anything, he had a gun pulled out and he was shooting at her and she had fallen."

Kent described the cars they were near in the parking lot. She said that Chino walked rapidly toward Lois, then stopped and shot her. Tindall asked her to describe the gun.

"I never expected to ever in my whole life, ever see anybody get shot," she said. "And on TV you see it like machine guns, but it looked like a fake gun. It looked real short and small, but it looked like a machine gun pretty much."

Tindall asked Kent to give a detailed description of Chino. The description given by all of the eyewitnesses was the same, and would be important at trial in proving that Chino was the killer. Tindall asked Kent to describe the woman coming down the stairs after Chino took Kokojan's car keys.

Kent told the detective that she was either white or Hispanic, eighteen to nineteen years old, about five feet six inches tall and weighed around 115 pounds, with long brown hair. She was wearing a camouflage shirt. She described the shooting and how she ran back inside her apartment and called 911.

"I grabbed the phone and called nine-one-one," Kent said. "I sat right there, crouched down, and looked out the window to see what was going on.

"I was pretty much freaking out at the time because I was crying and upset," Kent continued. "Like, my kid and my brother was there and they wanted to watch. But I didn't want them to. The operator on the phone was trying to get me to calm down and I was trying to explain what was going on."

"Did you see any other police officers fire at this individual who had the gun?" Tindall asked. "Or any of those people?"

"I never saw anyone. . . . After I had seen her lying there, and the operator had asked me if she was alive, I told her that I didn't think so because she . . . looked lifeless. . . . I told her that I saw another officer over her crying hysterically. She told me to stay away from the window."

Tindall asked her if it appeared that Paula and Chino were together.

"Yes. It . . . I mean, if I were to walk out and see that (shooting), I wouldn't just stand there. I would have ran or had some shock in my face, where they just kind of looked like it was expected."

Kent said she could identify Chino but wasn't sure about Paula because she didn't get a good look at her. Earlier, Kent had given a description of Paula to the police. Perhaps, after all of the stress and danger, she was less certain. "There was tons of cop cars out there," she said. "There was fire trucks. There was ambulances, helicopters, SWAT teams."

Kent said, "This is just something you don't expect, you know. Especially in your own front yard."

Chapter 15

Lissette Santiago, Chino's mother, told a reporter a day after her son's suicide that she was "shocked" at Paula's involvement in an armed robbery and the shooting of a police officer.

"I would expect that from my son because he was angry at the world," Santiago said. "But her? No way. She was very delicate. Shy. Like a piece of glass."

Mark Ober, state attorney for the Thirteenth Judicial Circuit—usually referred to as the Hillsborough County state attorney (SA)—was getting a much different picture. Ober's investigation led him to think that far from being a shrinking violet, Paula was manipulative, greedy, and was an equal partner in both robberies.

"Paula is all about money," Raymond Caraballo, a former friend of Santiago's told Ober. "She was constantly nagging him for things." As for Chino, Caraballo said, "He wanted everything yesterday."

The state charged Paula with two counts of armed robbery and one count of first-degree murder. Although Paula didn't fire a weapon, Ober said the law was clear on the murder charge: "The statutes say that anyone who commits a felony where someone is killed is guilty of murder, whether they pull the trigger or not."

The state attorney didn't buy into the scenario of Paula being brainwashed, or under so much duress that she couldn't resist Chino. Quite the opposite. He believed she goaded Chino into robbery because she wanted more than his paycheck could provide. Neither did Ober believe Paula's claim that Chino beat her.

"Detective Gene Black interviewed Paula right after her arrest," he said. "Chino was dead. If she had been abused, that would have been the time for her to say, 'He beat the hell out of me.' She didn't say anything like that. Everything she said was for her own self-interests."

Ober thought that Paula's behavior before Chino's suicide belied her claim of being terrorized by him. Ober had watched it on the police television-telephone. "Before he committed suicide, she kissed him on the lips and called him 'Sweetie,' her pet name for him," he said. "There was no indication that she was afraid of him."

Ober hired a detective to find out what problems Chino had at the last job he held. The former employer was kinder to Chino than Paula, who said he didn't want to work. The man who fired him said different. Raymond Suitt, owner of Building Services Network, said that Chino was a good worker until the time he quit without notice. Suitt said he was aware of "marital problems" Chino was having with Paula, whom Chino referred to as his wife.

Chino told Suitt that "Paula always wanted something he couldn't afford on his salary." Paula also wanted to live in New York, Chino said, and would take all of his money and go there. Suitt loaned Chino money when Paula did this, he said, and noted that Chino always paid him back promptly.

This was a much different perspective on Chino's character than Paula described. Ober tended to believe the former employer's version.

The state attorney was not easily swayed by appearances. During his career he had tried more than three hundred capital crimes as both a prosecutor and defense attorney. Even so, he believed it might be difficult to find a jury that would look at Paula without being influenced by her appearance.

"She's this tiny, sweet-looking woman," he said. "She looks more like an elementary-school kid than an adult. It's hard to reconcile what she did with how she looks."

Pruner's concern was not without cause. Although Paula was five feet six inches, her thin, well proportioned body gave her an appealing, waiflike appearance. Paula's curly dark hair, soft brown eyes and sweet expression made her seem innocent and vulnerable.

Ober chose Jay Pruner, assistant state attorney (ASA), who prosecuted only first-degree murder cases. In 2001, Pruner won twelve convictions in just four months. Known as "the prosecutor who sends killers to prison," Pruner was given the Outstanding Advocacy Award in capital cases by the Florida Prosecuting Attorneys Association. The defense would be up against the best prosecutorial team that Tampa had to offer.

It's hard to imagine two people more unlike than Ober and Deeann Athan. Ober is six feet four inches and built like a Bradley tank. Athan is petite, barely breaking the five-foot barrier, and she has a hummingbird-like energy. Athan wouldn't want to be a prosecutor and Ober, having been a defense attorney, chose to be a prosecutor. Ober had been a university law professor while Athan taught junior high school.

The one thing they had in common was love for the law. Although they were on opposite sides in the courtroom, they liked and respected one another.

Athan graduated from law school in 1983 and went to work as a prosecutor "for the blink of an eye." After being with the state attorney for six months, she went into private practice. She practiced general law, but concentrated on criminal defense and family law. She later worked in appellate law, but was burned out after nine years.

Athan's children were young and she was working long hours and couldn't devote as much time to them as she wanted. Athan went on vacation following a six-month trial in federal court only to return and find that she was held in contempt of court for missing a hearing to show cause.

Athan thought she had arranged for another lawyer to stand in for her. She said it was a nightmare. After that, she lost all desire to do appellate work. One day she had lunch with the public defender and asked for a job. She was immediately hired. She swore she would never try homicide cases. "I didn't like the thought of dealing with someone's death," she said. "But, as it turns out, those are really the most interesting cases, plus your clients are the most in need of someone looking after their interests."

Dr. Maher, who ventured inside the Orient Road Jail again on July 16 to continue Paula's psychological eval-

uation, discovered that she was still frightened of
Chino and hearing his voice. She was still under a suicide watch, and in addition to the antipsychotic drug
Trilafon, an antidepressant (Pamelor) and antianxi-
ety medication (Visiril) had been prescribed.

"She is very anxious," he said. "I think [she] probably would have qualified for a diagnosis of adjustment disorder when she became pregnant with her
daughter, Ashley." There was no diagnosis or treatment at that time, he noted, but her condition still
improved. Maher determined that the condition
had returned and Paula suffered from adjustment
disorder for at least a couple of months.

In psychological terms an adjustment disorder
occurs when a person develops emotional or behav-
ioral symptoms in response to a stressful situation.
Stressors can be anything that causes duress. Maher
believed that in Paula's case it was caused by abuse
from Chino. A patient with adjustment disorder is
depressed, and her ability both to think clearly and
to concentrate are impaired. A person who has the
symptoms for more than six months often has an
anxiety or mood disorder.

Maher believed that Paula suffered from post-
traumatic stress disorder, a recognized psychiatric illness. Some of the symptoms Paula displayed were
anxiety, difficulty sleeping, excessive worry, feelings
of being trapped or being unable to escape her situation, nightmares, and depression. Under the right
circumstances, he said, anyone can develop PTSD.

A diagnosis for PTSD is reached by identifying anything in a patient's life that causes enough stress or
trauma to form the base for the disorder. If there is
enough stress to cause anxiety and make a patient
relive an event, and if there is a relationship between

those and a mood disorder, the patient meets the criteria for a diagnosis of PTSD.

Maher believed that Paula suffered from battered spouse syndrome, a psychological disorder that is a subset of PTSD. BSS is associated with the consistent abuse of one person by another, usually within a marriage or an exclusive relationship. The abuse has to be severe enough to cause psychological and emotional disorders. From the way Paula said Chino abused her, she easily fit into a diagnosis of BSS. Maher thought Paula suffered from PTSD and BSS at least as far back as the robbery at Flowers By Patricia.

Paula was of average intelligence, Maher noted, but said she showed intellectual inconsistency. Maher believed Paula's psychological problems began when she became pregnant with Ashley. Paula was anxious and depressed, Maher said, because she believed herself too immature to care for a child, and she had doubts as to whether or not Chino would help out.

Up until then, he said, Paula seemed to adjust to the stresses of being sent back to Colombia and her first pregnancy and subsequent abortion. She went "a little overboard" in high school, experimenting with sex and drugs. Paula felt like she didn't "fit in" when she returned from Colombia, and she was angry with her parents for sending her away.

Paula told Maher how she met Chino, and how she liked it that he always had pot and money. During the interview Maher asked Paula if Chino was her first love.

"I still love him," she said, and then broke down and wept. "I know that doesn't make any sense. He's dead, and the terrible things that happened. It doesn't make sense, but I still love him."

Paula told Maher how the relationship with Chino had started off well, but deteriorated into

The inside of Flowers By Patricia, the scene of Chino and Paula's first robbery. *(Courtesy of the Tampa Police Department)*

The tape Chino used to bind Catherine Haddad during the flower shop robbery. *(Courtesy of the Tampa Police Department)*

After having her hands and legs restrained by duct tape, Catherine Haddad was left in the flower shop cooler. *(Courtesy of The Tampa Tribune)*

Paula *(standing)* wields the Mac 11 while employees and customers are forced to lie face down at the Bank of America. *(Courtesy of the Tampa Police Department)*

Chino *(wearing hat at upper left)* searches for cash during the robbery at the Bank of America. *(Courtesy of the Tampa Police Department)*

Officer Lois Marrero. *(Courtesy of the Tampa Police Department)*

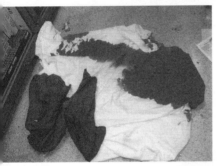

The blood-stained undershirt worn by Officer Lois Marrero. The fatal bullet struck her just above her protective vest. *(Courtesy of the Tampa Police Department)*

The radio that fell from Lois Marrero's hand when Chino killed her. *(Courtesy of the Tampa Police Department)*

This SUV was used in both robberies.
(Courtesy of the Tampa Police Department)

Stained cash litters the street after Chino threw it away when a dye pack exploded. *(Courtesy of the Tampa Police Department)*

The Crossings apartment complex where Chino and Paula holed up with hostage Isaac Davis and held police at bay for more than three hours. *(Courtesy of the Tampa Police Department)*

Bullets fired by Chino slammed into the police car driven by Officer Gary Metzger when he pulled up to The Crossings apartment complex. *(Courtesy of the Tampa Police Department)*

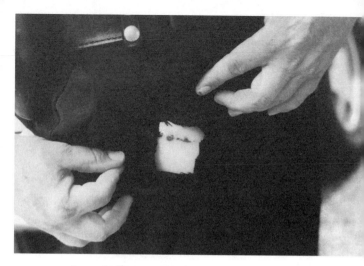

Chino's bullet grazed Officer Cole Scudder's thigh.
(Courtesy of the Tampa Police Department)

Members of a SWAT team hold a position during the hostage
stand-off. *(Courtesy of* The Tampa Tribune*)*

Detective Roberto Batista negotiated with Chino and Paula for almost three hours in an attempt to prevent further bloodshed. *(Courtesy of the Tampa Police Department)*

Chino's slumped body after he killed himself during a hostage stand-off with police. *(Courtesy of the Tampa Police Department)*

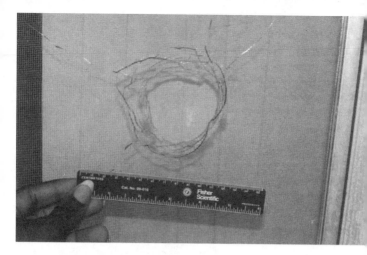

A forensic technician measures a bullet hole in a window at Sherry Williams's apartment. *(Courtesy of the Tampa Police Department)*

Bullet casings litter the walkway at The Crossings. *(Courtesy of the Tampa Police Department)*

Rubber gloves lie on a bathroom counter where Paula tried to clean red dye from cash robbed from the Bank of America. *(Courtesy of the Tampa Police Department)*

The 9mm Glock that Paula took from murdered police officer Lois Marrero. *(Courtesy of the Tampa Police Department)*

A fully-loaded magazine for Chino's Mac 11, which he used in two robberies and to kill Officer Lois Marrero.
(Courtesy of the Tampa Police Department)

After Chino killed himself, the Mac 11, magazine, 9mm round, and shoulder strap lay splattered with blood. *(Courtesy of the Tampa Police Department)*

A note that Paula wrote and tore up. It reads, "Mamacita, I love you so much! Please forgive us for messing up! We (heart) you! Mamacita, I will miss you!" *(Courtesy of the Tampa Police Department)*

Paula during a break in a police interview following her surrender. *(Courtesy of the Tampa Police Department)*

Public defender Deeann Athan fought hard for Paula.
(Author's photo)

Hillsborough County State Attorney Mark Ober led the prosecution in its case against Paula.
(Courtesy of the Tampa Police Department)

Paula hides her face after being taken into custody at The Crossings. *(Courtesy of* The Tampa Tribune*)*

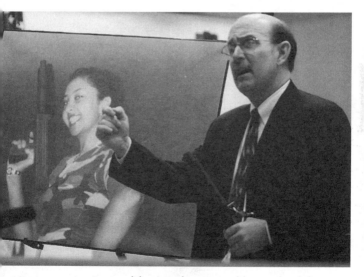

Prosecutor Jay Pruner delivers a devastating blow to the defense during Paula's trial. *(Courtesy of* The Tampa Tribune*)*

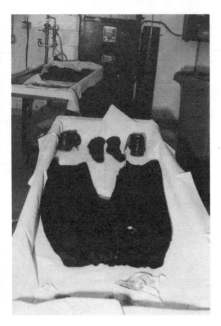

Chino's clothing on a morgue body tray.
(Courtesy of the Tampa Police Department)

Paula at Tampa Police Department headquarters after her arrest.
(Courtesy of the Tampa Police Department)

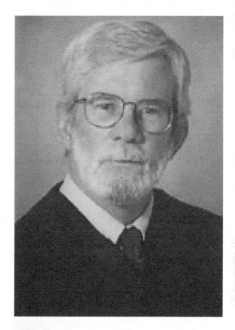

Circuit Court Judge J. Rogers Padgett presided over Paula's trial. *(Courtesy of the Hillsborough County Public Information Office)*

Mickie Mashburn struggles to keep her composure at Lois's funeral. *(Courtesy of The Tampa Tribune)*

A police honor guard carries the flag-draped casket containing the body of Lois Marrero. *(Courtesy of* The Tampa Tribune*)*

Police officers throughout Florida paid their last respects to their fallen comrade. *(Courtesy of* The Tampa Tribune*)*

abuse and control. She said she tried to get away from him.

"I told him I didn't want to see him anymore and that I didn't want him coming around," she said. "He would say, 'No, we're not going to break up.' Sometimes he grabbed me by the neck and said, 'I'll kill you if you leave me.' Then he knocked me down and ran away from me."

Paula told Maher about Chino's pattern of abusing her and then apologizing. But the apology always came with a condition: they would stay together.

Paula said she was worried and angry about not being able to break up with Chino. "I felt, 'Oh, my God, if I don't act right, if I don't do the right thing here, something really, really bad is going to happen,'" she said. "Maybe it's going to happen to me or maybe it's going to happen to him, or maybe it's going to happen to somebody else, but we're not playing games anymore."

Paula said she was relieved when Chino moved to Florida, but she missed him, too. "I was worried that he would show up at any moment," she said.

Maher noticed that Paula had trouble keeping the timeline straight. She jumped from one subject to the next, and thought it was because Chino was still trying to control and manipulate her.

During her teenage years, Maher said, Paula was "very immature and impulsive" and wanted adult privileges. But, he noted, "she never established herself as an independent adult. She was never self-supporting."

Paula had limited social skills, but "she knew how to flirt as a woman, and how to make herself attractive and appealing to men."

When Paula went to Florida in 1998, she wanted to maintain a platonic relationship with a friend named Felix, who lived in New York. This caused a conflict with Chino, but they stayed together four months in Tampa, and then went back to New York to live with Paula's parents. Luis, Paula's father, saw her kissing Chino and angrily told her to do that in private because it disrespected him.

"Who the hell are you to tell me what to do in relationships when you're cheating on my mother?" Paula responded angrily.

The argument represented a traumatic break with Paula's family and left her feeling uncertain about being able to rely on them, stay with them, or depend on them in the future.

At the jail Paula was frightened. She continued to hear voices and wasn't sure where they came from. Paula didn't understand why the deputies watched her all the time.

"They say that I killed a cop, that policewoman, that police lady," she said. "I don't understand. I didn't want anybody to die. I didn't kill anybody."

Paula wasn't certain why she was in jail. "I don't see how all this happened," she said. "It happened so fast. I knew Chino could get out of hand, but I never imagined it could be like this. Who are you?"

"I'm a doctor."

"Can you prescribe medicine for me?"

Maher told her no, but she asked several times.

The psychiatrist wanted to know about the bank robbery. He asked if she had shot anyone.

"No, I didn't shoot anybody," she said.

"Did Chino shoot her?"

"Well, I guess he had to. I didn't see him. Who else would have?"

Paula was concerned about their hostage. "What about Isaac?" she asked. "He didn't get hurt, did he?"

Paula rambled incoherently sometimes. Maher "definitely" concluded that she was an abused spouse and suffered from BSS, and that she was deeply depressed because of it. He believed Paula suffered from BSS for at least "a couple of months" before the flower shop robbery. Her emotional and psychological problems probably went back much farther.

Paula was sure she was going to die in the apartment before Chino killed himself.

"I believe that she was terrified of him at the time they were in the apartment together, where he killed himself, and for several months leading up to that," Maher said.

She became so accustomed to Chino pushing her around. "After a while, I didn't pay any attention to it," she said. "I didn't think it was abusive at the time." When Paula started to think more clearly, she said, she realized that this behavior was violent and abusive.

Paula said Chino thought she would marry him after she became pregnant. "He used the pregnancy to try to get me to marry him," she said. "'Now that you're pregnant, we're going to have a baby, we have to get married.'"

Paula refused. Marrying Chino, she said, would just make him more controlling. He would expect her to be even more obedient. Maher believed that Chino became angry whenever anyone challenged or contradicted him. If Paula wanted to be with other people, Chino became furious. Should Paula criticize him in any way, Chino hit the ceiling.

"He thought he was this big macho guy," she said, "and anything that didn't go along with that would set him off or upset him."

They argued in the Bronx, where he worked as an air-conditioning technician, that he wasn't a good provider for his wife and daughter. In response, Chino started to shoplift clothes for Paula and Ashley. Paula said she wanted him to stop, to earn money legitimately. She wanted to go back to school or to work, but Chino didn't want that. Paula said he had such a short fuse that she "walked on eggs" around him. "Things kept getting out of hand," she said.

He told her, "If you let go, baby, I'll hit you."

Following Ashley's birth, Paula didn't want to have sex, but she "went along with Chino to avoid trouble." When she moved to Florida in December 1999, she said she was miserable.

"I felt lonely and isolated. I cried a lot and I felt trapped, like there was no way out," she said. "I had a baby and Chino was the father, I felt like I was stuck with him forever, even though I wasn't married to him. I just decided to make the best of things and do whatever I could to make things okay."

At that time Ashley was the only positive thing in her life. She wondered what the future would be like for the baby, but put it out of her mind. She tried to focus on the present, hoping that Chino would change, become more mature, and they would have a normal life.

Paula told Maher about the fight they had after visiting the beach when her family was visiting. The fight went on for several days, she said, and she hit her head when Chino shoved her to the floor. He grabbed her by the throat and said, "I'm going to kill you."

Paula said she gave up all hope of Chino changing. She felt more discouraged, frightened, anxious, and had headaches and constant stomach pain. After Ashley was born, Paula had hoped things would be better with Chino. Now she felt more hopeless and trapped: she couldn't just leave because she had to take care of Ashley.

Paula sought refuge in marijuana. She mellowed out when she smoked and could sleep. But not for long. Chino got angry over nothing. He punched holes in the wall when he became angry with her. Melba, her mother, tried to convince Paula to leave Chino and come home. Paula said he grabbed Ashley and yanked her out of her seat: "You'll never take her away from me." Then he left, taking Ashley with him.

Paula said that she called the police. After police officers arrived, she told them what had happened, but they couldn't do anything because no crime was committed. He was the father, they told her, and he had a right to pick his baby up and take her.

Paula said she fled to New York several times. She hated their life together, but didn't hate Chino. If she could only change, she said, everything would be okay. If she could just do what Chino expected and be the person he wanted her to be, things would be okay.

Paula told Maher that she went to New York several times in 2000 because she was depressed and wanted to see her family. The visits were for two or three weeks at a time. Early 2001, Paula said, she felt so depressed and hopeless that it was difficult to take care of Ashley. Paula did the best she could, but still didn't feel good about herself.

During the first part of 2001, Paula believed, Chino was cheating on her. He stayed out late and tried to make connections with other women. Paula found that he had pornography from the Internet. Chino didn't approach her for sex as often. After discovering the pornography, Paula thought he might

have another woman. Paula said their fighting intensified, and Chino started to include Ashley in his
threats. "You'll never leave with Ashley," he said.
"I'll never let you have Ashley. You'll never take her
away from me."

Paula told Maher that Chino hit her harder and
more frequently. "I never knew what would set him
off," she said. "I tried so hard not to. I tried so hard
to avoid this, but you could just never tell what he
was going to do. Things were bad then and everything might have set him off."

Paula seemed confused at times. She said she lost
interest in sex. Then Paula said Chino didn't approach her for sex. She contradicted herself by
saying he approached often, and although she wasn't
interested, she always gave in. All the while, Paula
continued to blame herself for their problems. Her
emotions were in turmoil.

Paula had not been worried about Chino hurting
Ashley, but in early 2001, she feared that he would.
Paula said she couldn't get away from Chino and
couldn't protect herself from him. How could she
behave so that he wouldn't beat her? Paula didn't
understand why he would beat her in the first place,
since she wasn't doing anything wrong.

Paula said the robberies occurred because Chino
lost his job for stealing a check. They were broke, had
bills to pay, and no food for themselves or the baby.
Paula said she was scared when Chino told her to get
in the car—they were going to get some money.
Since she had known him, Chino had talked about
getting money through criminal activity. Chino
bragged to her, "I can get money whenever I want
it." Paula believed Chino was planning to rob a drug
dealer.

Paula knew that Chino was a shoplifter, but she liked the things he got for Ashley and the house. She made no comment about the things Chino stole for her. But maybe there was more to what he did than shoplifting, she thought.

Paula described the flower shop robbery, and indicated that she was an unwilling participant. She said it surprised her when he threatened the saleslady. Did she think of not participating? Maher asked. "No, he told me I had to be there and I felt I had to stay there with him."

Paula's auditory hallucinations continued to haunt her in spite of the psychotropic medicines that she took. In addition, she heard Chino tell her he was sorry, and then she heard him laugh at her. The bed shook, she said, and the entire room turned green.

The medical staff at the jail reported that she suffered from "major depression."

Maher saw Paula again on August 1, 2001. "Patient interviewed briefly in her cell," he noted. "Crying uncontrollably. Some of her speech is garbled secondary to crying. She makes eye contact and then asked the interviewer his name. Alert, oriented, and *extremely* anxious." The symptoms Paula experienced, Maher said, "go beyond normal feelings of being in jail."

On the day of the bank robbery, Paula said, she didn't know what was going on; she just did what Chino told her to do.

Maher asked, "Were you going to threaten people or hold the gun on people or that kind of thing?"

"Pretty much. I don't know. I don't remember. He told me I was going to hold the gun, so I held the gun."

She didn't think about refusing. "I just did what he told me to do. I wasn't thinking about anything.

I wasn't thinking about that. I wasn't thinking about what I could do. He said I needed to hold the gun and go in the bank, so that's what I did."

Maher noted that people who are experiencing great fear have a sense of numbness and indifference to their environment. He believed that was Paula's situation throughout the day of the bank robbery, and probably for a few weeks before that.

"She was scared all the time," he said. "She was afraid of what he was going to do next. She was afraid of being hit or other violent acts against her. It was a culmination of all the things he had done before, smacking her, hitting her, pushing her, beating her up in some way or another. She was terrified because he was angry about the dye pack exploding. She was doing everything she could to keep it from getting worse."

Paula was able to give only fuzzy details of the robberies and the shootings. Maher said it was because she was in a "disassociative state of mind. Disassociative state is a condition where some aspects of the brain function are either disconnected from other elements of brain functioning," Maher continued, "or are in some way put on hold and don't work at all. A person in a disassociative state may be able to process information of an emotionally meaningful character, but not have any idea what their feelings are about it. Alternatively, they may experience overwhelming feelings that they can only describe in the most primary and basic terms without saying why or what it is related to [in] the events that caused them to have those feelings."

Maher was "very certain" that Paula was suffering from a memory disturbance. Paula suffered from "overwhelming duress" because of psychological and emotional effects of BSS during both robberies and the shooting, he said. Paula displayed classic symptoms of this psychological disorder. Paula wasn't malingering—pretending that she was mentally unstable—or the jail's doctor would not have prescribed the antidepressant Trilafon.

Maher found that Paula's psychological condition had "deteriorated significantly" when he interviewed her again, on July 30. He said that Paula was "agitated and distressed." Paula's voice sounded as if she were on the verge of hysteria, and her body language was that of a frightened person. The chanting, music, and voices were constant. She couldn't understand what the voices said, but it was frightening.

"It just seems like there's a bad spirit, something bad, something evil that's connected to all of this," she said. Everything that had happened seemed to crash in on her. "I'm sorry for what happened," she said. "I'm sorry that Chino died and sorry the police officer died. I'm thinking about this all of the time. In spite of everything, I still love Chino."

Paula's feelings for Chino weren't unusual, Maher noted. A battered spouse often mourned the loss of a relationship, even though they were abused.

Paula talked for the first time about how the abuse had been a part of sex with Chino. "He forced me to have sex," she said. "It aroused him when I cried. Sometimes he would strangle me for his sexual pleasure. He told me that I liked it. I kept telling him I didn't, but he said I did. After a while, I stopped thinking about it and just heard him telling me that I liked it."

Paula said she was in the bedroom crying after

Chino beat her. "He would come with a hard-on and just do it," she said. "He would strangle me until all I could see was like tunnel vision. He would do it until I passed out."

Paula told Maher that Chino forced her to have sex with him. Maher said Paula didn't realize that she was being raped. "It was very clear she didn't want to have sex with him," Maher said. "She thought it would have been clear to him because she was crying and upset. She thought that her crying was sexually stimulating to him."

Five months after Paula was arrested, Maher noticed a marked change in her.

"Most people look worse after being in jail," he said. "Paula looked better. She had gained weight, she made eye contact more often, and even smiled once when she was talking about Ashley. It was from living in a safe environment without abuse."

The voices had stopped by then, but Paula continued to hear "scary sounds." But they weren't as frightening as before.

Paula was concerned that Chino was being presented in a bad light. "We're always saying these bad things about Chino," she said. "Deep down, he was a good person. He did a lot of positive things."

In the next breath Paula told Maher that Chino threatened to kill her and her parents. Her ambivalence showed in other ways. "I stayed with him because I was afraid to leave," she said. "But when I did leave, I came back because I thought I loved him and could help him change."

Maher said Paula's contradictions were consistent with BSS. The psychological duress she lived with, the psychiatrist said, made it impossible for her to think like a reasonable person. Paula had been conditioned to take everything Chino wanted as an order, Maher said.

Chapter 16

The facts for Paula's prosecution were indisputable: she held a gun while the Bank of America was robbed; was with Chino when Flowers By Patricia was robbed; she was present when Chino shot and killed Officer Lois Marrero; she was with Chino when Isaac Davis was taken hostage.

Even though these facts seemed obvious, the state still had to prove it beyond a reasonable doubt. Ober and Pruner also had to anticipate how to counter the defense. What the defense wanted was to show that Paula was not guilty because she was under duress from BSS and that Lois was killed after the felony ended.

As Pruner said previously, a person who helps commit a felony is guilty of murder if murder is committed during the felony. The law is a little tricky. It states that if a person committing a felony has found a "temporary safe haven," even momentarily, then the felony is over. Whether or not Paula had reached a safe haven before Lois was killed was a major point for both the defense and prosecution.

The defense contended that Paula had reached a safe haven when Lissette dropped her and Chino off at their apartment in the Crossings. They had showered, changed clothes, and Paula thought it was finished. The state would try to prove that the pursuit of the robbers began while the robbery was in progress and was ongoing when Lois was killed.

A timeline for both the defense and prosecution would be critical to their cases.

Using BSS as a defense was problematic. Prosecutors often call it the "he didn't deserve to live" defense. In most successful BSS defenses, the battered spouse killed the person who battered her. Paula didn't do that, but the defense wanted to show how the emotional and psychological duress she suffered prevented her from defying Chino.

The state also intended to show that Paula was not a meek or passive participant in the crimes with which she was charged. Ober and Pruner believed that Paula was fully aware of what she did, and that she had actually goaded Chino into committing the crimes. They wanted to show her as greedy, a liar, and a manipulator.

While depositions were being taken, a blizzard of paper was flying to the Thirteenth Judicial Circuit Court, where the trial would be presided over by Judge Rogers Padgett. A motion was made for a change of venue to move the trial outside Tampa. The defense argued that emotions were inflamed, there had been too much media coverage, and that Paula could not receive a fair trial. The motion was denied.

A gag order, to keep court officers from speaking to the press about the case, was struck down after a challenge by several newspapers and television stations.

Sometimes depositions taken by the state seemed to help the defense, while defense depositions sometimes bolstered the prosecution. Lissette Santiago,

Chino's mother, was deposed by Athan, with Pruner conducting the cross-examination.

Santiago presented Chino as being headstrong, always wanting his own way, and that she was afraid of him. On the other hand, she indicated that it was Paula who tried to isolate Chino, not the other way around.

"Chino, Paula, and Ashley pretty much kept to themselves," Santiago said. "At the beginning, when they came down here, Chino was okay, you know. Then Paula came down with the baby."

In the beginning, Santiago said, Paula tried to isolate her from Chino and Ashley. "I couldn't spend time with Ashley because Paula didn't want me to," Santiago said.

"What did Chino have to say about it?" Athan asked.

"Chino used to say, 'Ma, Paula doesn't want you in the apartment.'"

Paula stayed home to take care of Ashley most of the time, until Lissette helped Chino buy a new Xterra SUV because Paula wanted to get out of the house. Rather than being ordered to stay in the house, Santiago said, Paula went regularly to a health club after Chino bought her a membership. Chino was almost "obsessive," she said, about keeping the Xterra clean for Paula.

Neither was Chino as poor a provider as Paula claimed, Santiago said. She noted that he made $30,000 in 2000, a good income for Tampa; furthermore, she said, he didn't have to pay rent.

Despite the fact the Lissette provided the apartment Paula lived in free of charge, Santiago said Paula tried to keep her from visiting.

"I couldn't spend time with Ashley because Paula didn't want me to," Santiago said. Chino deferred to Paula, Pruner noted, contrary to her contention that Chino dominated *her*. Paula had convinced Chino, Santiago said, that she wasn't to be trusted to take care of Ashley.

"I got to see Ashley, but I had to see her when they were here," she said. "Like, if I wanted to take her out, they wouldn't let me. They wouldn't leave her with me if they went out, they took Ashley. I said, 'Leave the baby with me.' They wouldn't. She didn't trust me. She told me, 'I don't trust you with my baby.'"

The theme that dominated was that Paula was in control, not Chino. She was the one who determined what they did, not him. This was strengthened as Santiago's deposition continued. Santiago said that once they got the Xterra, Paula wanted her to take care of Ashley.

Santiago picked Ashley up in the morning and kept her almost all day. The little girl walked with her around the four properties where Santiago worked. Santiago loved having her granddaughter with her as she went from job to job.

It seemed from Santiago's deposition that Paula tried to separate Chino and his mother as soon as she arrived in Tampa. "I saw my son every day because he worked for me," Santiago said. "Paula didn't like me very much because I was close to Chino. Paula was very unfriendly. She didn't speak to me."

Paula's contention that Chino made her avoid speaking and making eye contact with anyone was also challenged. "She didn't talk to nobody," Lissette said. "She looked around, but was quiet. Paula's been that way since I've known her."

Santiago also maintained that it was Paula who went into jealous rages, not Chino, even though he was possessive, too. "He came to me one day with a twelve-pack and he said to me, 'Ma, let's drink. We've got to talk.' I said, 'Fine.'"

Paula was angry with him, Santiago said, because she found a telephone number in the van. Paula assumed it was a girlfriend's number. "She started arguing with him, saying there was another girl," Santiago said. "She was very jealous. That's why he wanted a couple of drinks." Santiago said Paula was always jealous of Chino. "Like, my friends talk to him, my girlfriends, and stuff like that," Santiago said. "She used to get jealous."

Instead of being submissive, Santiago said, Paula baited Chino into getting angry. She would push him until he exploded. Santiago testified that was why Chino knocked so many holes in the walls with his fist. "She was pushing him to a certain point and [he] didn't want to hit her, you know," Santiago said. "So he hit the wall and walked off."

In March 2001, about four months before the robberies, Santiago testified that Paula and Chino had a fight that resulted in Paula getting a black eye. She asked Chino about it, and he said that he had slapped Paula's face.

"I told her she can't take that from him," Santiago said. "It could be anything, but don't hit her. I don't go for that. You don't hit a woman. Because look at his size compared to her. I mean, she's so small."

After this fight, Santiago said, Paula telephoned and asked her to stop by. She found Paula in the bedroom with Ashley. Paula was crying and packing her things because she wanted to go to New York. Santiago bought Paula a one-way ticket to New York, because she couldn't afford the return fare.

"She wanted to leave," Santiago said. "She didn't

want to come back. Chino came back before I took her to the airport, but they didn't speak."

Where was the helpless woman who was dominated by Chino? Pruner wondered. It seemed to him that Paula was in charge. Chino bought her a membership in a health club and a vehicle to get around in. Was that domination? And every time Paula went to New York, who paid for it? Chino or his mother always picked up the tab. The facts convinced them that Chino, far from dominating Paula, tried his best to do whatever would make her happy.

"Did you ever feel that Paula was under Nestor's control?" Athan asked.

"No."

"Never?"

"No."

Lissette testified that Chino was suicidal and that he wanted fast money. "He'd tell me, 'Ma, I'm going to rob a bank.' I said, 'Go ahead. I'll see you in jail.' I thought it was a joke."

Paula had said she wanted to work, but that Chino wouldn't let her. Santiago disputed this. "Paula didn't want to work, because they didn't want to leave Ashley with nobody," Santiago said. "Chino wanted her to work. When she came down here the first time, she told Chino she already had a job. That's why I gave him the money for her to come down."

Athan asked, "What kind of tastes did she have in personal items?"

"They wanted everything expensive, you know. All they wore were Polo and Tommy (Hilfiger), and stuff like that."

"Did she ever describe her tastes about Tommy or Polo?"

"Yes. A lot of times when something comes out, they get it."

"How about the clothing for Ashley?"

"Well, Ashley was The Gap. I'm not sure. Paula is the one that usually goes shopping."

Pruner cross-examined. "Since her (Paula's) arrest, she indicated that your son told you during the car ride that they had committed a bank robbery, and at that point, you became angry and started to chastise them, telling them it was stupid, asking them why they did that."

"When Chino called me on the phone and told me he had robbed a bank, yeah, I told him. I was screaming at him on the phone."

The inconsistencies in the testimony, police interviews and depositions mounted. Paula had said earlier that Chino told Lissette about the robbery while she drove them from the Regency to the Crossings. In a previous deposition, Lissette said she learned about the robbery from the Regency manager. The truth was as illusive as a coin in a carnival shell game.

Pruner turned his attention to the timeline to build his case that the pursuit after the robbery had not ended, and that Paula had not found even a momentary "safe haven."

"You picked them up at the Regency Apartments?" he asked.

Santiago said she did.

"How long did it take you before you dropped them off at the Crossings?"

"Well, it depends. Five minutes."

"Did you go straight down Kennedy?"

"Kennedy, yeah, and then I turned on Church."

Pruner backtracked to when Chino had called Santiago from the Regency and established that it took her about ten minutes to get there. The ASA had no further questions. He had established that only fifteen minutes had passed between the time Chino telephoned his mother and she dropped them off at the Crossings.

Ashley. Think about Ashley.

Concern about what would happen to her daughter was what kept Paula from killing herself. Now Chino was dead and Paula was in jail. What was to happen to Ashley?

Santiago, who had kept the little girl with her almost every day, had no legal right to be Ashley's guardian. For several weeks Ashley stayed with her. Santiago visited Paula in jail frequently, and Paula, who had never liked her, started to become friendly with Chino's mother. Santiago wanted to raise Ashley, but a custody dispute arose between her and Paula's parents.

Deeann Athan, Paula's attorney, noticed that this changed the nature of testimony given by Chino's relatives. Before the custody dispute, Athan found that they supported her contention that Paula was battered by Chino. This changed after the custody dispute.

"They were testifying for the defense," Athan said. "They were talking about how violent, domineering, and abusive Nestor (Chino) was. After the custody dispute, I found witnesses I thought were defense witnesses turning up on the state's witness list."

Athan, who felt that the cards were already stacked against Paula, was particularly upset about testimony for the state to be given by one of Chino's relatives. She said to Mark Ober, "If you bring him in to testify, I'll impeach him with his deposition." The state dropped the prospective witness.

Paula's mother was granted custody of Ashley. She adopted the little girl and took her to live in New York—but not in the big city. She had lost one child to its temptations and wasn't about to lose Ashley the same way.

On April 9, 2003, Judge Padgett struck Athan's motion to use battered spouse syndrome as a defense. She resubmitted it on April 14. The judge took it under advisement.

The hearing on April 9 was to hear Athan's motion to suppress Paula's interview with Detective Black following her arrest on July 6, 2001. Athan maintained that the confession to the bank robbery was made without an attorney being present to represent Paula.

Patricia Turpin, assistant state attorney, conducted the direct examination. Black identified an audiotape of the interview and said Paula signed a Miranda consent form stating she understood her rights. After having the tape entered into evidence, Turpin received permission from the court to play parts of it.

On the tape Black identified himself, other law enforcement officers present, and Paula. "We're gonna read you your constitutional rights," Black said on the tape. "You have the right to remain silent. Do you understand that?"

"Yes," Paula answered.

Paula said she understood that anything she said could be used against her in court, and that she had a right to talk to a lawyer before answering any questions. Paula affirmed that she understood all of her rights, and that she could invoke them at any time.

A section of the tape that Athan considered crucial to her motion to strike was played.

Paula said, "Um, I don't know. I've never been in this situation. I don't know if I should talk to a lawyer first."

"If you wish, you can," Black said. "We mentioned that. If you wanted to talk with one, you have that opportunity."

"Yeah, I wanna cooperate, but I don't really— I don't wanna go to jail."

"Well, you know, the point of going to jail is on the basis of evidence. . . . You have to make that decision. I can't make it for you. You know, I'm not going to lie to you. There's a possibility you will go to jail . . . but you would go to jail even if you didn't talk to us right now, okay?"

"Do you have a lawyer here?"

"No, we don't have one here," Black said. "That's the only problem."

"Okay. I'll go with it."

Judge Padgett interrupted. "Are we going to listen to the whole interview?"

"No, Your Honor," Turpin replied. "There is just a little more that will be important."

On the tape Paula told Black a little about her background and said she had not used drugs or alcohol in the past twenty-four hours. Paula said she had not been hit in the head or experienced anything else that would impair her memory.

Turpin questioned Black when the tape session concluded. The detective said he had not coerced or intimidated Paula. Turpin noted the "significant" pause from the time he told her there were no lawyers available and her agreeing to continue. Why was that? Turpin asked.

"Because I didn't want her to think that I wanted her to answer either way," Black said. "I wanted to do what she wanted to do. . . . There was no intent on my part to intimidate her. . . ."

The detective testified that Paula wanted to cooperate. Then Turpin entered the Miranda documents that Paula had signed into evidence.

On cross-examination Athan reviewed the traumas that Paula experienced during the hours before she was interviewed. Specifically, Athan mentioned the bank robbery, the escape, the dye pack explosion, being a few feet away when Lois was killed, a shoot-out with police, breaking into Isaac Davis's apartment and taking him hostage, Chino trying to convince her to take her life before he shot himself in the head.

"As soon as he's (Chino) dead, she's coming out the door with her hands up, right?" Athan asked.

"Yes."

"So knowing all that she's been through that day," Athan said, "you must have had some concerns as to her mental state . . . as well?"

Black said there was some concern, but that Paula did "quite well."

Athan wanted him to discuss Paula's demeanor. "She sounds a little meek on the tape," she said. "Would you agree with that?"

"Oh, definitely, yes."

Black said he realized that the interview was Paula's first experience with the police. Athan showed him a copy of the form Paula had signed consenting to the interview. Black identified it as a standard form used by the TPD.

Athan received permission to approach the witness. "On the top of that form, it's got a check mark, 'Consent to be interviewed concerning an offense of,' and then there's a blank line," Athan noted.

"Right."

"And nothing has been filled in that blank?"

Black agreed.

"Isn't it the usual custom for police officers, detectives, to fill in the offense for which they're interrogating the suspect . . . ?" Athan asked.

"It's optional, but normally it is filled in."

Athan asked Black why it was left blank. The detective said he didn't know what the charges against Paula would be, or even if she *would* be charged. Athan attacked that position.

"You're telling Ms. Gutierrez . . . that we want information," she asked. "Is that what you said?"

"Yes, in regard to specific items; one, the bank robbery, and, two, the death of Officer Marrero."

"You're saying . . . you hadn't decided whether or not she was going to be arrested for any of that?"

"It's not my decision," Black said. "It's the state attorney's decision."

"But Ms. Gutierrez was . . . in custody?"

Black said yes, and admitted that Paula was handcuffed when she was arrested and taken to police headquarters. The handcuffs were removed when Paula was brought into the conference room to be interviewed. The handcuffs weren't put back on until Paula was transported to jail, Black testified.

"Was she free to leave?" Athan asked.

"No, she was not. No, she is not."

"So she is in custody?"

Black said that was true and verified that Paula knew she was in custody and couldn't leave. At no time was Paula left alone without a guard, Black said. Black verified that among them, he and Detectives Hevel and Lease were "very experienced."

"Nobody is on her side in that room, right?" Athan asked.

Black testified that this was obvious. Athan wondered why the interview was on audiotape rather than videotape.

"Is there any reason why . . . so we could see what you were doing, what she was doing, how people looked?"

Black said the video equipment had not been available. He added that in his years as a detective, he had never videotaped an interview. Black answered yes to Athan's questions about Paula understanding her right to an attorney and, if she couldn't afford an attorney, one would be appointed to represent her. Black agreed that he told Paula she could exercise her rights at any point.

Athan attacked the detective for not allowing Paula to see a lawyer when she said, "I don't know if I should talk to a lawyer first."

"You don't have to give her advice about a lawyer because that's not your job, correct?"

"That's correct."

Athan mentioned Paula's long pause before continuing. "We don't have the videotape," she said. "Could you tell if she was thinking about it?"

"It was obvious she was thinking about it."

After Paula understood that Black couldn't give her advice about whether or not she needed a lawyer, she said, "'I want to cooperate, but I don't really want to go to jail?' . . . And you say, 'Well, you know, the point of going to jail is on the basis of evidence.' And that's what you're trained to tell her, correct?"

"And that's the facts."

Athan questioned him about what he meant when he told Paula there was a "good possibility" that she would go to jail, with or without a lawyer. Black said he couldn't give percentages, but he thought Paula's chances of being jailed were better than fifty-fifty.

The detective admitted that the reason Paula asked if a lawyer was available was so she could consult with him. "And you say, 'We don't have one here,'" Athan said. "And then you say, 'That's the only problem.'"

"What's the problem with that?" Athan asked.

"If she wanted to talk with one . . . there was no possibility of getting an attorney then."

"No possibility of getting an attorney?" Athan asked, surprised.

"Not then."

"Well, do we mean in five minutes, ten minutes, a day? What are we talking about 'not then'?"

Black testified that there was "no way" an attorney could be obtained in the time allotted for the interview. Under more questioning, Black said that a lawyer could not have been obtained in a half hour.

"You just told her that if [she] couldn't afford an attorney, one would be appointed to her without cost of any kind; is that correct?" Athan asked.

Black agreed, and Athan asked him if he knew Hillsborough County had a public defender office. Black said he knew that, but had no way of knowing if there were attorneys available then. Athan showed the detective Defense Exhibit 2, which was an aerial photograph of downtown Tampa.

Athan pointed out the location of the police department headquarters and the public defender's office on the photograph. The buildings were three to four blocks away. Surely, Athan said, a public defender could have been called.

"I guess . . . she could have called," Black said. "I wouldn't have called for her. . . . She also had the knowledge that she didn't have to talk to us without an attorney."

"Would you agree that the whole situation is at least a little coercive?" Athan asked.

Black disagreed, and said Paula was free to speak or not, but that he and the other detectives did nothing to force her to make a statement.

Athan hammered away. "She's a young woman, no experience with police, having gone through a horrendous and terrifying day, and now she finds herself in a room with three detectives being questioned," Athan said. "Do you find that at all coercive? Just in and of itself, not that anyone is coercing her to do anything."

Black said he didn't believe so. Paula was an intelligent woman who indicated that she was fully aware of her situation. Athan asked him what he meant when he told Paula "that's the only problem," when he said there was no attorney there.

"What's the problem about that?" she asked. "What's the problem about letting her exercise her right to speak to a lawyer before she's questioned?"

Black said there was no problem, and that Paula could speak or not speak. She had chosen to make the statement.

"Was there a problem in your mind?" Athan asked.

"The only problem was she wanted to know if there was an attorney there now," Black said. "There wasn't one there now. That is the only problem."

Black said he didn't believe he could have found an attorney for Paula within an hour because it was a Friday afternoon. He said a lot of people had taken time off.

"Are you aware that the office of the public defender has, since 1996 at least, given Tampa police and other law enforcement agencies notice that we are on call twenty-four hours a day?"

"Uh-huh."

"Didn't you understand that if she wanted an attorney right then and there, all you had to do is pick up the phone and say, 'Would you walk over those four blocks and send a lawyer over?'"

Black doggedly maintained that Paula only had asked if an attorney was available; she didn't say she wanted to speak to one.

"Detective Black, a member of the office of the public defender could have been available within ten minutes, right?"

"I'm not sure."

"Why?"

"Because I don't know who is in the office over there, or if there's anybody to answer a call."

"Let's again make sure you understand—"

"He's already said he's not going to call the public defender's office," Judge Padgett said. "It doesn't really matter who was there."

Athan had no more questions to ask after the judge's statement. Turpin took the floor for redirect examination. She asked Black if he knew how many Tampa police officers had been killed in the line of duty since the 1980s. Athan objected, saying the question was irrelevant, but Padgett overruled.

Black said four or five officers had been killed. Turpin asked specifically if Black knew about the deaths of Detectives Childers and Bell. Athan objected again, as to relevance.

"We'll see," Padgett said. "It's not a trial."

Black knew that Bernice Bowen was charged in connection with the killing of Detectives Childers and Bell. Turpin asked if he knew the public defender's office had refused to represent Bowen. He testified that he also knew that Lois was the next police officer to be killed in the line of duty.

"Based on the Bernice Bowen case, did you have any reasonable expectation that the public defender's office would be willing to represent this woman, who is charged in the killing of a Tampa police officer?" Turpin asked.

Athan objected that the question was irrelevant and speculative. Judge Padgett overruled her. "I'm sure he didn't even think about it that afternoon. . . . No police officer is ever going to call an attorney," he continued. "They'll let the person call an attorney if they want to. They're not going to do it."

Athan called Paula to testify and she was sworn in. Paula testified that after her arrest, she was handcuffed, and people were guarding her. Athan asked how she felt that afternoon when she was arrested. Paula said she was in shock. In the conference room, Paula testified, she was nervous and "really scared."

Paula testified that she had understood all of her rights before she was questioned. But she said she wanted to talk to a lawyer, but she thought the statement had to be made that day. Paula said she thought she would get a lawyer before the interview.

"I was scared," she testified. "I knew they (detectives) wanted to talk to me. I wanted things to get cleared up and I thought I wanted to speak to somebody that would help me out."

After more conversation, Paula said, Black told her she would probably go to jail—even if she had a lawyer. That was why she asked, "Do you have a lawyer here?" Paula said she didn't understand the process for getting an attorney from the public defender's office.

Paula explained the long pause on the tape after Black told her there was no lawyer there and that was the only problem. "I felt all alone," she testified. "I just wanted to go home. I just decided to talk because I didn't have a lawyer, so I didn't have any choice. . . . I was stuck there."

Athan asked why she suddenly felt she didn't have a right to a lawyer.

"Because he (Black) told me that there was a problem and he made that face, like, 'Well, we can't get you one.'"

On cross-examination Turpin noted the discrepancies in Paula's testimony. Paula had said she understood her rights, including a right to an attorney, and that she could invoke her rights at any time.

"You replied 'yes,'" Turpin said. "You're saying you did not, in fact, understand that?"

"I understood . . . but I just—"

"You understood that, right? And you did not feel intimidated by Detective Black? In fact, you were more than forthcoming in asking any questions that you had. This was not a situation where you're going to stand just meekly by during advisement of rights," Turpin said. "Whenever you had a question, you were willing to speak up, correct?"

Athan said Turpin had just asked a compound question.

"Yeah, it is," Padgett said. "One question at a time."

Turpin asked if Paula had felt free to ask Black questions if she didn't understand something.

"Well, I was scared, but I asked him, yeah, for a lawyer."

Turpin said that Paula wasn't scared of Black, and that he honored all of her questions. "You had to go to the bathroom; you took a break," Turpin said.

"You wanted a drink of water; you took a break. You were hungry; he ordered pizza. You wanted to see your daughter, Ashley; he provided Ashley to you."

"I didn't ask for those things," Paula said. "I asked for water, for the bathroom. Pizza came because they wanted it. I wasn't hungry, and they were the ones who told me we're going to bring Ashley to see you, but I never told them I wanted to see my daughter. I didn't know what was happening so—"

"When you asked for something, you received what you asked for; is that correct?"

Paula said it was.

"There was nothing coercive or intimidating about Detective Black's questioning to you; is that true?"

"Yes."

Paula testified that she knew, before the interview began, that Lois was dead, and that she would be questioned about that and the bank robbery.

"And you're able to recall all of the persons who were in that interview room," Turpin said. "You recall Detective Black, Detective Hevel, and a gentleman with white hair?"

"Yes."

Turpin went for the kill. "So you were certainly not numb to the point of not knowing who was surrounding you at the time this interview began," she said. "Would you agree with that statement?"

"Yes . . . but I felt numb. . . ."

Turpin had scored. She had no other questions.

Julianne Holt, public defender for the Thirteenth Judicial Circuit, in Tampa, was called by Athan. Holt testified to the closeness of her office to the police station, and that the office was open the

Friday afternoon that Paula was interviewed. Criminal defense is available twenty-four hours a day, including holidays, Holt said. She acknowledged that memoranda were circulated to Tampa agencies, including the Tampa Police Department, with instructions on how to contact the public defender's office during emergencies.

Turpin noted that there were procedures mandated by law for the appointment of a public defender, and that Holt's memoranda had not included a list of "emergencies."

"People have to use their common sense," Holt said.

Turpin asked if it was true that the public defender's office had refused to represent Bernice Bowen in the killings of Detectives Bell and Childers.

"We had an ethical conflict of interest, ma'am," Holt said. In fact, Holt testified that she was on the telephone speaking with a highway patrolman during a high-speed pursuit of Bowen, who had killed his own son, in addition to the two Tampa detectives.

"It would have been inappropriate for me to use information achieved on a personal basis during the representation of Ms. Bowen," Holt testified.

When Turpin had no more questions, Athan wanted to clarify parts of Holt's testimony under cross-examination.

Athan began, "Since Ms. Turpin brought up Florida Rule of Criminal Procedure—"

"No, we're not going there," Padgett interrupted. "That doesn't kick in until someone has been arrested and booked, and the possibility of the public defender is appointed. The public defender is never appointed to represent somebody still at the police station."

Athan fought to win the point. She asked the judge

to take a look at statutes pertaining to a booking officer: "The officer who commits the defendant to custody has the following duties," Athan said. "Number two—"

"This is a booking officer," Padgett said. "We don't have any booking officers here."

"The—" Athan started.

"That's the booking officer."

"Has the following duties," Athan said.

"That's the booking officer," Padgett said again, "not arresting officer."

"The rule—"

Padgett cut Athan off sharply. "I'm not going to argue. Anything else?"

Athan was deflated. "No, Your Honor."

"Is there anything else, anything you want to say?" Padgett asked.

"I think my argument is clear," Athan said. "I won't repeat it."

Athan told the judge that she didn't think the state's responses to her memorandum cited pertinent law, and pointed out the examples. Padgett was ready to make his ruling.

"I've never seen a case that hinged on whether the detective has to assess how the person feels or what they're thinking," he said. "She (Paula) made an ambiguous reference to an attorney. I'm not even sure it was an ambiguous request for an attorney, just an ambiguous request if there was an attorney present. Detective Black's response was straightforward and truthful. I'm going to deny the motion."

The hearing was adjourned. Athan had lost again. Paula, looking tiny and childlike in an orange Hillsborough County Jail jumpsuit that was several sizes too big, was escorted from the courtroom.

Chapter 17

Jay Pruner wasted no time in setting a dramatic tone for the prosecution's case against Paula. He stood before the jury and began: "Officer Lois Marrero bled to death on the sunbaked asphalt parking lot of the apartment complex at church and Cleveland on July 6, 2001. Her life was taken from her because, a few short hours before, Paula Gutierrez and Nestor DeJesus awakened to find that they had a dollar between them, they had a two-year-old child, no food in the refrigerator, and a sports SUV ready to be possessed.

"Officer Lois Marrero, the evidence will show you, had her life robbed from her, less than one mile away from and forty-four minutes after this defendant and Nestor DeJesus robbed the Bank of America on Church and Neptune Street."

Pruner told the jury that the state's evidence would show that "elaborate steps" were taken by Paula and Chino to commit the robbery, to make their getaway, and to avoid being arrested.

He described how Paula and Chino were dressed at 2:31 P.M. on July 6, 2001, and how they had tried to disguise themselves by wearing hats, bandannas over their faces, and the baggy clothing Paula wore to conceal her feminine figure. Pruner pointed out that it was Paula who carried the MAC-11 semiautomatic pistol. The prosecutor noted that the pursuit of Paula and Chino actually began before the robbery was over and didn't stop until they were captured.

Anticipating the defense's contention that Paula was an unwilling participant in the robbery and murder, Pruner stressed that immediately after Chino entered the bank and ordered everybody to get down on the floor, "this defendant entered, carrying that semiautomatic firearm, and as she stood at a position in the lobby with that firearm raised, repeated Nestor DeJesus' command that people get down and stay down."

While Chino grabbed almost $10,000, Pruner told the jury, Paula was just a few feet away providing cover. Pruner used a large map to show the route they had taken from the bank to the Regency Apartments, and told the jury how they discarded most of the money when a dye pack exploded "spewing red dye and tear gas within the Xterra, causing great consternation and concern."

Pruner said that even before Paula and Chino left the bank, calls were made to 911 and that an alarm had been tripped. "Within a matter of moments, police officers from two separate squads of Tampa Police Department began to search for a bright yellow SUV."

Pruner said witnesses reported seeing the SUV and money being thrown out the window and that these witnesses called 911. Within minutes, he said, police are collecting the money and taking statements, and continuing the pursuit of the bank robbers.

Officer John Martin took off in a helicopter, 10:50 A.M., to help look for the SUV. Martin, Pruner said, directed police units to check on four or five SUVs in various parts of South Tampa.

Pruner told the jury that the evidence would show a relentless pursuit. Chino and Paula were only in their apartment at the Crossings "a few short minutes," Pruner said. "Paula Gutierrez and Nestor DeJesus . . . knew they weren't safe from pursuit," Pruner said, "and so they left that apartment after changing clothes."

Lois confronted Chino in the courtyard by the pool, Pruner said, with Paula standing only a few feet away with a bag containing the MAC-11 on the ground beside her. Pruner described the foot pursuit across the parking lot, through the veteran's cemetery, then back to the parking lot. The ASA described how Lois was killed before the suspects burst into an apartment and took Isaac Davis hostage.

"You will also see from the evidence, like a trail of bread crumbs the defendant left, dye pack–stained currency at separate locations," Pruner said. ". . . Nestor DeJesus was a very troubled young man. . . . [He] was not the type of young man that any parent in the world would wish to have to be the suitor of their daughter . . . that he had a hot temper."

Pruner said the evidence would show beyond a reasonable doubt that Paula was guilty of bank robbery, the murder of Officer Lois Marrero, and armed burglary. Pruner thanked the jury and took his seat.

Deeann Athan stood to address the jury. She knew she was fighting an uphill battle to convince them that Paula was not guilty. Athan was convinced that Paula was totally under Chino's thrall, and was so totally dominated that she was an unwilling accomplice in the crimes with which she was charged. In the months that Athan had been Paula's attorney, she had grown to like the young woman, and intended to fight hard to get Paula acquitted. She intended to show that Paula wasn't operating under her own free will.

"Ladies and gentlemen of the jury, meet Mr. De-Jesus," Athan began. "Make no mistake, on July 6, 2001, he gunned down Officer Lois Marrero in cold blood. For the previous three years, he had mentally, physically, and sexually abused Paula Gutierrez. This reign of terror culminated . . . when he killed Officer Lois Marrero in front of her eyes.

"Later, when he put a bullet in his head, ending his life of violence, he committed the ultimate act of abuse against Paula Gutierrez," Athan said. "He left her holding the bag."

Athan said there was no doubt that Paula was not guilty. She told the jury that Chino forced Paula to look down and not make eye contact with anyone. Athan said Chino would pick fights with Paula, anyone on the streets, and total strangers.

"He would just snap, Athan said. "He became physically violent to Paula Gutierrez. When she told him they should cool it, he threatened to kill himself or to kill her." Athan talked about Chino stalking Paula, and how, after they got together in Tampa, his abuse became worse. Once, when Paula was pregnant, Athan told the jury, Chino held a knife to Paula's swollen stomach and said, "If you weren't carrying my child, I would kill you right now."

Athan told the jury that the violence escalated. "Paula [was] trapped. He would hit and kick and punch her," she said. "He would demand sex and choke her until she blacked out. When she said she didn't like that, he told her she did."

Athan talked about Chino's episodes of violence with strangers and his episodes of road rage. Paula's family tried to get her to come home or move into a shelter for battered women, Athan said, but Paula was too afraid. "After all, Nestor DeJesus has told her she'll never leave him," Athan said. "She'll never take Ashley away from him. He'll kill her, he'll find her family and he'll kill them, too. She has witnessed his violence and she believes him."

Athan described a violent attack on Paula just three months before the bank robbery. "She experiences the most violent assault against her . . . ," Athan told the jury. "She questions why he has pornographic materials in his van. He is furious. He physically and verbally attacks her. She protects herself by getting in a fetal position. He kicks her everywhere, leaving bruises on her arm and leg."

Athan told the jury that Chino's mother found Paula crying, following that attack, and bought her a ticket to New York, where her parents lived. But Chino convinced her to come back by promising to get counseling, Athan told the jury.

Athan said that evidence would show that Paula didn't want to rob that Bank of America, but was psychologically conditioned to obey Chino. "He places the gun in her hand and tells her, 'You're going into the bank. You will hold the gun,'" Athan said. "She is very afraid. She says she doesn't want to do it. He says it is too late. She knows that look, that tone, that violent threat. She decides to go into the bank. He tells her to put on a hat and a bandanna to cover her face. She does it. She believes that what he will do to her if she does not follow him into that bank is worse than anything that could happen in the bank."

Although Paula followed Chino into the bank

and held the gun, Athan said, none of it seemed real to her. "To Paula Gutierrez, it seems like a dream," Athan said. "This can't be happening. In an instant he is leaving the bank. She follows him. They get into the Xterra and leave the parking lot. Half a block away, a dye pack explodes, spewing smoke and fumes. They throw the money out the window. They can't see, they can't breathe. The next thing Paula Gutierrez knows, she's at the Regency Apartments."

Athan tried to establish an important timeline for the events that followed the robbery. She pointed out that Paula didn't remember how they got to the Regency, but changed clothes as Chino instructed. She rode back to their apartment with Chino's mother, who came to give them a ride, bringing Ashley with her, Athan said. Once they arrived at their apartment at the Crossings, Athan said, "[Paula] feels safe. It is over. She's at home."

Athan wanted the jury to remember this chain of events because it was critical to her defense. "She takes a shower," Athan said. "She begins to relax, savoring it. It doesn't last long because the next thing she knows, DeJesus is telling her to get dressed, come on. She thinks, 'What now? What's going on? Where are we going?'"

She told the jury that the next series of events were "very foggy" for Paula. She remembered some, others she didn't. But it was clear, Athan said, that Chino was chased on foot by Officer Lois Marrero, across the street, through the cemetery, and back again. Athan said that Chino "got away" momentarily, saw Paula with Mark Kokojan, grabbed his keys, and tried to get into Kokojan's car, when Lois appeared and told him to put down the gun or she would shoot.

"Nestor DeJesus grabbed his gun and fires, hitting

Officer Marrero twice," Athan said. "She stumbled toward Paula Gutierrez. For Paula, everything is in slow motion, like a movie. Officer Marrero and she lock eyes. It appears to her that Officer Marrero is asking 'Why?' Officer Marrero falls to the pavement. Paula Gutierrez is in shock. She has seen Nestor DeJesus commit the ultimate act of violence. He has killed a police officer.

"She hears him yell at her, 'Get the gun.' Officer Marrero's gun has fallen out of her hand onto the pavement. There's a large pool of blood already formed. Paula, in a daze, reaches for the gun and picks it up."

Athan's delivery was rapid-fire as she related the events and she spoke in the present tense to give it a sense of urgency, trying to draw the jurors in.

"Nestor DeJesus is screaming at her to follow," Athan said. "Other officers are arriving. They're shooting at DeJesus. He fires back. They all run into the complex. Nestor DeJesus runs up a flight of stairs and Paula Gutierrez follows him. She is unaware of the gun battle that has taken place and continues.

"As police fire at DeJesus, he fires back; then he takes Paula by the neck, in a choke hold, and uses her as a human shield against the police officers' bullets," Athan continued. "She is hysterically screaming. This is according to Officer Shepler. To this day, Paula Gutierrez does not remember this horrifying experience."

Athan told the jury how Chino kicked the door to another apartment until it broke off its hinges; then, still holding Paula in a choke hold, "throws" her into that apartment. When Isaac Davis, the occupant, was terrified, Athan said, it was Paula who assured him that he wouldn't be hurt.

Athan related Detective Batista's attempts to talk Chino into coming out, and that Chino told him they were going to commit suicide. "He has convinced Paula Gutierrez to kill herself with him," Athan said. "She calls home to say good-bye to her family. She asks them to take care of Ashley. She tells her mother how much she loves her. Her mother begged her not to do it. . . . Eventually she agrees not to kill herself. Her maternal instinct comes through."

Athan said that Paula tried to convince Chino to surrender, but he refused, and he insisted that they kill themselves. "He shows them how they will do it," Athan said. "Put the gun under your chin: one, two, pow."

When Detective Batista, who tried to talk Chino into surrendering, realized what was happening, he became frantic and pleaded with them not to do it. "DeJesus counts—one, two—drops the gun," Athan said. "He curses. He doesn't kill himself. He puts down the phone, leans back against the wall, and says, 'Ready, Paula? One, two,' and puts a bullet into his brain.

"Paula could not kill herself. She is in shock. Batista calls, 'Paula, pick up the phone. Paula, pick up the phone.' She finally does. She surrenders and is taken into custody." Athan paused for a moment, then said, "Nestor DeJesus' reign of terror is over, but a new nightmare is about to begin for Paula Gutierrez."

Athan insisted that Paula was not guilty of felony murder. "The robbery simply was over," she told the jury. "They had effectively escaped from the immediate area of the robbery. Although the police started to look for them, they were never pursued. . . . They had reached a place of safety in their home."

Paula acted out of duress, Athan said. A medical expert would help them understand how this happened. Athan criticized the way Paula's interview was conducted by the police, who, she said, steered Paula away from having a lawyer present. The jury would find Paula not guilty of all charges if it listened closely, Athan said, because Paula was compelled to act out of duress.

"She was not a willing participant," Athan said. "Her fear was real. It was imminent. It was impending. Her life was lived in real and imminent and impending fear. Never knowing when he was going to snap."

Athan concluded her remarks by reminding the jury that the trial was about justice, not vengeance, and "the law says Paula Gutierrez is not guilty."

The state began to build its case, brick by brick. Eyewitnesses testified about seeing the robbery in progress, the robbers' descriptions, the type of vehicle they used, dye-stained money thrown from a yellow Xterra SUV, the suspects' arrival at the Regency Apartments, and about their arrival at the Crossings, with Ashley and Chino's mother.

Most of the testimony was tedious as Ober and Pruner built a body of evidence they believed would convince the jury of Paula's guilt. Athan had few questions, for the most part. The first day of the trial ended with no surprises and little excitement outside of the opening arguments.

Chapter 18

The courtroom was jammed on May 9, 2003, the second day of testimony in Paula's trial. Paula wore a skirt, white blouse, and black sweater. She looked small and ethereal at the defense table beside Athan and Deborah Goins, another assistant public defender. On the state's side were Ober, Pruner, and Turpin.

The first witness to give testimony was Dr. Bernard Adams, chief medical examiner for Hillsborough County. As a police officer, Mickie Mashburn knew that the details of Lois's death would be described in horrifying detail. She was pale and tense as Adams took the stand for direct examination by Ober.

Ober handed Adams four photographs of Lois's body in the morgue. In murder cases autopsy photos are frequently blown up to almost life size so that the jury—and the gallery—can see the horror in startling detail. Only the jury would see the four photographs that Adams examined.

Ober established Adams's expert credentials, and had him explain in detail how he had conducted the autopsy. Then Ober asked him the question that would bring graphic testimony to the pain and trauma that Lois had suffered in the moments before she died.

"Would you describe . . . what wounds you saw on her and those wound paths?" Ober asked.

"She had two perforating gunshot wounds," Adams said. "Each of the wounds had an entrance and an exit. One of the wounds began with a scrape across the chin and then entered the throat, perforated the windpipe, the trachea, continued down . . . and tore across the subclavian artery and the vein right next to it, both major vessels, and then continued down and perforated the upper part of the lung and then exited on the right side after fracturing a couple of ribs."

Ober received permission for Adams to leave the witness stand so that he could demonstrate how the bullets had entered Lois's body. Ober questioned Adams in detail about the wounds while showing the autopsy photographs to the jury. Then, using Ober as a teaching aid, he pointed out how the bullet would have traveled through the state attorney's body.

The wound to the subclavian artery was particularly horrifying to hear about.

"In this case the blood would flow into the airway, fill the windpipe, the mouth, and leak out through the entrance wound . . . ," Adams said. "Then the blood filling the chest cavity could also leak out through the hole in the side of her chest. . . ."

Adams said that this single wound was fatal. Then he described the damage caused by the second bullet. Once again, Adams used Ober's body to describe how the bullet had torn through Lois. This bullet punctured a lung, diaphragm, spleen, kidney, liver, shattered the spinal column, and grazed the spinal cord. This would have caused almost immediate paralysis of Lois's legs, Adams said. The medical examiner said this was the first bullet to strike Lois. The second bullet was the one that killed Lois, Adams said.

Mashburn and Brenda Marrero, Lois's sister, looked visibly shaken during the medical examiner's testimony. Paula appeared dazed.

Patrolman Gary Metzgar testified about being on patrol and hearing the first radio reports of the robbery at Bank of America, and of a foot pursuit by a female police officer. At first, Metzgar didn't know who the police officer was, or where the pursuit was occurring.

"I kept talking to the radio, like 'Give me a location, give me a location,' because I couldn't help," Metzgar testified. "I thought like, 'Where the hell are you at?' Sorry, 'Where the heck are you at? I need a location. He's running, he's got a gun, help me, help me.'"

Metzgar described how he arrived at the Crossings apartment complex when he figured out where the chase was occurring. Metzgar arrived just after Officer David Shepler arrived to help. At that point, Metzgar testified, he jumped out of his car so he could help.

"I didn't make it far," Metzgar testified. "I got out of my car, and as soon as I opened my car door, I saw out of the peripheral side of my eyes, I saw a black object in the parking lot."

Metzgar said he had a quick glance at a man standing over a body in the parking lot. Later he learned that it was Lois's body.

"The instant I saw him, he opened up on me," Metzgar testified. "It was all open area. So he had a straight shot at my location." Metzgar said he found out later that ten shots had been fired at him and Shepler.

"My first instinct was to get cover," he testified. "I probably shouldn't be here because they just missed the top of my head. I could feel them and hear them, so I dove behind [a utility trailer] for cover."

Metzgar said he heard other shots fired as he rolled to a car for better cover, but when he lifted his head to return fire, the gunman was disappearing into the breezeway. The police officer testified that he didn't see anyone else in the breezeway. Ober asked Metzgar what he did next.

"It's almost like a tunnel vision," Metzgar said. "When you hone in on something like that, you don't believe it, you can't believe it, or then it could get downhill from there.

"I took off running. I wasn't sure what the object was. I still wasn't sure what it was laying on the ground. So I ran toward it and as I got closer, that's when I saw the bottom of her boot and recognized it as a police boot."

Metzgar told the court how he jumped over Lois's body and ran to the breezeway to make certain it was clear. He ran back to check on Lois.

"Was there any pulse?" Ober asked.

"It was obvious it was a massive wound, so I don't know why I was doing it," Metzgar testified. "I guess just doing it. There was no pulse."

Metzgar realized whoever shot at him had far more firepower than he, so he ran to the cruiser to get a shotgun. He saw spectators watching from an automobile shop next door. Metzgar warned them to get down, and asked them to throw him a blanket. They threw him a fender cover, he said, which he used to cover Lois's body.

The police officer used a pointer to indicate various locations in an aerial photograph of the apartment complex. Reliving that day caused Metzgar to tremble, and he had difficulty holding the pointer steady. Metzgar testified that he advised Shepler he was going to a different location to try and box in the gunman. That's when he heard a woman screaming, but he didn't see anyone at first.

"It was Officer Hill," he said. "She was standing, running around Lois's body, screaming. She just kind of lost it."

Metzgar said he was worried that Hill would be shot. "I knew there was nothing we could do for Lois, it was too late," Metzgar testified. "She needed to get cover. I didn't want a second one to get shot." Metzgar said he continued screaming at Hill to take cover, and she did.

Metzgar testified that he tried to evacuate a woman from an apartment he feared might be shot up. The woman inside was afraid to come out. Even after he ran to the living-room window, beat on the glass, and she saw his uniform, Metzgar said she was still afraid. He finally had to pull her out.

Athan stood for cross-examination. She established where Metzgar was before he heard any traffic on his radio regarding an officer chasing a suspected bank robber. Athan also established that Metzgar didn't hear any helicopters then, but that he did a few minutes later.

"He's already shooting before you even see he has a gun?"

"Yes."

"I think you described him as standing in the Rambo style?"

"It was like shooting from the waist, hip, stomach area. The rounds start walking up," Metzgar said. "That's why I think they missed me."

"'Walking up' means the muzzle of the gun faces upward or the bullets go upward?"

"The kick of the gun, the recoil of the gun, causes it to start," Metzgar said. "If you don't hold it down when you start shooting, it will start walking up on you if you're shooting rapidly."

"He was shooting very rapidly?"

"Yes. I was surprised how fast he got them off at me. I thought he had a fully automatic weapon."

"Clear to you that this guy knew how to handle this gun?"

"No . . . he would have hit me if he had known how to. He was shooting wildly . . . with no accuracy."

"But he was shooting at you, there's no doubt about that?"

"Toward us. Because I knew Dave Shepler was behind me somewhere, I could hear him. I could feel it almost touching my hair."

"And, as a matter of fact, you heard Officer Shepler say, 'He's up there, he's up there,' and you also heard him say—"

Jay Pruner jumped to his feet. "Objection, Judge."

"He said that on direct, Judge. It's an excited utterance."

"Yeah, we covered that," Padgett said.

Athan asked if they could approach the bench.

"Counsel, I'll sustain the objection," Padgett said.

"I don't understand. I'm sure what the pretrial order is on this. . . . It's all an excited utterance, Your Honor."

"Yeah . . . I'll buy that," Padgett said. "Overruled."

Athan knew there would be conflicting testimony between Shepler and Metzgar on what occurred on the balcony. She needed to bring this out for the jury to consider.

"You also heard Officer Shepler, 'He's got a hostage,' didn't you?"

Metzgar agreed.

"And that's the reason that when that blind kept peeking open, you didn't take your shot, correct?"

"Probably. It wasn't a clean shot, as much as I wanted to shoot."

Athan had no more questions. Pruner had only one or two points to clarify in his redirect.

Daniel M. Tatum, an employee at Lindell Honda, was the next witness for the state. Tatum told the jury that he had seen "the guy with the gun" shoot at Metzgar from the Crossings parking lot. He described the shooter as being Hispanic, with short hair, and a woman at the left front of the car, where the shooter stood.

As other police officers pulled up, the shooter turned his gun on them, Tatum said. "He was shooting in both directions." Tatum said the woman worked her way back to the breezeway, where the shooter had fled. Fifteen or twenty seconds later, Tatum said, the shooter unleashed another volley.

Tatum testified that a black police officer arrived by a fallen police officer and screamed for blankets.

During cross-examination Athan continued to work on the timeline. Tatum said he and a friend were at a convenience store getting something for lunch.

"While you were at the convenience store, or while you were driving to and from the convenience store, you didn't hear any helicopters, did you?" Athan asked. Tatum said no. "And before you got to the intersection of Cleveland and Church, you hadn't seen any police cars, either, had you?"

"No."

Athan asked if the young woman he saw shot at any of the police officers.

"No."

Athan had no more questions for Tatum, and Pruner had only a few on redirect. He asked Tatum if he could identify the woman.

"She's sitting right over there . . . ," he said. "She's wearing a black sweater with a white shirt."

Neither side had further questions for Tatum, so he was excused.

Next to take the stand for the state was Corporal James Hill. Hill testified about racing to the Crossings with his siren on and lights flashing, after he received a radio call about an officer in distress. When Hill pulled up to the Crossings, he saw a woman in a red pickup truck, whom he later discovered as Chino's mother.

"I motioned for her to leave the complex because I understand there is a gentleman with a gun," Hill testified. "She refused, like she was yelling at me, screaming at me. She had a bunch of kids in the truck. After several minutes of arguing with her, she finally drove away."

Hill said he heard gunfire and Shepler yelling. Hill said he lay Lois down and ran to a breezeway, where he thought he might intercept the shooter. "I'm thinking that the bad guy, the guy that just killed Lois, is inside the courtyard," Hill said. "They're probably chasing him southbound and I'm going to cut him off here."

Hill testified that Officer Cole Scudder yelled to warn him someone was above him. Hill scrambled for better cover. Although he didn't see anyone, Hill said he heard other police officers yelling that the gunman had taken a person hostage.

Neither the prosecution nor the defense had further questions for him. Hill was excused and Scudder was called to the witness stand.

Pruner started to establish a timeline that was crucial to both sides. Scudder told the court it took him only three or four minutes to get to the Crossings after he heard Lois's radio call. He described how he entered the glass doors to the Crossings and saw no one on the second-story landing. Scudder said he entered with his gun at "low ready," meaning he held it in a two-handed grip, pointed slightly downward. Almost immediately after he entered the Crossings, Scudder said he came under fire.

"As the gunshots first went off, because of the foyer, the echo, flashes, and muzzle flashes, I couldn't tell where the gunfire was coming from," Scudder said. "I looked up. I could see a tall, slender silhouette. The rapid muzzle flashes from the gun, there's gun smoke surrounding the person. I immediately crouched down and returned fire."

Scudder moved for cover, but not before a bullet hit him in the right leg. It was a minor wound, he said, so he kept moving. After he found cover, Scudder said, he saw the gunman standing at the railing shooting straight down at him. He testified that he had a full, clear view and was certain there wasn't a woman on the landing with the shooter.

Athan had only a few questions on cross-examination.

The state called several witnesses to testify about the physical evidence found at the scene. One point of conflict between the state and the defense concerned a disposable camera that had been taken from Chino and Paula's apartment. The camera contained the film with Paula posing with the MAC-11 right after she bought it. There were exposures of Chino with the gun alone and with Ashley. Other photographs were simply family-type snapshots. Athan didn't want the photograph with Paula holding the gun entered into evidence.

Sergeant James Simpson, a homicide detective, found the camera inside a Polo bag just outside Paula's apartment. Simpson verified that he had, at the state attorney's request, hand-carried the film from the camera to the photo lab for development. After Simpson identified the camera, the state entered it into evidence.

Then Pruner showed Simpson a larger-than-life photograph of Paula wearing a camouflage shirt and holding the MAC-11. Paula was turned three-quarters away from the camera and had turned to look into the lens. She wore heavy makeup, her hair was pulled back, and she smiled. Paula didn't look like an innocent little girl in the photograph; she looked seductive and dangerous. Simpson identified the photograph as having been from the camera he had found.

Pruner moved to have the photograph entered as evidence. Athan, who realized that the photograph severely damaged her defense, objected and asked if she could voir dire the witness. Padgett denied Athan's request and overruled her objection. Athan sat down, devastated.

The lawyers gathered at the bench after a break for lunch. Athan wanted to explain to the judge why she had asked to approach the bench during Metzgar's testimony.

"It was to ask Your Honor to take a break because

it was very clear that Officer Metzgar was very emotional," Athan said, "and to put on record that he was quite emotional and remained quite emotional throughout his testimony."

"The carpet over here, under the witness chair, is stained with tears," Padgett said. "It just happens. The best way to handle it is to . . . just keep it going."

Ober said that the defendant also had been emotional, but the state was trying to remain calm about it.

"I know," Padgett said. "We used two boxes of Kleenex in this courtroom."

"I know there is going to be a lot of boo-hooing in this trial," Athan said. "I feel bad. I don't have a problem with that. I felt bad for Officer Metzgar."

"I know, but that happens. You guys ready to roll?"

The lawyers were ready and Padgett had the bailiff call the jury.

Pruner questioned James S. Noblitt, who was retired from the TPD. He was a detective in the robbery division, on July 6, 2001, when the Bank of America was robbed. He testified that he found stained bills and baggy clothing in Paula's apartment.

The ASA turned his attention toward building a detailed timeline from the time the bank robbery was reported until Lois was shot and killed. He questioned Teresa Mellor, a communications technician, who was in charge of the care and custody of communications made over the police radio band.

Mellor had a record of the time various calls were made on July 6: robbery reported at 10:42 A.M.; description of suspects and their vehicle at 10:43 A.M.; Scudder at Church and Neptune, responding, 10:44 A.M.; report of money being thrown from a yellow Xterra, 10:45 A.M.; Officer Martin en route to

a call about a yellow Xterra, 10:55 A.M.; police officers arrived at the Regency to investigate yellow
Xterra, 11:12 A.M.; Bingle radios for officers to go to
the Crossings regarding a white male named Chino,
11:22 A.M.; request for officer to go to Cleveland and
Church, 11:23 A.M.; Officer Marrero radios that
she's in pursuit, 11:24 A.M.; Lois radioed that Chino
had doubled back from the cemetery, 11:25:19 A.M.;
Lois radioed "that gun," 11:25.44 A.M.; "Officer
down" broadcast, 11:25.52 A.M.

Only forty-three minutes elapsed from the first
police alert broadcast until Lois was shot and killed.
Pruner wanted the jury to know that the pursuit of
the two suspects, from the time of the robbery until
Lois was killed, was continuous. There was nothing
helpful Athan could get from Mellor and she did not
cross-examine the witness.

Detective Roberto Batista, who was the chief negotiator during the hostage standoff, was the next
witness for the state. Batista had been transferred to
internal affairs, but he still was a hostage negotiator
with the TRT. Batista identified a recording of his negotiations with Paula and Chino on July 6, which was
played for the jury. The transcripts included sixty-
four pages of the conversations.

"Did you have a complete understanding of what
Paula Gutierrez's involvement may have been during
that robbery?" Pruner asked.

"No, I did not."

Batista told the jury that a negotiator tries to build
rapport with the other person and keeps them on the
line. "As long as you keep it positive, there's always
hope," he said. "And as long as you keep him talking,
there's always hope that everyone will come out alive."

Batista said the reason he started talking about

Ashley with Paula was to make everything personal. "To bring someone into the picture, the daughter, the future, our daughter growing up," he said. "Them maybe not being there with her, maybe in prison . . . but they have something to look forward to."

The witness acknowledged sending in a telephone with the hidden video camera and transmitter. Pruner asked him to explain why this was done. "So we know what's going on inside the apartment, should we have to make an entry," Batista testified. "It will make it safer for (officers) to make that entry."

Athan had several questions on cross-examination. Batista told the jury that he was home when he heard about the situation, and that he was the first hostage negotiator to arrive. He told the jury that Officer Terry Mims was speaking to Chino on Lissette Santiago's cell phone.

"So Officer Mims is very happy to see you, a hostage negotiator," Athan said, "and hands the phone over to you?"

"Yes, ma'am, very quickly."

"And so now you begin to speak to this stranger on the other end, who you understand is a suspect in a bank robbery, correct?"

Batista said it was, and that he had never met Chino or Paula.

"So . . . you're talking to strangers . . . and it's a very dangerous situation because there's been a police shoot-out, right?"

"Yes, ma'am."

"An officer is dead?"

"I didn't know that at the time."

"Or was at least critically wounded?"

"I knew that an officer had been shot," Batista replied.

Batista testified that he didn't know immediately that there was a hostage in the apartment. But since it was the middle of the morning, he knew there was a chance someone had been home when the apartment was invaded.

The detective told the jury he was allowed to lie when he negotiated because he needed to say things that would bring everyone out unharmed.

"When you first started talking to Mr. DeJesus, he seemed kind of calm, right?" Athan asked.

Batista said that was true. He testified further that he wanted to keep Chino calm.

"So the first thing that you do is try to develop a rapport, correct?" Athan asked.

"That's correct."

Athan noted that Batista was Hispanic and Chino was Puerto Rican, and when he mentioned that to Chino, it was a way to make a connection. Again, Batista agreed. He testified that he was doing what he could to develop a personal relationship with Chino and Paula. Ashley, Batista said, was the most important thing he talked about with both of the suspects.

"Every time you brought up Ashley, Miss Gutierrez softened up and her voice cracked—"

"Yes, ma'am."

"You realized that that was an important thing to talk to Miss Gutierrez about," Athan asked, "that was something that was going to get to her?"

"That's an important thing to everybody."

"That maternal instinct?"

"Yes," Batista said.

"So you are talking to her about different things, 'Give yourself up,' on and on, some of them lies, some of them truths, but in any event, she eventually says . . . 'I want to turn myself in,' correct?"

"Yes."

Athan asked if he was optimistic that Paula would give up and surrender. He said he was always optimistic during negotiations, and at that point he thought both Paula and Chino would turn themselves in.

Athan asked if Batista ever thought that he had lost them, that they would never give up. The negotiator said he had remained optimistic. He testified that he thought Paula was ready to surrender and he wanted to keep her thinking in that vein.

"When you're talking to Paula, you can hear Nestor DeJesus talking in the background, right?"

Batista said yes and agreed that Chino seemed to be talking with someone on a cell phone. Sometimes he said he could hear Chino talking to Paula. Athan zeroed in on Chino's domination of Paula, which was a critical part of the defense strategy.

"When you're asking her certain things about Isaac Davis, he's telling her what to tell you, right?" Athan asked.

"In one case I remember hearing, yes."

"You heard him talking to her . . . just to be clear?" Athan asked. "You were talking to Paula Gutierrez, and you say, 'Okay, who else is in there besides you and Isaac and Chino?' And in the background, he (Chino) says, 'Is everything okay?' When you're talking to her, he's in the background?"

"Yes."

"She says, 'They want to know how many people are in here,'" Athan said. "Now, that implies that she's not talking to you . . . that she's talking to someone else, right?"

Batista agreed that was correct and that Paula's comments were to Chino. He agreed that he heard

Chino say in the background, "We don't want him to know that."

"Then she says, 'We can't let you know that'?"

"Yes."

"At times during the conversation you're having between yourself and Paula Gutierrez, Nestor DeJesus is telling her what to tell you, right?"

"Yes."

Athan asked Batista why Paula picked up the telephone when he was talking with DeJesus. Was it that Chino started to cry? she asked. The detective answered yes.

Athan asked, "Not just Hispanic men, but men in general, I suppose, feel like women cry, but men are a little more concerned about crying, don't you think? When he starts to cry, he hangs up, right?"

"Yes."

Athan questioned Batista about his actions from the time he first arrived at the scene, trying to find cover, then moving into the house to establish a command center. He said that Detective Gene Black was with him as the secondary negotiator, and that Black wrote things down for the record. Athan established that Black, who later questioned Paula about the robbery and shooting, had heard much of his conversations with Chino and Paula.

Athan reviewed Batista's testimony and reminded him that Chino had appeared calm at the beginning of the interview. She added that Batista had "softened him up" further by talking about Ashley.

"So he's kind of calm and rational, right . . . at the beginning?"

"Yes."

"Then, all of a sudden, he starts screaming. Remember that?"

"Yes, ma'am."

"So you must have been feeling that, okay, I need to calm this guy down, right?"

Batista agreed.

"So anytime he starts screaming or sounds really stressed, you need to calm him down, correct? And so you guys are talking and he's just kind of ranting, right?"

"At that point, yes."

"You say, 'What about Ashley?' He comes right back down, and that's when he starts crying, when you start talking about Ashley and Paula, correct? And he hangs up. And now you talk to Paula for a little while and it's obvious there at some point you want to talk to Isaac, right?"

"Once I found out there was somebody else in there, yes, I wanted to talk to him."

Athan's next few questions tried to establish that even though Batista was talking to Paula, it was clearly Chino who was in charge and telling her what to say.

"Part of the time, Miss Gutierrez is crying, correct?" Batista answered yes. "Part of the reason they're not wanting to come out," Athan said, "is this thing about not wanting to go to jail, right? . . . Nestor DeJesus is very clear about that, he is not going to go back?"

"He doesn't want to go back."

"And Paula says, 'I don't want to go to jail'?" Athan asked.

Batista agreed.

"So when you say to them, 'We're not going to destroy your entire family, you know, you got the father already going to prison, for sure he's going to prison because of the shooting and the robbery. . . . And then you say, 'And the mother may have to do some jail time, but not much'?"

"That's what I said, yes."

"You don't know how much time she's looking at because you don't even know what she's going to be charged with, do you?" Athan asked.

"No. First, I wasn't even sure she was involved in any type of crime."

"When you say to her, 'You weren't in there, were you,' she's kind of going along with that," Athan said. "You really didn't know what her involvement was?"

"That's correct."

"Eventually she fesses up and says, 'I was in there,' right?"

Batista said that was true. Athan continued to press the point, noting that Paula had said she was not only in the bank, but that she had the gun. Batista agreed that Paula volunteered the information, and that he wasn't trying to elicit it. Batista answered yes when Athan asked if Chino took the phone back when he told Paula that Chino could have a face-to-face conversation with his mother at the jail.

"He's a little upset with you, right?" Athan asked. "He's angry. You're trying to calm him down . . . and he's responding to you kind of in a hostile way, right? And you say, 'You know, if you want to talk to your mom, I can have you talk to your mom,' and he said, 'Yeah, I do, but you just interrupted.' So he goes from screaming to angry, and next you're talking to him about a lot of people in there, SWAT guys in the hot sun, and we hear Detective Black telling you in the background, 'Tell him we'll wait it out for as long as we need to,' right?"

"Yes."

"Then he goes from angry to 'they have itchy fingers,' and he kind of chuckles. So his mood just swung back to kind of calm, right?"

"Yes, it did."

Athan said that when he started to tell Paula to think about Ashley, "because he jumps right in and he says, 'She is an accessory,' and now he's all rational again, right? Then he launches right into the point system, and you must have been thinking, 'What is this guy talking about?'"

"Well, I have some knowledge of the point system."

"Then he goes on to educate you because you said, 'I'm just a burglary detective, I don't know about the point system.' Then he goes on to educate you about the point system in a very rational way?"

"Yes."

"He's concerned because he thinks his points are really high?" Athan asked. "He stays calm and he chuckles a little bit. Then he talks about going to jail and that kind of thing. And he remains very rational until he says to you in a very rational tone, 'What I did is a capital crime,' correct? And what did you understand that to mean?"

"Capital crime was death penalty crime."

"And he presses you. 'It's a capital crime.' And you say, 'It's a serious crime; yes, it's a serious crime.' And then he goes from 'Mr. Rational' to yelling at you, 'A cop died.'"

"How did he have this information?" Athan asked.

"I assume that he got it from television because I didn't find out that Lois had died until I heard it from him," Athan replied.

"So he's now yelling, 'A cop died.' And you finally calm him down. 'Yeah, it is, it is a capital crime.' But he continues to scream at you and you try to calm him down. You start talking more. And then, all of a sudden, he goes rational again," Athan said. "Because you said, 'I'm sure you didn't wake up this morning thinking you were going to kill a cop; it's not premeditated.' And totally rational, he says, 'When's the last time you saw a premeditated cop killer?' You said, 'It's never premeditated.' Then he goes on to screaming and being irrational. Would you agree with that?"

Batista did.

"At some point you learn that he and Miss Gutierrez are going to kill themselves. Then he must hear some footsteps on the roof and he's asking you about the SWAT team and you're telling him, 'Don't worry about that, man; there's nobody up there,' right?"

"Yes, ma'am."

"Then you have this conversation with him about the SWAT team and TV and media people are everywhere . . . and he says, 'What happened?' You say, 'Is Paula okay?' And he says, 'I think so.' So now he's distracted or coming way down, right?"

"Yes."

"So you talk to him about cigarettes. He wants an unopened pack, because he believes you guys are going to put something in the cigarettes to make him sick, sleepy, or kill him?"

"I did tell him that we don't do that," Batista said.

"Because you want him to trust you. He clearly is letting you know that he hasn't decided what's going to happen. At what point did you realize that he's going to commit suicide or there might be a suicide pact?"

"That's always on the back of my mind," Batista said. "From the very get-go, you always think that's a possibility."

"When the video camera goes in," Athan said, "you're not watching video, right? Because if you're

watching the video, you might let something slip that
lets him know that you can see him?"

"Correct."

"You say, 'I'll call you back.' Chino says he wanted
a private conversation with Miss Gutierrez and he
says, 'I'll call *you* back,' and you say, 'A few minutes,'
and he says, 'Give me five, ten minutes.' You say,
'Okay, a couple of minutes. I'll call you back.' You want
to get back in there?"

Batista said he wanted Chino to have some time,
but he wanted to resume the connection as soon as
possible. During this break the tape recorder was
turned off. There was no way of knowing how many
minutes it was not recording, Batista said. Batista said
he didn't speak to Paula again and didn't interview
her at the police station.

Athan finished her cross-examination and felt that
she had scored some points. She had helped establish that Paula was under Chino's control and that
Chino's fits of rage were unpredictable. At least that
was how she hoped the jury saw it. The state had no
further questions for Batista and he left the witness
stand.

Pruner called Corporal Lawrence McKinnon, a
hostage negotiator who was in charge of the audio
and video equipment during negotiations with Paula
and Chino. After McKinnon identified a videotape,
Pruner introduced it into evidence without objection
from the defense. Portions of the video and audiotape were played for the jury.

CHINO: Have to kill (inaudible). We made—it's
a mistake (inaudible). Uh, you know, who fuckin'
(inaudible). Blow off our faces, fuck, man.

BATISTA: You can surrender and we can get this

done, you know. Paula can see the little girl, I mean, Ashley. Ashley's at the babysitter's. You know she needs you. She's going to need you for a long time to come. You're her father and mother. Ashley is a two-year-old little baby. She's a beautiful baby. She's got her whole life ahead of her, you know. What do you say, man?

CHINO: Sounds good.

BATISTA: You want to come out first?

CHINO: I'll send Isaac out first.

Chino described what Davis was wearing and that he was a black man. Batista told Chino to have Davis wear only his shorts out because it would be safer. The police, he said, would know he wasn't carrying a concealed weapon. Chino said to give him a minute and he would call back. In the courtroom the tape was still running, showing what was happening on the camera the police had sneaked inside.

CHINO: What do you want to do? Tell me.

PAULA: Huh?

CHINO: I'm not giving myself up.

PAULA: You know she's been crying.

CHINO: I know. Just hear TV from where I'm sitting. I'm sitting behind the screen. I can't see what's going on.

(The telephone rang and Chino picked it up. Batista was on the line.)

BATISTA: How you coming along? Are you coming out?

CHINO: I'm just talking to Paula right now and—

BATISTA: Make sure when he comes out that he follows the instructions of the SWAT guy. Just listen to the guys. They'll give him instructions, where to walk, how to walk, what to do. Okay?

CHINO: Okay. Do you want him to just step out, get down on his knees?

BATISTA: Just listen to the SWAT guy. He'll tell him what to do.

CHINO: Let me talk to Paula. I'll get back to you in a minute on the telephone.

(Chino hung up and Batista called right back.)

BATISTA: Are we ready?

CHINO: Getting him ready.

BATISTA: I'll stay here with you and kind of walk you through this.

CHINO: Isaac, come on, man.

BATISTA: You going to be okay? We got to get through this. We got to resolve this. Your mother is here waiting for you. Ashley is down the street. We'll get Ashley to see you, okay. We're going to get through this. Just hang in there.

CHINO: Ashley is not here yet?

BATISTA: She's at the babysitter's, the last time I knew. She may be with your mother. Are you coming out soon?

CHINO: No.

BATISTA: Okay. George, we need to go get Ashley. We're going to send somebody to go get your mom and Ashley right now.

CHINO: Okay. Just once I see Ashley and my mother, then I'll come out. How does that sound?

BATISTA: Well, what about Isaac and Paula?

CHINO: I'll send Isaac out. I'll look out the window and see my mother and Ashley across the street by the truck.

(Batista told him he couldn't do that because it wouldn't be safe. He told Chino that he had sent someone to get Ashley.)

BATISTA: You're not going to back out on me, are you?

CHINO: No, I'm not backing out.

(Chino and Batista discussed getting Davis ready to exit the apartment. Chino said Davis had stripped down to gray shorts and told Batista that Davis had been vomiting.)

CHINO: He's been throwing up. There's no need to rough him up.

BATISTA: No, no. Believe me. Is he at the door yet?

CHINO: He's almost there.

BATISTA: No surprises.

CHINO: Isaac, lift up your chin.

CHINO: I'm going to put the phone down.

BATISTA: Why? Why? Just let me know what's going on.

CHINO: I need to take a leak first.

BATISTA: Let me talk to Paula.

CHINO: Okay, all right. Hold on.

BATISTA: Paula, Paula? Hey, Paula. You doing okay?

PAULA: Yeah. Isaac's doing it.

BATISTA: We're not going to rush anybody. We'll take it one step at a time. I sent somebody to go get Ashley. Come down and you can be with Ashley. Then you and Chino can spend some time together, okay?

PAULA: Spend time together, you know, you said, yeah. I know you won't let us see Ashley.

BATISTA: I promise you I will.

PAULA: Did Isaac make it to the door yet?

CHINO: He's holding it.

BATISTA: Is he all right?

CHINO: It's fine. He just feels really ill. . . . He's really sick. He's been throwing up for two weeks. He has had nothing [to eat] since yesterday and he's really ill.

BATISTA: He's probably dehydrated if he's throwing up a lot. We'll get him some medical help. Where is Isaac at this point?

CHINO: He's out the door.

BATISTA: How you doing on the cigarettes?

CHINO: They're gone.

BATISTA: Chino, we're not going to rush you. I cooperated with you. We don't want anybody to get hurt.

CHINO: You can't do it.

BATISTA: Is he out the door yet?

CHINO: Almost. I'm going to count to three, and on three he's going to go out the door.

BATISTA: Count to three, and on three he's going to go out the door?

CHINO: One, two, three. Okay, Paula? One, hey, fuck.

BATISTA: What happened?

CHINO: I'm going to kill her. I'm doing it.

BATISTA: Why you going to do that?

CHINO: I can't go to jail.

BATISTA: Come on, man. Don't do that. Chino, come on. You got too much going here. Come on. Is Isaac out the door?

CHINO: No.

BATISTA: Why not? Why don't you let Isaac go, man? I thought you said you were going to let him go on three?

CHINO: You didn't need to on three.

BATISTA: Let him go. Let Isaac go. He's got nothing to do with this. Chino, talk to me, man. You don't want to do this. I know you don't. It's a lot easier to surrender. Your mom is out here. Ashley, your little girl, is out here. Chino, pick up the phone, man?

CHINO: One, two (sound of gunshot).

BATISTA: One shot. Pick up the phone. Pick up the phone. Paula, Paula, pick up the phone. Paula, Paula, pick up the phone. She may be armed. . . . Paula, pick up the phone.

PAULA: Hello.

BATISTA: What happened?

PAULA: He's dead.

BATISTA: Paula, come on out. Paula, put your hands on your head and come on out. Just give yourself up. Paula, there is nothing you can do for him. Paula . . . it's over. Your daughter needs you. . . . Don't go out like him. Paula, it's over. Don't do what he did. . . . Your daughter is never going to forgive you if you kill yourself. Come on out, Paula.

PAULA: They're going to charge me with the killing of the officer.

BATISTA: No, they're not. You didn't kill the officer.

PAULA: I know I didn't.

BATISTA: You're not going to be charged with that. What about your daughter? Ashley needs you. Just come on out.

PAULA: All right.

BATISTA: Just hang on to that phone. Keep talking to me. I'll walk you through this.

PAULA: Why, to see this?

BATISTA: Close your eyes. Go up to the door and walk outside and follow the instructions of the SWAT guys. They're not going to hurt you. . . . Put your hands on your head and walk out the door.

PAULA: I'm scared.

BATISTA: I know you're scared. As soon as you get down, I'll talk to you. Everything will be fine.

SWAT TEAM MEMBER: Come to the door. Shut the door. Get there. Lay down. Don't move, ma'am, and do not fuckin' move. Keep going. Officer, this is a crime scene. Don't mess anything up. Don't move anything. Don't pick up the fuckin' gun.

The tape ended. The jury sat transfixed by what they had heard. Pruner ended his direct examination and Athan had no questions. The next witness for the state was Isaac Davis, who had been held hostage. Pruner said his testimony would be lengthy. Padgett said they would stop for the day and resume testimony the following Monday.

Padgett addressed the jury and told them not to watch, listen to, or talk about the case. "And something else I wanted to tell you, I haven't told you yet," Padgett said. "Don't anybody go by there looking at these places. You know, we don't need any detective on the jury. If one of you goes out and looks at the scene, that's information you're not getting in the courtroom. It's not fair for those people to do that. Refrain from doing that, too."

The court recessed for the weekend.

Chapter 19

Older faces peered from the gallery as Paula and her attorneys took their seats. Trial watching is a favorite pastime of certain Florida retirees and they become good at predicting a trial's outcome. But the trial watchers were undecided on Paula's guilt or innocence.

One of the jurors had called in sick, with a notification from her doctor that she couldn't continue. After she was replaced by an alternate, who had seen and heard all of the previous evidence, the trial resumed. Before taking the testimony of Isaac Davis, Pruner called Jacquelyn Rojas and Tangela Williams, both crime scene technicians with the TPD.

During their testimony they described pertinent items they found at the trial scene, including clothing that matched the description of what the robbers wore at the Bank of America. Piece by piece, Pruner built his body of evidence. But the testimony everyone was waiting for would come from Davis, the former hostage.

Davis was a slim, handsome black man, who had recently graduated with a bachelor's degree from the

University of Tampa. He was alert and clearly intelligent as he sat in the witness chair. Davis acknowledged Paula with the glimmer of a smile.

Davis testified that he was home, sick with the flu, in his apartment at the Crossings when he heard what he thought were firecrackers going off outside, followed by kicking on his door. The door was smashed open, and as he approached it, Davis testified, a woman came in holding a gun that was pointed at the floor. Almost simultaneously, Davis testified, a man with a gun burst through the door. He identified Paula, who wore a pretty bluish green dress, as the woman with the gun.

Davis described how he had run into the bedroom to jump out the window. But, he said, he was too weak from being sick. He tried to hide in the closet instead. That is where Paula found him, Davis testified, and both she and Chino took him back to the living room. Davis said he begged for his life and that Chino assured him he wouldn't be hurt.

Chino marched him to the door at gunpoint and yelled that he had a hostage, Davis said, and then opened fire. Davis said Chino barricaded the door and started talking at him when they went back into the apartment. He said it wasn't a conversation, just Chino talking.

"He was just saying, 'We did something really bad.' He never said what it was, but he was really frantic. He was 'Oh, my God, what are we going to do?'" Davis said that Chino was "confused and scared," and Paula was "more so calm, but still kind of scared."

Davis said Chino and Paula watched television news, showing the standoff. They became increasingly nervous, Davis said, when the newscaster talked about SWAT teams arriving.

"They got more wired," Davis said. "They were more scared than they were before. It was kind of like they were running out of time, like, 'What are we going to do?'"

Davis testified that when Chino entered the apartment, he held cash that was stained red. He testified that Chino asked about his health and how Davis was feeling about five times over the next few hours. Paula came to the bathroom once, Davis said, and asked if he wanted water.

Chino and Paula started to talk about committing suicide, Davis testified, when the television announced that a police officer had been shot, and Chino thought he had killed her. "He was explaining to Miss Gutierrez that either way they're going to die—they're either going to die in prison or they're going to die by their own gun.

"Either way, he's not going to let the state kill him," Davis continued. "He said he was going to kill himself. And he was saying how they had talked about it before, that if anything went wrong, that they were supposed to kill themselves."

Davis said Paula was trying to talk Chino out of it, saying that jail wouldn't be so bad. "And he was saying, 'No, this is the only way it has to happen.'"

Throughout the next few hours, Davis said, Chino and Paula continued to discuss suicide. Davis described how Chino had made him close the blinds, check the windows, and get the telephone the police delivered outside the door.

"Did you feel threatened for your own safety, feeling these strangers had the guns in your house?" Pruner asked.

"Yeah, he had the gun pointed at me every time I closed the blinds or looked out of a window."

During the approximate 3½ hours they were in the apartment, Davis said, he never saw Paula and Chino touch one another. Paula eventually agreed to commit suicide, Davis said, after prolonged discussions with Chino. Initially, he said, Paula had rejected suicide.

"It was like she changed her mind," Davis said.

"Did she show any demonstrable signs of fear when she agreed with him?"

"What do you mean by 'demonstrable'?"

"Crying, shaking. Did you notice any reluctance on her part to express a disagreement about committing suicide?"

"Yes. She didn't want to do it. She would rather go to jail."

Davis testified that Chino had a gun in his hand when they talked about suicide. Paula, he said, was unarmed, but the gun Paula had taken from Lois was within easy reach. Pruner asked if Davis had heard Chino tell Paula that something wasn't supposed to happen.

"I was sitting in the archway of the hallway and he was standing up, kind of pacing between the dining-room table and the television," Davis said. "She was sitting down at the end of the table and he was walking back and forth. And he was like 'This was not supposed to happen. You never said this would happen.'"

"What did she respond?"

"She would say, 'I know, I know.'" Davis put his hands on his forehead. "She put her hands like this, at the end of the dining-room table, as if she was thinking."

Davis said he had been sick for two weeks and hadn't been able to eat much. He said Chino went into the kitchen for juice and crackers, but didn't take the gun. Both guns were within Paula's reach.

They talked more about suicide, Davis said. "Miss Gutierrez said, 'Well, I was just there for the bank. I can just be there for the bank robbery.' And he was saying, 'Don't you understand? You're an accomplice.'"

Davis said Chino had the MAC-11 under his chin and was talking on the telephone and to Paula at the same time when they decided to release him. "He would talk on the phone, but at the same time, talking to Paula," Davis said. He added that Chino said he was going to let him go on the count of three. He said Chino mentioned it several times. Paula, he said, was in his bedroom with Lois's gun. Under Pruner's questioning, Davis described his eventual release and Chino's suicide.

The assistant state attorney was trying to establish several key points: Paula wasn't under Chino's domination; she could have run when he left the room; she could have armed herself with both guns. Pruner also raised doubt about Paula's claim that she didn't know about the robbery in advance. It appeared that she and Chino had previously discussed suicide if things went wrong.

On cross-examination, Athan did her best to show inconsistencies in the statement Davis gave to the police and the information he provided in a later deposition. Davis admitted that he had described Paula as being calmer than Chino, but Athan asked, "Did you describe her as looking like she was trapped like a dog?"

"I described both of them like that."

"As a matter of fact, you agreed, she looked like a deer caught in the headlights?"

"Yeah, that was further, when they were in the apartment, yes."

Davis admitted that he was confused when Chino and Paula first burst into his apartment. He said that when he was handcuffed and taken to police headquarters for an interview, he was "disheveled." Athan pounded at Davis's confusion, such as thinking gunshots were firecrackers. "You're sick and you're not really registering what's going on, right?" she asked.

Before his apartment was invaded, Davis said, he was watching television and didn't hear helicopters outside. He told Athan that he heard screaming and then somebody banged on his door. Davis said he was scared when the door frame came flying in.

"Adrenaline is pumping?" Athan asked.

"Yes."

"What's in your memory is the first thing you see is Miss Gutierrez, right?"

Davis agreed.

"But Mr. DeJesus is so close to you that you said they could have been touching, correct?"

"Yes, he could have touched her."

Davis said everything was happening fast. He said he didn't know if Chino and Paula had talked while he was running to the closet. "Isn't it true you said to her at that point, 'Please don't hurt me'?" Athan asked. "And she said, 'Don't worry, we're not going to hurt you.'"

"No, she did not say it," Davis answered. "He said it."

"He wasn't there, was he?"

"Yes, he was. He was right behind her."

Athan's questions established that Paula stayed in the bedroom while Chino gripped Davis's neck and escorted him to the living room at gunpoint. "He's the one telling you what to do?" she asked. Davis agreed.

"It's clear to you that he's in charge, right?" Athan asked.

Davis was reluctant to concede the point. "Well, at that moment he's in charge of me, yes."

"But he's not in charge of anything else, just you?"

Davis said that was his impression, but he admitted that it was Chino who had him peek out from the blinds several times. "Not only is he telling you, 'Go look out the blinds,' he's got a gun pointed at you?"

"Yes," Davis said.

Davis admitted that he had lost track of Paula because he was looking out the windows for Chino in all of the rooms, including the two bedrooms. Athan's questions established that at one point a police officer was pointing a gun straight at him when he looked out the window. Athan also established that Chino used Davis as a shield when he went to the door and shouted, "I have a hostage" before firing a burst of bullets.

Davis said he thought Chino's gun was silver, but he knew now that it was black.

"What jogged your memory?" Athan asked.

"I didn't remember the actual color. I remember exactly what it looked like, but the color, I did not know."

Davis agreed that Chino had the gun in his hand or at his side 99 percent of the time. He also agreed that his memory was foggy on some things. Davis said that Paula didn't talk much. Davis verified that some of the images he saw were reflected in the tiling as he lay in the bathtub. But he heard them talking. He said Paula cried several times.

"Nestor DeJesus is trying to persuade Miss Gutierrez to commit suicide with him, right?" Athan asked.

"Yes."

"Because she doesn't want to do it, right?"

"Yes."

"And she's telling him, 'Let's give up. Let's surrender'?"

Again, Davis agreed. He also agreed that Chino said he wouldn't give up and that she shouldn't, either. Davis said he missed some of the conversations Chino and Paula had even when he was in the same room with them.

"I would black out, or just not pay attention because I was focusing on myself," he said.

Athan reminded him that Chino was nervous and that Davis had testified that Chino rambled, not always making sense because he was scared and nervous. "For example, he would say, 'What are we going to do? This was not supposed to happen. You never said that was gonna . . . Oh, my God, do you know how much trouble we are in?' He was just saying stuff like that, right?"

"Yes."

"During that time Miss Gutierrez wasn't saying anything. Most of the time she sat at the table with her head in her hands, correct?"

"Yes."

Davis said that Chino had been "persuasive" when he tried to talk Paula into committing suicide. He said Chino explained why he shot a police officer.

Athan asked, "He says that she's pointing her gun at him, right? And he says that she had the nerve to tell him she was going to shoot him, right?"

"No, kill him."

"Kill him. And he was upset, angry? How would you describe that demeanor?"

"I would say, yeah, angry, more so angry."

"That this law enforcement officer would say such a thing to him, correct?"

Davis agreed.

"You would see him go from calm to upset, to angry, to crying, back to rational, and so on and so forth, while he was in the apartment with you. His mood changed a lot, didn't it?"

"Yes."

"Her mood didn't really change a lot, did it?"

"No."

"She was crying? She was quiet? She was scared?"

"Yes."

Davis said he was "kind of out of it" when Paula and Chino entered his apartment and that he didn't recognize them right away. Later, he said, he remembered that they were residents of the apartment complex and that he had seen them at the pool. Davis said that he and his roommate had nicknames for Chino and Ashley.

"Your roommate called him 'the monkey guy'? And you called Ashley 'the Star-Kist girl'?"

"Yes."

"You didn't have a name for Miss Gutierrez, right?"

"No."

Davis testified that every time he saw Paula and Ashley at the pool, Chino was with them. He had never seen Ashley with anyone but her parents. Switching back to the apartment, Athan established that Davis was in the bathtub when Chino gave him the telephone to talk with the police. He admitted that he didn't know what Paula was doing.

Paula was in the bedroom just before he was released, Davis testified, adding that Chino kept looking at her while he talked with Batista.

"Now, you understood at 'three' they were supposed to kill themselves, right?" Athan asked.

"Yes."

"Did you hear him say, like this, 'One, two, pow'?"

"No, it was not 'one, two, pow.' It was, 'On the count of three, I'm going to let him go.' You can put two and two together to gather what was supposed to happen."

"But after that, he kept saying on the count of three . . . and kept telling you on the count of three, out of here?"

"Yes."

"And you understood by that they're going to commit suicide. When you say he was trying to persuade Miss Gutierrez to commit suicide, she was reluctant to do it, right?"

Davis agreed.

"And in order to persuade her, he kept telling her what big trouble they were both in, right?"

Davis said, "They were both making their cases. He was trying to persuade her to do that and she was trying to persuade him to give up."

Athan emphasized the fact that Davis was ill and didn't remember everything clearly, and that he had even blacked out at times. She asked if Paula might have said, "I was *not* there" when she talked about the bank robbery, instead of saying, "I *was* there." She emphasized that Davis's memory might be faulty because he was remembering things that happened two years ago.

On redirect Pruner moved quickly into damage control. Davis testified that Chino never verbally or physically mistreated Paula. Davis described them as being "just a regular couple." Pruner asked if Paula stumbled into the apartment or seemed disoriented. Davis said no.

"Mr. DeJesus spoke about he's going to leave in a

body bag one way or the other, something along those lines?" Pruner asked.

"Yes."

"Did you ever hear Mr. DeJesus tell Paula Gutierrez you, too, are going to leave in a body bag one way or the other?"

"No, he only spoke of himself."

Pruner asked if Chino said to Paula, "You never said this was going to happen."

"Yes."

"Was her response silent or to say, 'Right, right'?"

"Her response was silence."

Both Davis and Pruner seemed confused. Pruner tried to clarify.

"On direct examination, did you tell me 'right, right' is what she said?"

Athan stood. "Objection, improper impeachment."

"No, that's okay," Padgett said.

Pruner tried again.

"Remember when I asked you this question on direct, you answering she said, 'Right, right'?"

Davis was still confused.

"I'm not trying to trip you up," Pruner said. "Just tell us what you remember, at the time Mr. DeJesus is saying, 'You never told me this would happen'?"

"When he said, 'You never told me this would happen,' her expression was silence," Davis said. "When he said, 'This was not supposed to happen, this was not supposed to go this way,' her answer was, 'Right, right.'"

"Did you see or sense any hesitancy on Miss Gutierrez's part in trying to persuade not to commit suicide?"

"No."

"She didn't show any hesitancy to express a contrary opinion?"

"No," Davis said. "She spoke freely."

Pruner had no further questions for Davis and he was released.

In building a homicide case, the state can't just hit the highlights. Every little detail must be presented and proved, even the obvious fact that the victim was dead. Ober relieved Pruner to do some of the grunt work. He questioned a police officer about evidence found at the apartment and asked John Romeo, an officer with the Florida Department of Law Enforcement (FDLE), to describe the MAC-11 that was used in the bank robbery and murder.

Detective Aubrey Black was the next witness for the state. Athan would also have some pointed questions for the detective who elicited Paula's confession to the Bank of America robbery. Black, a twenty-five-year veteran with the Tampa Police Department, was with the hostage-negotiating team and interviewed Paula after she surrendered.

Pruner entered into evidence the "consent to interview" form that Paula signed. Black said the conference room, where the interviewed had occurred, was comfortable. He said he noticed red stains on Paula's shirt, which proved to be Chino's blood. After Black identified the audiotapes of Paula's interview, Pruner entered those as evidence and played the interview for the jury. After more than an hour of listening to the interview, it was time for Athan to cross-examine Black.

She presented Paula as a meek, tired, and traumatized young woman who was overwhelmed by the day's events and by the presence of three seasoned detectives with fifty years of combined experience.

Black testified that he wasn't tired, and he had started a long day as a hostage negotiator at the Crossings. As Athan had done during deposition, she elucidated Paula's traumatic day, which ended with seeing a suicide. "I don't think she physically witnessed it," Black said. "Obviously, she came upon him shortly after he had shot himself . . . and saw the gore and all the things that go with a suicide case."

Athan established that Paula was further traumatized by being "taken down" by the SWAT team, handcuffed, put in a police cruiser, and taken to police headquarters. She established further that Paula knew she was a suspect in armed robbery and first-degree murder. Black said he wanted to conduct the interview while everything was still fresh in Paula's mind.

"After this horrendous day? Not tomorrow?" Athan asked.

"Oh, definitely."

Athan asked Black if he could have booked Paula on the information he had before the interview. He answered yes. Had that been done, Athan asked, wouldn't Paula have seen a judge, and a public defender would give her a form that said, "I don't want to speak to anybody without a lawyer present"?

"That's correct."

Black said he realized that once Paula signed the form, police could not question her without a lawyer present, unless she specifically asked to be interviewed.

"So it's important that you talk to her and get a statement before she actually goes to court for the first time?" Athan asked.

"You remember things fresher in your mind from talking to somebody immediately instead of waiting several months later," Black said.

"But you knew that if you didn't get a statement this day that you probably weren't getting one, right?"

"That's a good possibility."

Black agreed with Athan that Paula's memory could have been affected by her "horrendous day," which included seeing two violent deaths. Pruner objected on the grounds that the question was too vague and Padgett sustained the motion, saying the question called for speculation.

Athan continued to hammer away: Black wanted to get a statement "now"; Paula was all alone with experienced detectives; the police didn't want the statement to appear coerced; there were different levels of coercion.

"You don't have to be holding a gun to somebody's head to coerce them, do you?" Athan asked.

"If you're talking about whether or not we coerced her to make a statement, I don't think we did."

Athan established that Black had been a detective for twenty years and had taken more than a hundred statements. "I've taken it from people who have cried, boo-hooed throughout the tape," Black said. "I've taken it from persons who cursed me throughout the course of the interview. So I've taken it from all extremes." Black said he had no doubt that Paula made her statement without coercion.

Athan asked if Black had taken courses on interrogation techniques and Black said yes. Black agreed that getting a suspect into a room, using a calm voice, and "being very nice" to a suspect was one of the techniques. Black affirmed that an interview would not have helped Paula "unless she wanted to go to jail."

Black had told Paula there was a "good possibility" that she would go to jail whether she made a statement or not. Athan insisted that it was an undisputable fact that she was going to jail, not just a possibility. Black agreed: "There was no possibility that she was going to go home that day." The detective said a reasonable person would have known she would go to jail if he told her there was a "good possibility" that she would.

"A better way to say it would have been: 'Miss Gutierrez, you're going to jail, no ifs, ands, or buts about it,'" Athan said. "Because that, Detective Black, was the truth, wasn't it?"

"Semantics," Black replied.

Athan showed Black the form Paula signed to give her consent to an interview. The form stated her constitutional rights. The form read, "Consent to be interviewed concerning an offense of . . . ," Athan said. "And there's a blank?"

Black said the offense was left blank because he didn't know what the charges against Paula were, but he was certain that Paula knew the offenses were for armed robbery and the murder of a police officer.

"So you don't write here what the offense is," Athan said, "that it's a homicide, it's a bank robbery. But you *do* write she's a high-school graduate, she has two years of technical, et cetera, et cetera?"

Athan wanted to know why Paula's interview wasn't taped on video. Black said he preferred audiotapes.

"But we can't really see what's going on?" Athan asked.

"That's true," Black replied.

Athan asked about how Paula looked when Black told her she had a right to see a lawyer before answering questions. "Now, almost two years later, you probably can't sit there and tell us what the look on her face was when you said that to her, can you?"

"I don't think her expression changed. . . . She was looking right at me," Black said.

The defense attorney contrasted how Paula was treated, with regard to her constitutional rights, as opposed to how police officers involved in the shoot-out were treated.

"As a matter of fact, it's so important that the police union requires a lawyer to be present when the officers are being questioned about the events of that day, right?" Athan asked. She mentioned Scudder, Shepler, Metzgar, and Bingle, in particular. "They all had a lawyer present that day, didn't they?"

"They had that option."

Black said he was aware that the police attorney went to the Crossings before the officers were questioned. "Because the right to a lawyer is that important for the police, yes?" Athan asked.

"Yes, it is."

"For Miss Gutierrez?"

"That's correct."

"She doesn't have a union contract. . . . She's just listening to you . . . and then you say . . . 'Now, at this particular time, what I'm going to ask you to do is talk to us and tell us about what happened today, if you will?'" Athan said. "And you're going to have her sign the form, right?"

Black agreed.

"You didn't ask her, 'Do you want a lawyer present?' or, 'Do you have any questions?'"

"I'm not allowed to get her a lawyer."

Athan pointed out that Black asked Paula to sign the consent form before it was filled in.

"I asked her if she was willing to talk to us without an attorney and she said yes," Black replied. "And she signed it."

"You didn't say, 'Without an attorney'; you just said, 'Are you willing to talk to us?'"

Black said that he read Paula her rights and that she asked if there was an attorney present. "I said, 'No, that's the problem, we don't have one.' But I said, 'You have to make the decision.' After a few seconds she made the decision. We're talking about a community-college student. We're not talking about somebody that is not educated. She made a conscious decision that she was willing to talk without an attorney being present."

Athan emphasized once again that Paula had no experience with the police before her arrest. "She says, 'Okay, I have a question,'" Athan said. "She doesn't say it as loud as I said it; she said it kind of meekly?"

"She told me exactly what she wanted."

"When somebody says, 'I don't know. I've never been in this situation. I don't know if I should talk to a lawyer first,' your antenna goes right up, doesn't it?"

"It's obvious."

"The interview is going to be way different if a lawyer isn't there, right?"

Black said that if a lawyer told Paula not to talk to the police, the interview would have ended. But, he said, Paula thought it over and told him that she wanted to go on, not that she wanted an attorney.

"When any suspect says the word 'lawyer,' there's a possibility that he or she may be invoking his or her right to counsel, right?"

Black said the suspect had to ask for a lawyer specifically. Athan asked why the police didn't get a public defender for Paula. She insisted that Black knew Paula could have had a public defender in less than an hour. Black contended that it wasn't his job to get an attorney for Paula. He said he wasn't sure a public defender would be available on a Friday afternoon.

"Detective Black, what's the point of telling her you can have an attorney if you are not allowed to let her make a phone call to an attorney or call an attorney for her?" Athan asked.

Athan continued to ask the question and Black continued to be evasive. It had gone on long enough for Pruner. He stood to object. "Objection, Judge. This is argumentative at this point."

Padgett said, "It's getting to be. . . ."

"I've told you before, I'm not going to get her an attorney," Black told Athan firmly. "That's not my job. I don't go around getting defense attorneys." Black said if Paula had said specifically, "I want a lawyer," he would have stopped the interview.

"If she was deluded about her right to an attorney, it wouldn't be a voluntary and intelligent statement, would it?" Athan asked.

Pruner objected, but Padgett overruled him. "Deluded by? What do you mean?" Black asked.

"Tricked."

"I think you can hear the tape. I didn't try to trick her."

Judge Padgett interrupted: "She's saying *if.*"

"I apologize," Black said. "*If* I was trying to trick her, then, yes, it would be. I was not trying to trick her."

"When you say, 'That's the only problem,' she's sitting there for twenty seconds thinking, correct?"

"She's thinking. She's making a conscious decision."

"Detective Black?" Athan said impatiently.

"Mrs. Athan, I'm trying to answer you fully," Black said sharply. "Just take a moment and wait and let me answer, please. Okay?"

Black reiterated his previous testimony that it was Paula's decision to decide whether or not she wanted a lawyer, and that he was simply waiting for her to make up her mind.

"So when she is thinking for twenty seconds, which is a long pause, you can't, to this day, tell us what she was thinking, can you?"

Black wouldn't concede the point. "Yes, I can, because she says, 'Okay, I'll go with it.'"

"And you got the result that you intended when you told her that it would be a problem bringing an attorney there at that moment?"

"Right. That is correct."

Pruner objected when Athan asked if Black had an opinion as a detective of twenty years if the day's trauma had affected Paula. Padgett overruled him. Black said it would affect anyone, but he didn't think it would change what Paula would tell him.

Black said that when he asked Paula if she had any mental illnesses, she told him she was depressed. Athan asked him if he wasn't really looking for schizophrenia, hearing voices, hallucinating, or something more serious because "depression doesn't set off any bells or whistles." Black answered that he didn't think depression was "a big deal. You get depressed over a bad grade in school."

"Or being beaten by your paramour who lives with you?" Athan asked.

"She didn't say that."

"You don't ask her what that meant, did you?"

Athan tried to show that the interview had not been conducted properly. Sometimes Black tried so hard to confuse Paula that he asked more than one question at a time, Athan said. She read one instance where Black had framed five questions as one. Black claimed that the questions were all related and that one answer would suffice.

Athan asked about the Bank of America robbery. "It's a pretty stupid thing they did that day, wasn't it?"

"Yes. And it cost so dearly."

The detective and the lawyer continued to duel over Black's interrogation techniques. Athan said that Black had not met Paula before the interview and asked if his assessments about her were made "in a vacuum." Black said that Paula's actions that day told him what he needed to know. He added that Paula had several opportunities to get away from Chino.

"This isn't a whodunit," Athan said. "This is a 'why did it happen,' right?"

"And a 'why it happened,' why she did what she did after it happened," Black answered.

Athan said, "The reason that we're here is for this jury to determine why this happened, that's it."

Pruner objected, saying that Athan had made a statement, not asked a question. Padgett sustained the objection. Athan and Black continued a heated duel over the nature of Black's questions during Paula's interview.

"So Paula said, 'I got to do it, I got to go there,'" Athan said. "Your next question was 'So he *asked* you to go along?'"

Black disagreed, saying it was obvious that Paula "had" to go once she was committed to the robbery.

"Did you change what she said to something different?" Athan asked. "That's the question—"

The judge interrupted. "Please don't let this get out of control."

Black agreed that Paula told him Chino gave her the gun outside the bank. "He told me to hold it (the gun). I was scared. I didn't want to go in."

"You didn't ask her what she was scared of?" Athan asked.

"I think it's fairly obvious she was scared because there is a possibility they could get caught and they would be in the situation that they're in right now."

Black admitted that he kept asking Paula the same question until he got the answer he wanted.

Athan asked, "So you want to make sure that she says, 'He didn't force me.' You wanted that in the statement. That's why you say to her, 'He didn't force you to go in, though.' Right?"

"That's correct."

"You didn't ask her if she was scared of Chino, did you?"

"I asked her if she was forced by Chino to do this. She said no. Chino is dead and presents no danger to her. If there is ever a time to come forward and say, 'Yes, he threatened me'—that would be the time to do it. She didn't."

After a few more heated exchanges that seemed to go nowhere, Black was excused. Athan sat down and looked exasperated. She knew that Black was a seasoned detective who knew how to get a confession. She wasn't pleased about it.

Chapter 20

The state showed that Paula purchased the MAC-11 from Robert P. Henderson, manager of University Gun and Pawn. Under cross-examination Henderson said that even though Paula bought the gun, Chino showed the most interest in the weapon. Henderson said he didn't think that it was a "straw man" purchase—that Paula was buying the gun for Chino with Chino's money. Henderson said all the paperwork for the gun purchase was in order.

For the state, linking Paula to the MAC-11 was just part of the tedium of building a case. The prosecution rested after Henderson's testimony. Athan was getting ready to set off some fireworks. She asked to approach the bench outside the jury's presence. Padgett sent the jury from the courtroom and Athan presented legal precedents dealing with felony. Although she had no good argument to the state's case for robbery, she didn't think Paula should be charged with felony murder.

"The felony was over," she said. "The actions that took place after Mr. DeJesus and Paula Gutierrez left the apartment were a completely separate incident."

Athan had several precedents to support her argument. She cited *Hornbrook* v. *State*, a case that was decided by the Florida Supreme Court in 1955. In that incident two gunmen robbed a bartender, made their getaway in a stolen car, and took hostages. When police spotted the stolen vehicle, a gunfight ensued and a police officer was killed. Hornbrook escaped, but was captured later. The Florida high court turned to a California case, *People* v. *Boss* for guidance, since it considered Florida law too vague.

If Paula had found a safe haven, Athan argued, the felony was over. The *Boss* case stipulated that a crime is not completed if the perpetrators have *not* found even a temporary place of safety. In that case, Athan argued, the *opposite* must be true.

"Paula Gutierrez had arrived at her home, the most secure place for her. The law looks at your home as your castle for purposes of defense," Athan said. "She was there. She had showered and changed her clothes. She won her way to a place of temporary safety, even if it was momentarily. The flight from the robbery was complete."

The Florida Supreme Court ruled that a felony continues from the time it is committed, even though the pursuit may technically be over. In the case of a felon making a getaway, the court stated that in considering *flight*, "the most important consideration is whether the fleeing felon has reached a place of temporary safety."

"In the case of Paula Gutierrez," Athan said, "she had not only reached her own apartment, but she had reached the Regency Apartments, where they were picked up by Lissette Santiago. But the most important fact in breaking the chain is that she had reached her home at the Crossings, where she took a shower and changed her clothes."

Athan argued that the flight from the robbery had ended. And because it had, Athan said, Chino's pursuit by Lois was "a new sequence of events." The defense attorney also argued that the Fourth District Court of Appeals ruled that, when evaluating flight, one of the most important things to consider is whether there's been a break in the chain of events and if the felon has reached a place of temporary safety.

Athan told the judge that the cases she presented were not "absolutely on point." But she maintained that Paula and Chino had "broken the chain" of events when they reached their home. "They were at a place of safety, even if it was just for five minutes or ten minutes or fifteen minutes," she said. "The chain is broken. The homicide committed by Mr. De-Jesus is not connected to the robbery . . . and the state has failed to prove a prima facie case."

Turpin said the state's argument relied on the same cases Athan presented, but interpreted them differently. The ASA said that Paula still was being pursued by the police when Lois was killed, and that the police officer's murder allowed her to continue her flight.

Turpin argued that Paula and Chino had only gone to the Regency to abandon the yellow Xterra because it was so noticeable. When they got to the Crossings, Turpin told the judge, both immediately showered to wash off red dye and tear gas residue. They only did this, Turpin said, so they could continue fleeing.

"They can't go walking around the city of Tampa with red dye, stinking of tear gas, and expect not to draw attention to themselves," Turpin said. "They kept the gun with them at all times because they were still fleeing." Lissette Santiago and Mark Kokojan both testified that Paula carried the bag containing the gun until minutes before Lois was murdered.

Paula and Chino had not reached a "place of temporary safety," Turpin said. "They were constantly on the move. They ditched their clothes. They ditched the red dye that was all over their persons, and then they were moving."

Paula and Chino heard the police helicopter circling long before anyone else did, Turpin told the judge. "They were listening for the helicopters because they were still on the run," Turpin said.

Padgett interrupted. "Okay. Okay."

"Just let me go on," Turpin said.

"No, that's all I need to hear," Padgett said. He said it was up to the jury to decide whether Paula had reached a safe haven. Padgett looked at Athan. "I submit that your client and Mr. DeJesus probably didn't even think they were home free." The judge said the evidence showed that Chino's mother was waiting downstairs for them and that Paula and Chino were "just going to get their stuff and go."

Padgett denied the defense's motion and told the bailiff to bring the jury back in. It was time for the defense to present its case. Athan called Shepler, who had already testified for the state, to the witness chair. She considered him one of her best witnesses.

Shepler's body trembled and his eyes teared up as he remembered the emotional events Athan asked about. She elicited testimony from the police officer from the time he heard radio traffic about the Bank of America robbery, through the search for the SUV, and the shoot-out at the Crossings. The key testimony Athan wanted from Shepler was what he saw Chino do on the balcony during the gunfight.

Athan showed Shepler photographs of the apartment complex and asked him to point out his and Chino's positions. The laser pointer the officer used wobbled over the map.

"I won't get anybody in the eyes with this," Shepler said in a trembling voice.

"Where is your car?"

"I can't stop shaking. That's my car right there. I stopped right there."

Shepler pointed to the photograph to show where he first had seen Lois pursuing Chino. Lois disappeared from his view and he heard her radio that Chino was doubling back. Shepler said he drove to an area where he might cut Chino off. Just as he got out of the car, "I hear, *boom, boom, boom, boom, boom,* and not a sound, not a sound, dead silence," Shepler said. "A string of gunfire."

Shepler said he ran to the parking lot, and other patrol cars pulled up. "Man, that gunfire is fresh," he said. As he looked around the parking lot, Shepler told Athan, he saw Lois's body lying on the ground with a pool of blood around her head and face.

Shepler said that his immediate thought was to help Lois, but he couldn't because he would be exposed. As he scanned the parking lot, Shepler said, he saw a man standing near Lois's body.

"As soon as I look at him, I'm trying to figure out who he is," Shepler said. "And all of a sudden, he's got his gun up and he's looking right at me like he had been waiting for me. And he just *boom, boom, boom,* and he started shooting at me. So I started returning fire against him."

Shepler said that he was wide open in the parking lot when the gunman ran toward the apartment buildings. "I realize I'm just standing in the wide open parking lot and this guy is trying to kill me, and I'm trying to kill him," he said. Shepler said he saw no other police officers and that he was "totally focused" on the gunman.

"I got him in the sight of my gun and I said, 'Let him stop running so I can kill him,'" Shepler said. "But he makes that corner and I put another round or two after him . . . and he gets into the breezeway."

Shepler said the gunman was alone. The police officer left his cover and ran after the shooter. As he ran through the parking lot, Shepler testified, he glanced at Lois. "There's nothing I can do to help you," he said. "I got to get this bastard."

As he ran to a better spot, Shepler said, he saw the gunman on the second-floor landing. Shepler said he had his gun out and was ready to fire another shot. The policeman testified that he held his fire when he saw a young female just a few feet from the gunman. Shepler said he had not seen the woman before.

"So what happens next?" Athan asked.

"He grabs the female around the throat."

"Did you point your gun at him?"

"Yeah, had my gun on him."

"How did he grab the female?"

"He grabbed her like this." Shepler demonstrated a choke hold that would put the gunman's forearm under the woman's windpipe. Shepler said he held his fire because he didn't want to hit the woman. "Within a second or two, it starts up again."

"Do you know who was shooting at him?"

"Yeah. At this point I see Cole Scudder coming right through there." Shepler pointed to a first-floor landing.

Shepler said the gunman looked away from him and started shooting at Scudder. Shepler said Scudder returned fire and took shelter. The gunman kicked a door in, Shepler said, and the woman in the choke hold was screaming. Shepler said that when the door was kicked in, the man and woman disappeared inside.

When Athan took her seat, she believed she had made her point: Chino had used Paula as a shield to protect himself. It wasn't an act that showed Chino had any great regard for Paula.

Pruner began his cross-examination and it was clear what he was up to. Employing the same chronological order that Athan had, Pruner used Shepler's activities to show that the pursuit of the bank robbers was continuing when Lois was killed. Pruner stumbled once when he asked: "Did that (the pursuit) appear to be in somewhat of an organized systematic search in a grid pattern?"

"I don't know what it was," Shepler replied. "I wasn't paying attention."

Shepler said that he didn't actually see Chino kick the door in, but he saw the foot up and kick something. "Or he was kicking the brick wall," he said, "and I don't think that's what he would be doing."

Athan asked Shepler on redirect how many times he had been in a gun battle. He answered that gunfight was his first and that he had never seen a fellow officer gunned down.

"You're still emotionally affected by that?" Athan asked.

Shepler could only nod in the affirmative.

"Were you affected by what you were seeing and experiencing while you were chasing this guy?"

"I didn't have a chance to be affected by it," he said. "I had to continue to function. I was trying to stay alive."

"Shepler had the most unobstructed view of the balcony," Athan said to a reporter when Pruner ended his cross-examination. "He knows what he saw and he saw Chino use her as a human shield. The state's trying to make Shepler look confused, but he wasn't."

Athan's next witness was Carey Forney, who was driving to work from a convenience store when he saw something horrifying at the Crossings apartments: a police officer and a man facing each other with guns aimed at each other. Forney said he braked to a stop.

"It seemed like a long time, but it only lasted a couple of seconds and he shot her," Forney said. "She fell. And the other cops busted loose. . . . When they ran into the breezeway, I heard a whole bunch of gunfire and I just backed my car up as much as I could."

Forney said he could see the gunman on the second-floor landing. He heard gunfire. "It sounded like a war," he said. Forney left his car and ran to the Lindell car dealership next door, where he worked. Besides the gunman, Forney said, he saw a woman pacing back and forth on the balcony.

"While you went to the convenience store, and on the way back, had you heard any helicopters?" Athan asked. Forney said no. "Had you seen any police cars in the area?" Athan asked. Forney again said that he had not. Athan took her seat beside Paula as Pruner rose to cross-examine the witness.

Forney said that when the shooting started, he ducked down in his car. "When the police started running through, crossing the street, and I mean, it was so quick, I backed up," Forney said. "I got down and stayed down while they were firing."

Pruner asked Forney if he took his eyes off the parking lot while he backed up. "No, I was just trying to get the hell out of there," Forney said. The witness added that after the gunman disappeared, it was the last he saw of him.

"Is it fair to say what you have is a snapshot image of what you saw?" Pruner asked.

"Oh yeah. It's been two years."

Leon Wynne, who had demonstrated the MAC-11 for Paula and Chino at University Gun and Pawn, told the jury that he had tried to convince Paula and Chino not to buy it. "They were pretty much knowing what they wanted," he said. "They pointed down at the MAC-eleven."

"Did both of them point?" Athan asked. Wynne answered that only Paula pointed. He walked to the display case, Wynne said, and told Paula and Chino that the MAC-11 wasn't a very good gun.

"I said, 'You can't hunt with it. It's not a target gun,'" Wynne testified. "'It's a very inaccurate gun.' And she said, 'Well, we're interested in that gun.' So I took it out of the case and told them, 'This is a good toy if you just want a toy to play with, but I wouldn't recommend it to anybody.'"

Athan showed Wynne a display case with two guns in it and asked if he could identify the guns. The witness identified a MAC-11 and a Glock. Wynne said the Glock was "a top-quality pistol with extreme accuracy. . . . The other one is for somebody who wants to play Rambo."

Wynne said he took the MAC-11 from the display case and handed it to Paula, who handed it to Chino, and then stepped back while they discussed the purchase. Paula asked Wynne if he had a layaway plan. He said Paula seemed nervous.

"She was kind of blinking a little bit and kind of looking at him," Wynne said. "Like you have the obvious sensation that he was in charge of the situation, but she was the actual buyer."

Athan asked if he remembered anything else. "I remember she was looking at him like she was waiting for his approval or something," Wynne said, "like he had the say-so of what was going on."

When Pruner cross-examined Wynne, he immediately tried to establish that Paula didn't seem to fear Chino. "Paula Gutierrez and the man appeared affectionate toward each other when they were in your shop?" Pruner asked.

"Yeah, I knew they were a couple."

Pruner established that Wynne was familiar with the "straw man purchase" of a firearm, or when one person buys a gun for someone else, which is not approved by the federal government. Wynne said he knew that was a felony.

At Pruner's request Wynne read from a standard gun purchase form: "'Are you the actual buyer of the firearm indicated on this form? If the answer is no to this question, the dealer cannot transfer the firearm to you.'" Wynne said, "She answered yes."

"Although you indicated it appeared that Paula Gutierrez was looking for the man's approval," Pruner said, "your concern didn't rise to the level that you thought she was buying the gun as a straw man, did you?"

"No, sir. By law we can refuse to sell a gun to anybody for any reason at all."

Wynne responded to more questions about the MAC-11. "It's for people who watch a lot of *Rambo* movies," Wynne said. "They think they can shoot nine thousand times by loading the gun just once. It's not a quality weapon."

"In fact, when she (Paula) was talking about the gun, she told you she wanted a gun that would shoot a lot?"

"I said I would not recommend this," he said, adding that a good used Glock would be about the same price as the MAC-11. "I said, 'The only good thing about this weapon is you can load it and shoot a lot before you have to reload it.'"

Wynne said Paula didn't want the gun for protection, but as "just something to play around with." Wynne said it was common for women who buy guns to bring men to give them advice. He testified there was nothing suspicious about Paula and Chino.

Although Paula didn't buy ammunition at the time, Wynne said, she asked how much it cost. Paula gave him $100 to hold the gun for her.

Athan called several witnesses in an attempt to show that Chino dominated Paula and that he was violent. Pruner, in cross-examination, elicited testimony that undermined the defense's position. One witness said that Chino "was a very friendly guy."

Chapter 21

In another bench conference, the attorneys were engaged in what passed for a bare-knuckle brawl in a courtroom. Athan and Goins hammered their points as they battled to have the jury hear testimony from April Hildreth, a girl Chino had beaten several years ago. Ober, Pruner, and Turpin were determined to block it. The judge listened to both sides argue outside the presence of the jury.

Goins told the judge that Hildreth's testimony was important because it went to the heart of why Paula was afraid of Chino, and because it was relevant to the duress defense. She said it was also relevant in corroborating evidence about Chino's violent nature.

"If she is not allowed to testify about what Mr. DeJesus did to her and the injuries that incurred as a result of that," Goins said, "we want to be in the position to be able to proffer her testimony."

"I didn't previously rule on this?" Padgett asked.

"Judge, I believe you did," Turpin said. She said Padgett had stated that Paula could testify only to what she actually knew about Hildreth's relationship with Chino. "I believe that was your court's ruling, that she could testify to what she knew, but the details were not coming in."

"That sounds like it," Padgett said. He looked at Goins. "But you want to go beyond that?"

Goins said that Chino had lied to Paula about his battering Hildreth and that she had not been able to tell the defense psychiatrist about it. Goins claimed it would be important for the defense medical expert to have this information.

"Hold on a second," Padgett said. "Is Dr. Maher here to tell us about Mr. DeJesus?"

Goins said Maher would testify that Paula suffered from PTSD, based on trauma she experienced from Chino. Goins said she had noticed that the state, during cross-examination, was trying to show that "Mr. DeJesus is a really friendly guy and he would never do anything to Miss Gutierrez."

Goins added that Maher relied heavily on what family and acquaintances had said in diagnosing Paula's condition. Padgett countered that everyone in the world could testify and that there would be no end to it. "He (the psychiatrist) can tell everything and anything he ever heard about this guy and maybe even read about this guy," Padgett said.

Goins countered, "If it relates to corroborating things he's already been told."

The defense attorney tried hard to convince the judge, but Padgett was unmoved. "We're not going to let anybody and everybody come down here to testify about anything and everything just because Dr. Maher knows about it," he said.

Goins kept pushing. Padgett said, "I think I'll stick with my previous ruling."

Even then, Goins kept at it. "For the purposes of

proving Miss Hildreth's testimony," she said, "it is very important that we are able to make a clear record on this about what she will testify to . . . by actually having her testify in court, on the record."

Padgett said he would allow the testimony, but not with the jury present. Athan countered the testimony should be heard by the jury.

"Just totally trash Mr. DeJesus," Padgett said.

Athan said that wasn't true. The state had already tried to paint DeJesus in a favorable light, she said. "'He was just a friendly guy, wasn't he?' In public he was a friendly guy. In private with a woman—"

Padgett said if Chino beat one woman, he probably beat another. That was the pattern. The judge wanted to continue the trial. "Get it going," he said. "We got to finish this trial this week. Bring her in. We'll hear what she has to say."

Hildreth, like Paula, looked like a vulnerable woman. She was a pretty blonde who wore a horizontally striped blue-and-white sweater. Hildreth fidgeted and seemed uncomfortable in the witness chair.

Hildreth testified that she was fifteen when she met Chino and moved in with him. She recounted details of beatings she had suffered at Chino's hands. At first, she testified, Chino was "nice," but then became domineering and physically and emotionally abusive. Chino never took her anywhere, Hildreth testified, and would not allow her to talk or look at people. If she did go out, he would beat her, Hildreth said.

The witness said Chino talked about Paula constantly, and made her wear perfume and lotions that Paula used. Hildreth said Chino wanted her to *be* Paula. She said that he became meaner as time passed.

"He used to hit me," she said. "He used to scream

at me, slap my face, scratch me, and belittle me." Hildreth said she didn't do anything to provoke this type of behavior. "I didn't do anything to deserve what he did to me."

Once when she left the apartment, Hildreth said, Chino slapped her and "tossed me around, screaming at me." Another time, Hildreth said, he banged my head on the floor. "I was laying down and he was straddling me and he took both of his hands like this"—Hildreth demonstrated—"on my ears and was banging my head, kicking me in front of his friend, who did nothing but sit and watch."

Chino made her feel "nasty," Hildreth testified, because he belittled her so much. Hildreth said Chino never took her to the movies or a store, and that he only showed affection when he wanted something from her. Hildreth said Chino was always "throwing Paula in my face" and making her feel worthless.

Athan showed Hildreth the damning photograph of Paula holding the MAC-11. "Would you have taken a picture like that for Nestor DeJesus?" she asked.

"Probably."

"Why?"

"Because he told me to."

Athan asked questions to determine what happened that caused Hildreth's mother to file an assault and battery charge against Chino. Hildreth said they were standing by the Slurpee machines behind the 7-Eleven where Chino worked. She was smoking, and Chino didn't like the way she did it. He told Hildreth she held the smoke too long when she inhaled. "He told me if I didn't stop holding it longer than I was supposed to, he was going to punch me," Hildreth said.

"He told you don't inhale so long?" Athan asked.

"He said, 'Inhale it and blow it back out. If you don't, I'm going to punch you.'"

Hildreth inhaled in a way Chino didn't like, she said, and he punched her in the breast, hard. Although she didn't tell anyone about it immediately, Hildreth said, her breast started to hurt "really bad and it got real swollen." Hildreth said she lifted her shirt to show her ex-stepmother "and when I did, it busted."

Athan asked her to be more specific. "All kinds of stuff started pouring out of it," Hildreth said. "It was like thick, maybe like a yellowish color, yellowish red."

Police picked Chino up after Hildreth's former stepmother filed a complaint, and a police officer photographed Hildreth's injured breast. Athan introduced the photographs into evidence. Chino was never tried on the assault charge, Hildreth testified, because she went back to live with him.

A month later, Hildreth testified, Chino insisted that he hadn't hit her. An argument followed while they were at Lissette's house, Hildreth said, and Chino made here take off all her clothes and sit on the couch. "He said the only way I was leaving him . . . was in a body bag," Hildreth said. "I was scared."

Athan asked if Hildreth had been diagnosed with any mental disorders. The witness answered, "Posttraumatic stress syndrome." The parallels between the way Chino treated Hildreth and Paula were uncanny. If only the jury could hear it, Athan thought.

Under cross-examination, Hildreth told Pruner that her post-traumatic stress syndrome wasn't caused solely by Chino's treatment, but by abuse from her father and another man. Although Chino abused her, Pruner established that Hildreth had not committed any crimes and Chino had not asked her to.

* * *

Lissette Santiago didn't look happy. Sitting in the witness chair, Chino's mother gave Deeann Athan a hard look. She blamed the defense attorney, at least in part, for Paula's parents gaining custody of Ashley. Santiago had testified earlier for the state and now Athan had called her for the defense.

Athan knew that Santiago would be a difficult witness. In Santiago's words she was "pissed off" at Athan. The defense attorney said earlier, "She was absolutely devoted to her son. I think she would have done anything for him."

Athan established through her direct that Santiago was Chino's mother, and that she babysat with Ashley. Santiago said that Chino had a "very bad temper," but she wasn't afraid of him. "Sometimes it has to be his way or no way."

Athan asked what she meant.

"With his temper, that's all." Santiago said that Chino never lost his temper with Paula in front of her. Athan asked about the holes that Chino had punched in the wall, but Santiago was careful with her answer.

"I didn't see him do it," she said. "I can't say he did it, because I didn't see him."

Santiago admitted that she had heard Chino talk about committing suicide once when Paula was present. "He said, 'If I got to go to jail, I got to kill myself first,'" Santiago said.

Although Chino lost his temper with Paula and her parents, Santiago said, he never threatened them. Athan asked Santiago about the argument between Paula and Chino in April 2001, when Chino knocked the bedroom door down. Santiago downplayed the incident.

"She said she had an argument with Chino," she said. "She was crying. She was upset. There was toys around and stuff."

"How about the bedroom door?" Athan asked.

"I didn't notice that."

Athan asked Santiago several times if she had noticed anything about the bedroom door. Santiago answered that she didn't remember. Later, Santiago said, Chino told her that he had kicked the door down.

Santiago denied that she wanted Paula to leave after that fight with Chino. Instead, Santiago said, she offered to let Chino stay with her until they cooled off. She said that Paula wanted to go to New York.

"Isn't it true that he had kicked her out?"

"No. He didn't kick her out."

"When he came back, did he tell you, 'Get this bitch out of here'?"

"No. He was quiet. He sat down in the living room."

Santiago admitted that she bought Paula a one-way ticket to New York, but hedged when asked if Paula said that Chino slapped her. "Yes, but she didn't make it specific," she said. "She was crying. I don't know."

Pushed further, Santiago admitted, "Nestor told me he slapped her. My son told me."

Santiago said she didn't remember if she spoke to Paula's parents on the telephone. She denied telling them that Chino would kill Paula if she stayed.

Chino's mother said she didn't spend much time with him or Paula, and that Paula had no friends. "She didn't talk to nobody." Santiago said Paula never left the apartment until she and Chino got the Xterra for her. Then Paula would take Ashley to the park and the beach, Santiago said.

Asked to describe her relationship with Chino, Santiago said, "He was my son. It was okay."

"Isn't it true that you were very close to your son?"

Santiago said that was true. She testified that she bought the ticket for Paula to return to Tampa. "She was mad at me because I sent her to New York," Santiago said.

"She never told you that, did she?"

"She didn't have to. Chino [told me]." Santiago said Paula wouldn't speak to her, acted "real cold," and told Chino she didn't want Santiago in the apartment. Santiago admitted that Paula didn't tell her that, but that Chino relayed the message.

"Have you ever described Nestor "Chino" DeJesus by saying that he could snap at any time?" Athan asked. "He was very unpredictable."

Santiago answered yes, and Athan had no more questions for her. The lawyer sat down feeling that she had been questioning a stump.

Under ASA Jay Pruner's cross-examination, Santiago said Chino had been steadily employed until he was fired a week or so before July 6, 2001. She said that her son had tried to be a good provider for Paula and Ashley.

"When she wanted to join a health club, he signed her up for a health club," Pruner said. "Is that right?"

"Yes."

Athan objected, but Padgett overruled. Pruner asked, "She wanted to go; he signed her up and got the membership?" Athan once more objected and was overruled by the judge.

Pruner asked Santiago if she and Chino got Paula a car because she never went anywhere. "Nestor got Paula the car because she was, like, bored in the house," Santiago said. "No place to go, and stuff.

And so he spoke to me and he said, 'Mother, get a car so Paula could take the baby out and go to the beach, and stuff like that.'"

Santiago said Chino had a van from work and didn't need a car for himself. Before she bought a ticket for Paula to go back to New York, Santiago said, she offered to let Paula stay in the apartment. Chino did not object to her buying Paula's ticket to visit her family in New York.

Padgett gave the lawyers permission to approach the bench when Pruner asked. The prosecutor wondered if some testimony should be taken without the jury. The questions he wanted to ask centered on Santiago's answer when Athan asked if Chino had ever threatened to commit suicide. Santiago answered yes, and qualified it: "'They were talking about her doing something and I am saying before he would go to jail, he would kill himself,'" Pruner quoted. "The implication is that they were talking about committing a crime. I don't know if they're talking about committing this crime or the flower shop. . . ."

Padgett had already ruled that the flower shop robbery could not be used in this trial. Athan was outraged at the answer Santiago had given to her question. "Your Honor, for the record, I find this really interesting that this is the first time after several hours of deposition that she has come up with this big whopper."

Padgett told Pruner to ask Santiago if Chino talked about suicide before the robbery.

"Yes," she said. "A lot of times."

"And is that what you were referring to when you indicated that your son had talked about committing suicide rather than going to jail?"

"Yes."

Pruner finished and Athan rose for redirect examination. Athan elicited testimony indicating that Chino talked often about robbing a bank, adding that Paula did, too. Athan asked if Santiago remembered giving almost five hours of depositions. Santiago said she remembered.

"And you understood that these depositions were to find out everything that you knew about this case, right?" she asked. "So that I could find out everything that you knew. And nowhere in any of these depositions did you say that Paula Gutierrez ever talked about a bank robbery before July 6, 2001, right?"

"A bank robbery, yes."

Santiago testified that Chino talked about a bank robbery all the time, but she thought he was joking. Athan asked if it wasn't Chino who did all of the talking. "Not on that day," Santiago said.

Athan was exasperated. "Where, in all these hours of depositions, did you say that, Ms. Santiago?" she asked. "Where did you say it?"

"I don't remember."

Athan asked the question several times and got the same answer from Santiago. Pruner objected that it was all argumentative and Padgett sustained the objection. Neither Athan nor Pruner had further questions for Santiago and she was excused.

Court was recessed for twenty minutes. Knots of spectators huddled and talked about the case. There was a buzz of excitement as everyone waited for Paula Gutierrez to testify. During the proceedings she had never wept, but with her soft curls and soulful eyes, she projected an almost angelic aura. What would she be like in the witness chair? Especially under Pruner's astute cross-examination?

* * *

Court reconvened and Paula was called to testify. She approached the witness chair tentatively. She wore a skirt, white blouse, and a pale blue sweater. Paula seemed to float across the floor. She sat down and was sworn in. Athan had to ask her to speak louder so the jury could hear her.

Paula said that she was born in Colombia and moved to the United States with her parents and sister. She described her childhood as "fun" until she was thirteen. Paula said she had a boyfriend and became pregnant the first time they had sex. After having an abortion, Paula testified, she and her two sisters were sent to live in Colombia with their grandparents.

Paula described the difficulty she had adjusting to life in Colombia and how her parents returned the three sisters to the United States after Paula wrote them a letter threatening to kill herself if she remained in Colombia. Once back in the United States, Paula said, the family lived in a better neighborhood in Queens.

Paula said that she was fifteen when she met Chino, who was sixteen. After telling her parents she was going to a movie with Chino, Paula said, she spent the weekend with him. She gave her parents the number of Chino's beeper. When it beeped two days later, Paula said, she and Chino went to a pay phone. Paula's parents, sisters, and grandparents were all waiting for her. Paula said her mother "threw" her into the car and told Chino to stay away from her.

Chino came unexpectedly to her school, Paula said, and got angry because he thought she was flirting with other guys. Paula said she fell in love with

Chino, but the relationship went downhill because he was too possessive. She said he told her not to look at anybody. If Chino thought a man looked at her, Paula said, Chino would punch him.

Paula said when she tried to "cool it," Chino got mad and accused her of seeing other men. "[He was] in my face. Really loud, upset, angry. When he got angry, he was in my face."

Paula described numerous attempts to break up with Chino, but said she always went back to him. She testified about the Thanksgiving dinner where Chino put a razor blade in his mouth, cut his throat, and went into the bathroom after saying he intended to kill himself because Paula wanted to break up.

She said Chino attacked another guest, and then tried to break back into the house after Paula's mother asked him to leave. Paula said she went back with Chino because she feared he would hurt the family. Chino became increasingly violent toward her, Paula said, and she described an incident at a train station.

"He was choking me," she said. "He was mad. He was like, 'I'm going to kill you if you don't want to be with me.' He just kept repeating that he was going to kill me." Paula said Chino released her when her family came to join them.

Chino went home with them, Paula said, and told her parents that she was a slut. She said Chino described their sexual activities in detail. Finally, Paula said, she was so humiliated that she ran out of the house.

Paula talked about several occasions when Chino was violent and abusive, but he always apologized and promised to change. Chino moved to Florida in 1994 through 1997, Paula said. During that time, Paula said, she felt safe.

While working at a shop in Manhattan in 1996, Paula said, she looked up and saw Chino. She said it scared her to see him. She told the jury that she said hi and then asked security to make him leave. Paula said Chino went back to Florida and she didn't hear from him until he telephoned and asked her to testify for him in court.

"His girlfriend charged him with domestic abuse," Paula said. "He was hitting her." Paula said she believed Chino was guilty "because of what he did to me." She didn't see Chino again until the beginning of 1998. Goins wrote the date down on a large sheet of paper for the jury to see.

Paula wrote to Chino in Florida because she didn't know he was back in New York. Santiago forwarded the letter to Chino and he met her at Macy's. Chino said he still loved her and that they could make it work. Paula said her old feelings of love for him came back and she decided to give it another try. She believed Chino had matured.

Paula had an explosive argument with her father about kissing Chino in her family's home, she said. Her father, Paula said, thought it was disrespectful. She told her father he had no right to make her feel like a slut because he had had an affair. Not able to stay at home after that, Paula said, she went to Chino.

A few months later, Paula said, she told Chino she was late on her menstrual cycle. Chino was shooting pool when Paula told him she was pregnant. "He just looks at me and he says, 'Well, I already knew that; I planned it,'" Paula said. "I felt trapped."

Chapter 22

The lawyers argued again at the bench. This time they were fighting over whether the defense could enter into evidence all of the photos that were on the same roll of film that had the damning photograph of Paula holding the MAC-11. Athan wanted the jury to see another photograph.

"She's sitting there like a bump on a log," Athan said earlier. "She looks retarded."

Athan's point was that Paula had no will of her own and was like a zombie until Chino told her what to do. The defense attorney argued hard to have the other pictures admitted because they showed Paula in a different light. But Padgett sustained the prosecution's objection. The trial was almost finished and the judge had ruled against Athan on every major argument.

Paula returned to the witness stand and testified at length as to Chino's volatile nature, explosive temper, bullying ways, his abuse of her, and how she was frightened of him. The testimony was repetitive, but Athan was trying to build a duress defense.

Athan questioned Paula about her intent to commit suicide and her confusion during the interview she gave to Detectives Black, Hevel, and Lease.

Shortly after they entered Isaac Davis's apartment, Paula testified, "Chino started telling me that we had to kill ourselves. That's what we were going to do. I didn't want to, but he kept saying that we had to."

Paula said that before March 2001, Chino talked about killing himself "all the time. He told me when I was pregnant, 'I bet you that I'm not going to live to see my baby after she's two years old.' And when we came to Florida, he kept telling me that he just wanted to put a bullet in his head."

At Davis's apartment, Paula said, she was in a state of shock and didn't remember everything that transpired. Paula remembered that her mother and sister Louisa telephoned and convinced her not to kill herself.

"So when did you change your mind about committing suicide?" Athan asked.

"When I had the gun under my chin."

Paula said they agreed to commit suicide on the count of three.

"It was when I'm ready, I kiss him, and then he knew I was ready."

"So when you were ready, you were supposed to kiss him? That was your agreement?"

Paula said that she was in Davis's room and Chino was in the hall, sitting on the floor so that they could see one another. "He was telling me he was going to let Davis go and then we were going to do it. And I kissed him and—"

"So you kiss him. Then did you pick up the gun?"

"Yes."

"What happened next?"

"I put it under my chin." Paula demonstrated how she held the gun with both hands.

"How did you feel with that gun under your chin?"

"I don't know what I felt. Just—I don't know. I was just scared. And I heard him count two. When he got two, that's when I screamed and I said, 'I can't do it.'"

"Is that the first time he counted?"

"Yes. That's where you heard him say—he said 'Fuck.' He cursed. He got mad at me and then he did it."

Paula said she didn't remember Chino saying, "Ready, Paula?" But she remembered him counting: "'One, two,' and then he pulled the trigger."

"Did you watch him kill himself?" Athan asked. "What happened next?"

"I saw blood coming out of his head," Paula said. "It was just real slow at the moment and I just remember sitting there watching him die."

"Do you remember crying in the room?"

"I don't remember. I was sitting there watching him. He was trying to move his arm. I think he wanted me to touch him or something. I remember I couldn't touch him."

Paula's testimony that she kissed Chino as a signal that she was ready to kill herself conflicts with other testimony. Before Chino's death, Paula was outside the police surveillance camera's range when he did the countdown to suicide and the suicide itself. Paula appeared in the video after Chino shot himself. Paula kissed him, and said, "Good-bye, Sweetie," and patted his arm. Defense attorney Deeann Athan explained that Paula had a garbled recollection of memories because of PTSD.

Paula said she remembered leaving the apartment and being arrested by the SWAT team. The SWAT team "threw her on the ground," handcuffed her, put her in a car, and took her to the police station. Paula said the police put her in a small room with a police officer to watch her. She was still handcuffed.

"How were you feeling when you were surrendering?" Athan asked.

"Felt relieved that it was over." At the police station, Paula said, "I'm in shock. I'm feeling, was it true, or was it not true? Was this a dream?"

Athan wanted to show that Paula had been too tired and upset to give an interview with the police that day. The attorney tried to convince the jury that events of the day and lack of food had overwhelmed Paula, and that her confession was not valid.

"What had you had to eat that day?"

"I didn't eat anything. Ashley and Chino ate oatmeal."

Paula said she was terrified when she went to the conference room for an interview with three detectives. "I didn't know if it was a dream. I just kept playing it over in my head. Did this happen or not? I felt like I just wanted to wake up."

Paula said she was tired, exhausted, and in shock when she was interviewed. It never occurred to her that she could stop the interview, Paula said. When Black read her constitutional rights, Paula said, she understood them. Athan asked if she remembered being told she had the right to talk with a lawyer before questioning.

"Yes. I started thinking about a lawyer." Athan asked why. "Because he told me I could have a lawyer."

Athan asked why she wanted a lawyer. "To help me. I was alone in there. I wanted help." Paula said she thought the police would get a lawyer for her when she asked for one.

Athan established that Black gave Paula the form to sign, but he didn't ask her if she had any questions first. "But, you say to him, 'Okay, I have a question'?"

"Yes. I wanted a lawyer."

"Did you think you were entitled to one?"

"He just told me I could have one."

"You say, 'I don't know. I've never been in this situation. I don't know if I should talk to a lawyer first.' Were you kind of asking for his advice?"

Paula said that she was.

"And then you say, 'Yeah, I want to cooperate, but I don't want to go to jail.'" Black told her she would go to jail if she didn't talk to them "right now," Paula said. The defendant said she thought that cooperating with the police would keep her out of jail.

"Then you ask, 'Do you have a lawyer here?'" Athan said. "Do you remember that?" Paula said she did. Athan continued: "And he says, 'No, we don't have one here. That's the only problem.' This is all on tape and there's a twenty-second pause. Were you thinking? What were you doing?"

"I was confused," Paula said. "They're telling me that I can have a lawyer and then when I ask about one, I can't have one. So then I said, 'Well, I have no choice then.'"

"Talk or get a lawyer?" Athan asked.

"Talk. There's no lawyer, so I have to talk."

"But he had just told you, you had a right to a lawyer."

"That didn't matter because he said I couldn't."

Paula said that on the day of the bank robbery, Chino woke up "real stressed" and "told" her they were going to rob a bank. Chino didn't ask her, she said, he "forced" her. Because of shock, Paula testified, she wasn't able to explain this very well during the interview with Black.

Athan asked what Paula meant when she told Black that Chino told her they "needed" to rob the bank. "He forced me," Paula replied. Athan asked, "So he (Black) said, 'So he (Chino) asks you to go along.' You started to say, 'Said that we . . .' and he (Black) says, 'So he asked you to go along with him.' And you said, 'Yeah.' Did he ask you or did he tell you?"

"He told me."

Paula said she went into the bank and held the gun because she was afraid of what would happen if she didn't do as Chino told her. "What are you afraid of about him?" Athan asked.

"Everything about him."

Paula implied that Black put words in her mouth and didn't let her explain things the way she wanted. In the days following the interview, Paula said, "I started hearing like devil chanting and gospel music," she said. "A week passes and it gets louder. It gets louder by the end of the week. It was real loud. I could tell it was devil chanting and gospel music together, and with that music, I heard a voice talking to me, telling me that he was Chino and that he was just apologizing, that he was sorry for putting me in this situation."

Paula said she talked with the voice for about two weeks because it got worse. "Every time I looked at the TV, I would just see flames and the floor would turn like a bright red. It was driving me crazy, because it was just demons, just laughing at me, would shake my mattress at night, and wouldn't let me sleep. It was just twenty-four hours a day."

When Chino shot Lois, Paula said, she didn't

know he was going to do it. "I just couldn't believe he did that," she said. "I kept thinking, 'Please don't do it, don't do it.' Every time she (Lois) said, 'Put your gun down.' I wanted to scream it out, but I couldn't. I couldn't say anything. I was stuck."

Athan had no more questions for Paula and turned the witness over to the state. Jay Pruner, who tried only homicide cases for the state, was a master at cross-examination. Both Pruner and Ober had been listening to Athan's direct and advising one another. Pruner was nothing, if not prepared.

He said, "You helped Nestor DeJesus rob the bank, didn't you?"

"No."

"You're telling this jury that by going in with a gun when your unarmed boyfriend is snatching money and you're telling patrons and bank employees to stay down that you aren't helping him commit the robbery?"

Paula said that was the case, but that Chino made her do it. Pruner asked if she did anything in the bank that helped Chino with the robbery. "The reason I told people to keep their heads down," Paula said, "was because they kept looking up and I was scared for them."

Pruner asked if Paula felt so desperate and despondent from having been in the bank that she was ready to put a bullet in her head. Paula said yes.

"You knew you were in deep trouble for being part of this bank robbery, right?" Pruner asked.

"I was thinking about the murder he did."

"That's not what you told your parents on the tape that you left for them. You said, 'We went to do a bank robbery.' You didn't say anything about a cop, did you?"

Pruner hammered relentlessly on Paula's testimony about the interview with Black. Paula admitted that she knew she could stop talking at any time. She wanted a lawyer before she talked, but said Black left her no choice.

"He didn't give me a lawyer, so there was no choice," she said.

"You could have stayed silent," Pruner said. "You knew that; isn't that true?"

"I was confused. When he told me about the lawyer, that's why I asked him if I needed one, and he told me that I couldn't have none, so that's why I spoke."

Paula admitted that her parents did a good job providing for her, and that she broke their rules before she ever met Chino. Paula said she ran away from home, took illegal drugs, skipped school, and got pregnant at age thirteen.

"Each of these acts was a conscious choice that you made before you ever met Nestor DeJesus; isn't that right?"

Paula answered yes. Pruner asked, "And your parents decided to send you to Colombia because of your decisions and misconduct before you met Nestor DeJesus; isn't that correct?"

Paula admitted that. When she confronted Chino at Macy's years later, Paula admitted, Chino had not threatened her for having security throw him out. Pruner asked if anyone in her family was hurt, or threatened, by Chino on the Thanksgiving when they had him picked up by the police. Paula again answered no.

Pruner pounded away at incongruities in Paula's testimony. Paula had broken up with Chino before he moved to Florida in 1994 through 1997; each year he had asked her to join him, and she said no. They had broken up. There were no repercussions. She felt safe when Chino was one thousand miles away in Florida.

Paula said she had another boyfriend, but when he "dumped" her in 1997, she wrote to Chino in Florida.

"You remembered how terrible it had been, how fearful you were, and you still reached out to him over the thousands of miles to initiate contact with him, didn't you?" Pruner asked.

Paula said yes.

"You knew old Nestor DeJesus told [you] he was going to 'love me forever and he would also be there for me'; isn't that right?"

"No."

"Isn't it true that only after you had been dumped, you decided that the risk of communicating with this hot-tempered maniac was outweighed by whatever benefit you might get personally from the contact?" Pruner asked. "You made that decision, didn't you?"

"I wasn't afraid of writing him. I thought he was here in Florida."

In fact, Chino had been back in New York for some time and had not even been in contact with Paula. "He was telling you he loved you. When you rejected him, he said, 'Okay, I'm on my way out of here,'" Pruner said. "Isn't that what happened?"

"Yes."

"Never any threat of 'I'm going to kill you; I'm going to kill your parents; I'm going to send demons down on you' on any of those occasion over the four years he tried to get you to come with him?" Pruner asked.

Paula agreed and said she decided to go back

with Chino following the letter she wrote to him in Florida. The old feelings of love emerged and were rekindled, she said. But Pruner showed that Paula couldn't stay at home because of the argument she had with her father, where she told him he had to leave his own house.

"You threw an iron at him, didn't you?" Pruner asked.

"Yes."

"Because you have a temper, too, don't you?"

"Well, out there I did."

"That one isolated incident?"

"I'm no angel. I got mad at my father."

"You got mad at your father to the extent that you told your mother that your father shouldn't live in the same house; isn't that correct?"

The court called a twenty-minute recess before Pruner resumed his cross-examination. He picked up where he had left off, with the argument between Paula and her father. "Explain to the ladies and gentlemen of the jury where you believed, as a sixteen-year-old, that you had the power, authority, to tell your father that he has to leave his house?" Pruner asked. "What was your mind-set?"

"I was very hurt that my father betrayed my mother. She had forgiven him, but I hadn't—"

"You wanted to hurt your father, didn't you?"

"I didn't do it on purpose to hurt him," Paula said. "Just things got out of control that day."

But things didn't go the way Paula had planned, Pruner brought out. Paula's mother wouldn't make her father move and Paula's boyfriend had dumped her.

"Who did you turn to?" Pruner asked.

"Chino."

When Paula knew she couldn't live with Felix, and she had burned bridges at home, she needed a place to stay. "You went back to your old standby, Nestor De-Jesus, who, a few hours earlier, had left with the idea that things weren't working. It was over, right?"

"I turned to Chino."

"When you needed Chino, you decided that you would be with Chino, right?" Pruner asked. "This was your decision at the time and place when you wanted it, right? To be with him in any type of relationship. Because the motivation was all about Paula Gutierrez and what Paula Gutierrez wanted and needed. And when you had needs and you had wants, that's when you reached out to Nestor DeJesus every time in your relationship; isn't that a fact?"

"No, no, no."

"Nestor DeJesus wanted you to live with him since 1994, but you determined when you went to live with him, right?"

Paula answered yes.

"And that was the same way it was after Ashley's birth in 1999 in College Point, right?"

Paula agreed again.

The defendant admitted she knew that Chino shoplifted, that she enjoyed the items he stole for her, and that she was with him once when he got caught at Macy's. Chino lost his job because Paula told his boss he had been arrested. Paula testified that Chino didn't get angry with her.

Pruner pointed out that Paula had testified that Chino didn't want her to have a close relationship with her family after she moved to Florida. "But isn't it a fact that you flew to New York from Florida to visit your parents so many times that you can't recall a number?" Pruner asked.

"I flew many times, yes."

"Did you pay for those trips, since you weren't working?"

"He paid for them."

"So, even though in your view he discouraged you from having a close relationship with your family, he never isolated you from your family, did he? He paid for your trips from Florida to New York in 1999, 2000, and 2001, correct?"

"Not all those trips. Most of them."

Paula admitted that Chino had paid for her to take Ashley to New York to celebrate her first birthday with Paula's family. She said he had encouraged her to go.

"He sacrificed that time away from his daughter on her first birthday to help you with your depression," Pruner said, "so you could be closer with your family; isn't that true?"

Paula said yes.

No matter what else Chino had been, Paula said, she never doubted that he loved Ashley without reservation or limitation. Pruner mentioned that Paula said Chino threatened to kill her and her family in 2001 and that he had made many similar threats over the past seven years. Pruner asked if Chino had ever followed through on the threats. Paula said he had not.

Pruner asked about the numerous times Paula chose to stay away from people, including Chino's relatives. "You decided who you were going to spend time with, right?" Pruner asked. "Not Nestor DeJesus, this controlling and abusive man you describe in your testimony. It was you who made these types of decisions?"

"Yes, I made the decision."

Pruner reminded Paula of her testimony about confronting Chino regarding pornography she found in his work van. "You accused him of having another woman in his life, didn't you?" he asked. "You accused him of this even though you expected a strong, if not violent, response, right?"

"I didn't know . . . how he was going to react at the moment."

"Well, Miss Gutierrez," Pruner said, "you've just told this jury a few hours ago how [Chino] reacted when you saw him looking at other women while you were pregnant, and how he violently reacted. Now, are you telling this jury that you didn't know what to expect when you confronted him with your suspicions that he was running around on you?"

"It was just phone numbers—"

"You didn't think, in the world, he would become violent or argumentative with you, did you?"

"Not that bad, no," Paula said.

"He told you, 'Pack your shit and get out of here.' He kicked you out of the house, didn't he?" Paula answered yes. "Nestor DeJesus wanted you out of his life, didn't he?" Pruner asked.

"That day he kicked me out."

Paula said she went to live with her parents following this incident and stayed about five weeks. She said she felt safe. Chino started e-mailing her and telephoning almost immediately, Paula said, and then they went to videoconferencing so they could see one another while they talked. Paula said she refused Chino's pleas to come back, for five weeks, before she finally agreed to return.

"You had no fear that [Chino] was going to kill you or kill your family because you stayed up there, did you?" Pruner asked. "You had no fear . . . that he would use your mom's Social Security number to find you and her and your father and kill you?"

"No, not at that time."

Paula's portrayal of herself as a woman dominated and terrified by Chino unraveled, thread by thread, under Pruner's meticulous cross-examination: *Who drove the Xterra SUV?* Paula. *Did Chino keep it spotless for her?* Yes. *Did he buy her a membership in a health club?* Yes. *Did he pay for Paula to have her hair done weekly?* Yes. *Were all of the credit cards in Paula's name?* Yes. *Did she use the credit cards?* Yes. *Was the hair salon two blocks from the Bank of America?* Yes. *Did she make several trips to the bank to use the ATM?* Yes. *Who bought the MAC-11?* She did.

You like nice things, nice clothes, right? Yes. *Your clothes are either Ralph Lauren or Polo, right?* Yes. *You and [Chino] lived beyond your means, didn't you?* Yes.

Paula testified that it wasn't a surprise that she and Chino were broke the day they robbed the Bank of America. Paula admitted that their belongings were packed and they intended to move permanently to New York. She was worried about the Xterra being repossessed, Paula said, because they planned on leaving Tampa as soon as possible.

"Is it your testimony to this jury that you had no idea that Nestor DeJesus intended to commit bank robbery at the Bank of America until you found yourself in the parking lot?" Pruner asked.

"Yes, sir."

"You had absolutely no idea that this was where you were going to get money?"

"Yes."

Alarmed at where these questions might be going, Athan got to her feet and objected. She asked if counsel could approach the bench. She was worried that the previous flower shop robbery was going to be introduced. If so, Paula wouldn't be tried for that, but it could have an impact on the jury that would be devastating for the defense. Once they were huddled with the judge, Athan said, "I'm very cautious about not opening the door to anything else—"

"You ought to be," Padgett said.

"I'm not sure where these questions are going. I don't want to stop Mr. Pruner from asking the questions that are relevant. . . . However, I'm making an objection at this point. It sounds like we're getting real close."

"Whatever happens happens," the judge replied.

"I'll tell you where I'm going to go right now, so there's no confusion," Pruner said.

"You don't have to."

Pruner said he was coming to a stopping point, at which time he would ask the judge if they could have a conference outside the jury's presence. "We believe the door has already been opened wide," he said. "I'm not going there now."

Pruner continued cross-examination after the bench conference. Paula's statement to Detective Black, Pruner said, indicated that Paula didn't know where they were going the morning they robbed the bank.

"Where did you think you were going when you left the apartment that morning?" he asked.

"I was scared. I didn't know where we were going."

Pruner zeroed in with surgical precision. *Did you think you were going to Lissette Santiago to borrow money?* No. *You didn't think you were going to a day labor job, did you?* No. *You didn't think you won the lottery, did you?* No. *Tell me what he gave you to wear inside the bank.* A bandanna, a hat, a gun. *Did Nestor DeJesus threaten you?* No.

Paula admitted that she knew they were robbing the Bank of America before they entered it. It was wrong,

Paula said, and she didn't want to do it. "When you're terrified about somebody telling you we're going to go do this, you know, I wasn't thinking then."

Paula testified that she had the gun and waved it around inside the bank to cover Chino. They had the gun in the Xterra when they fled, Paula said. "You knew there was a possibility that the cops would pursue you?" Pruner asked.

"No, I didn't think about that."

"Not even after the dye packs go off and tear gas is spread in the Xterra?"

"No. What I was thinking was that I was going to die because you can't breathe."

Paula testified that she changed clothes in the Regency parking lot because Chino told her to, not to get out of her dye-stained clothing. Paula testified that she didn't listen to Chino and his mother's conversation when she picked them up, even though she told Detective Black that she heard him tell Lissette, "We robbed a bank."

Paula admitted under Pruner's cross-examination that she had no intention of surrendering to the police until after Chino killed himself. But Paula denied knowing that the police were looking for them.

"You get into your apartment and you immediately shower, don't you?" Pruner asked.

"Nestor was telling me to go shower and I go."

"You shower to get off all that bank dye?"

"I don't know if it was on. I just showered."

"You showered because you had bank dye on you, didn't you?"

"I had it on, but I didn't do it because of that. I was just so out of it and he said, 'Go shower,' and that's what I did."

Paula testified that in the shower she didn't concentrate on cleaning bank dye off herself. "I just cried in the shower. I didn't really wash up."

"You didn't even have enough time to dry off fully, did you?"

Paula said that was true.

"You didn't have time to even put underwear on before you and Nestor DeJesus left, right?"

"True."

Paula said she didn't know how long they were in the apartment, five or ten minutes. All she heard was Chino screaming, "Hurry, hurry, get dressed," Paula said.

"He was telling you, you need to get out of there because he heard the helicopters?" Then Pruner asked, "Isn't it true that, even before this robbery, you and [Chino] had spoken or thought about how to deal with the police?"

"No. He said he never liked cops, that he would never go to jail."

"That he would rather die?"

"Yes. He always said that."

Paula said at no time did she think the police were pursuing them. When they left Lissette's apartment, Paula said, Chino went first and she followed with the gun in a blue bag. When Chino was first pursued by Lois, Paula said, he didn't have the gun.

"Isn't it a fact that the gun was still in the bag after [Chino] doubled back from the cemetery?" Pruner asked.

"Everything happened so fast. I remember he came back and he got the gun and he ran across the cemetery with it."

"Isn't it a fact that you told Detective Black that you started going upstairs, meaning to Mr. Kokojan's, and you didn't want to get between that, meaning Officer Marrero and [Chino]?"

Paula explained that was two years ago and now "I remember it differently."

"The gun was still in the blue bag in the breezeway at the time [Chino] came running back from the cemetery, yelling, 'Paula, Paula, Paula'?"

"No, that's not how it happened."

"You didn't want to get between Officer Marrero and Mr. DeJesus because you didn't want to get caught, right?"

"No, I was just scared. He's got the gun. She's an officer."

Paula testified that she was not thinking of running from the police when Chino tried to open Mark Kokojan's car. Instead, she was going to get into the car "because that's what he wanted."

"Just a passive observer; is that it?" Pruner asked. Paula said no, she would have gotten into the car.

Paula testified that she saw Lois take two or three steps after she was shot, even though the medical examiner had testified previously that Lois would have been paralyzed immediately. Lois was still holding the gun when she fell, Paula said, and told the jury she took it from her.

"She was still gushing blood at that point, wasn't she?"

"Yeah. The blood was out, yes."

In the gallery Brenda Marrero, Lois's sister, and Mickie Mashburn, her life companion, were white-knuckled and grim as they heard the testimony about Lois's death.

"You paced in that breezeway as [Chino] fired shots at officers after Officer Marrero was killed; isn't that correct?" Pruner asked.

Paula said she just started running after Chino. She didn't remember pacing.

But Paula said she didn't run because she thought the police might be pursuing her or Chino. She answered no. "That thought never crossed your mind?" Pruner asked incredulously. No, Paula said again.

"Are you telling this jury you didn't have any concern that you may be apprehended by or pursued by police after a police officer was shot within a few feet of you?"

"I was in shock."

Paula's interview with Detective Black indicated that she entered Isaac Davis's apartment with Chino. Now she testified, "He (Chino) threw me in there."

Did you see Isaac Davis running? Yes. *Did you say, "He's in here"?* Yes. *Were you still in shock?* Yeah. *But you had the presence of mind to alert Chino?* Yes. *Are you still in shock in this courtroom?* Yes.

The sharp and devastating cross-examination continued until 5:30 P.M. Padgett adjourned the court until the next morning.

Chapter 23

A nightmare for the defense unfolded at a bench conference when court reconvened. One of Athan's greatest fears was materializing in spite of her best efforts.

Patricia Turpin put it into words: "The defendant, through her testimony, both on direct and cross-examination, has opened the door to the evidence of the flower shop robbery that occurred three days before."

This was what Athan had foreseen when she asked for a bench conference the day before. She knew where the state was heading. Introducing a previous armed robbery into the testimony, committed just days before the bank robbery, would leave Paula's defense in rubble.

At the beginning of the trial, Padgett reserved a ruling on whether or not that evidence intertwined. Turpin gave the judge twenty-one examples of how Paula's testimony paved the way for inclusion of the armed robbery at Flowers By Patricia. She said Paula should not have been unaware that she and Chino were going to rob the bank, because they had done it before.

Turpin maintained that Paula and Chino's bags were packed and that they intended to leave town after the July 3 robbery, but didn't get enough cash at the flower shop. The Bank of America was closed July 4 and 5, Turpin said, so Paula and Chino had to wait until July 6 to strike again. The state should be allowed to make that argument, she said.

Turpin noted that Paula was afraid of what Chino would do to her if she didn't help rob the bank. On the other hand, Turpin argued, nothing had happened to Paula when Chino blamed her for failing to get enough cash at the flower shop.

"She's creating a false impression that, in her twenty-two years of life, she had never committed a violent act that resulted in this dazed and confused state," Turpin said, "rather than the fact that she was actually dazed and confused because this time they had been caught and they were running from the police."

Turpin was just getting warmed up. "The jury has been deluded into believing that she is a person who had absolutely no knowledge that the gun was going to be used for any criminal purpose," she said, "that she was a person who could not even contemplate that a violent robbery would ever occur by herself or by Nestor DeJesus."

Turpin argued that the duress defense Paula used required that the jury know all the circumstances that contributed to Paula's psychological state. "This clearly goes to the lack of duress," Turpin said. "It goes to the lack of imminent threat. She wants them to believe she didn't have time to react because she had never before found herself in this situation. A jury might be able to believe that someone can be paralyzed by fear once, but twice?" Turpin continued. "So it goes to the heart of the duress defense."

Arguing against the motion, Athan cited the same case law the state used, but interpreted it to favor the defense. Athan argued that if she had made a mistake in her direct examination of Paula, "let's call it a mistrial right now and I'll confess that I've been ineffective. Everything that she said was consistent with being afraid, knowing they were going to get money. That's her defense, Judge. If we can't present that, we can't present a defense."

Athan accused the state of trying to "cripple" the defense at every point of the trial. "They don't want us to present a defense," she said. "Now they're going to take every little thing she said and say, 'Oh, guess what, she opened the door.'" The defense attorney pointed out that Paula had every reason to believe no one would be hurt at the bank because no one was injured during the flower shop robbery.

Athan was emotional and argued with passion. She pointed out that Paula and Chino had pulled the flower shop robbery without being caught. They weren't pursued by the police. Paula had every reason to believe they wouldn't be pursued after the bank robbery, Athan said.

"If that's what she was thinking, then that kind of flies in the face of your duress defense," Padgett said.

"She wasn't thinking that," Athan replied.

"You just suggested she was."

Athan said the state believed that, not her. She argued that the two robberies weren't intertwined. "We didn't talk about it in voir dire," Athan said. "We didn't talk about it in opening. All of a sudden, surprise, there's another robbery. I might as well pack up and go home, because this jury is going to go, 'Wow, what is this about?'"

"The point Mrs. Turpin makes about the jury being

kind of deluded or fooled is big," Padgett said. "We're telling the jury just part of the story because, if they knew she had done this before, your argument would be that both were done under duress."

"Absolutely. To spring it on this jury can only prejudice us."

"It's bombshell evidence, no question about that."

"She didn't know there was a plan to rob the bank. She was afraid from the minute she got in the car. She was afraid when he told her to get up and get dressed."

Padgett said that it wasn't likely Paula didn't know she and Chino were going to rob a bank. "The jury is being fooled in thinking that's the truth when it more than likely is not the truth," he said.

"You know what the problem is with this case, Judge?" Athan asked. "The connection Miss Gutierrez has to felony murder is slim at best. That's why the state now wants to throw as much mud against the wall as they can to see what sticks. That's not what our judicial system is all about. Our judicial system is about fairness to everybody, including and utmost to the defendant."

Athan expressed displeasure that the picture of Paula with the MAC-11 was introduced into evidence, but that the jury didn't see the other photos on the roll of film. She said the gun was a toy.

"I'm tired of you talking about it," Padgett said. "Just receive that in evidence, mark that as one of your exhibits."

Turpin interjected that the trial was about truth, not fairness. "When witnesses come in here, they swear to tell the truth, not to tell what is fair."

"We're having a heated discussion about this," Athan said. "But you know what? I'm offended that the implication is that I'm trying to delude this jury.

I'm seeking the truth, too, because I think that the more facts the jury has, the better it is for them to make a decision."

Goins added her opinion to the defense. "What the state wants to do is deny this woman a fair trial," she said.

"I don't know how the defense can say they were utterly unprepared for the introduction of the flower shop robbery when you reserved ruling on that," Turpin said. "You said you would address that at the time that it became relevant." For Paula to say she committed the bank robbery because she was afraid of being beaten or killed, Turpin said, was not the truth.

Athan, known to be an aggressive defense attorney, drew herself up to her full height of five feet. "To throw in the flower shop robbery for the reasons that they say is ludicrous at this point."

Padgett had heard enough. He denied the state's motion and the jury was called back in. Athan sat down. The defense attorney had won a victory, but was not sure it would do her client much good. The only defense Athan had was duress and it was unsuccessful 90 percent of the time.

The break in Paula's testimony did not throw Pruner off stride. His cross-examination continued to pick at the defense's underpinnings. Pruner hammered away at Paula's weakening defenses. *Did she tell Detective Black that she went inside after Chino kicked Isaac Davis's door in?* Yes. *Did she previously testify that she was on the landing when there was a shoot-out?* Yes. *Did she later testify that she was inside the apartment during the shoot-out?* Yes.

The inconsistencies in Paula's testimony were important. If Paula had been inside the apartment during the shoot-out, Chino could not have used her as a human shield. Davis had testified, too, that Paula was inside and that *he* was Chino's human shield.

Mr. DeJesus wanted to marry you when you got pregnant, didn't he? Yes. *Did he ask you more than once?* Yes. *You weren't too afraid to tell him no, were you?* Well, we didn't have money. *You didn't agree to marry him, did you?* No. *You didn't want to marry him, period?* Yes. *It wasn't because of fear, was it?* Not too much.

Pruner brought the hammer down and severely damaged the defense case of duress. Padgett gave Pruner permission to play Paula's confession to the robbery at Flowers By Patricia. The judge told the jury they could only consider the previous robbery as it related to Paula's duress when she robbed the Bank of America two days later. It was a hard loss, but Athan's expression didn't show how much it hurt.

The jury listened to Paula's confession. Several gave her disapproving glances. Paula's defenses crumbled all around her.

When Pruner finished his cross-examination, Athan had no questions on redirect.

Athan called Paula's mother, father, two sisters, and two other witnesses. They all testified about Chino's temper, incidents of road rage, and times they had seen him attack Paula, physically and verbally.

Athan called Dr. Michael Maher, the forensic and clinical psychologist who had interviewed Paula in jail, as her next witness. Maher noted that he had interviewed Paula on nine different occasions, read medical records and depositions from her friends and family.

"Having reviewed the material and interviews, have

you formed an opinion as to whether Paula Gutierrez suffers from any mental disorders?" Athan asked.

"Yes, I have," Maher said. "Post-traumatic stress disorder is the first diagnosis; the second disorder is major depressive disorder."

Maher testified that he believed Paula suffered from PTSD as far back as December 2000. Paula, he testified, was disabled by mood disorder and PTSD. He said she had thoughts of hopelessness, suicide, difficulty sleeping, trouble with memory, and difficulty in making rational decisions. At times, the psychiatrist said, Paula was "barely able to drag herself through her life."

Maher said that Paula's condition was worsened by the abuse she experienced at the hands of Nestor DeJesus. Under such duress, he testified, Paula could not make reasonable decisions because fear caused a disassociation from reality.

The defense rested following Maher's testimony. Dr. Donald R. Taylor, the psychiatrist who testified for the state, had also concluded that Paula suffered from PTSD. The critical difference was the time frame each gave. If the jury accepted Maher's diagnosis, Paula would have been impaired at the time of the robbery and murder. Taylor believed that the murder and Chino's suicide were the stressors that pushed Paula over the edge. If so, Paula would not have been impaired by PTSD when she and Chino robbed the bank.

Mark Ober and Jay Pruner pondered over the points they wanted to stress in the prosecution's closing argument:

- None of the defense witnesses, except for Paula, testified that Chino made her keep her eyes downcast in public.

- Paula claimed that Chino didn't want her to be close to friends and family, yet Chino or his mother paid for all of her trips to New York.

- Defendant claimed to feel safe at home, but took a shower to wash red dye off herself, didn't hear helicopters everyone else heard (because she was listening for them), and left the apartment carrying the gun.

- Paula put on sweatpants in July before the bank robbery. She claimed they were more comfortable, but they were to disguise her figure. She did this before she left the house.

- Inside the bank, only Paula said, "Do not look up" and "We will be out of here in a few minutes." Chino never said this, so either they talked about what she would say before or she thought of it on her own and was not simply following mindlessly.

- Duress requires that the crime avoided be greater than the crime committed. The witnesses were terrified of being shot. Someone being killed during an armed bank robbery was a very real threat. Defendant could articulate no broken bones, no loss of consciousness, no hospital visits. Was the harm avoided greater than that committed, or did the defendant simply choose she would rather put others at significant risk than herself?

- Money was being thrown out of the driver's side. This was because the defendant was holding tight to the money she had, and she intended to clean it with peroxide and use it.

- Defense tried to show they were at the Crossings a substantial period of time. Lissette Santiago testified it took her between ten and fifteen minutes to pick them up and take them to the Crossings because she had a two-year-old and had finished a plumbing job before getting them.
- Lissette was angry when she saw the MAC-11 and Paula laughed at her.
- Motive: Paula and Chino were getting ready to move to New York, and Paula asked Lissette for a loan because her parents were being evicted. Paula's parents made an offer on a house that didn't close until October. They would be happy to have Paula, Chino, and Ashley move in with them.
- Daniel Tatum saw Paula pacing in the breezeway after Officer Marrero was shot. She looked from side to side. When Chino ran through the breezeway, she ran after him. *She was watching his back.* This clearly showed more than anything else her degree of cooperation, her desire to succeed in this robbery, and her willingness to protect Nestor DeJesus.
- Detective Batista said "Ashley" was the key word that snapped Chino back. Paula didn't mention Ashley to dissuade Chino from robbing the bank.
- Defendant denied involvement in bank robbery until it occurred to her that security tapes were going to show that she was there.
- Videotape inside apartment. This was actual evidence of their relationship under stress. How did Chino treat her? Deferentially, kind,

inquisitive. How did she treat him? She initi-
ated a long sexual kiss and called him sweetie
twice before he was dead, and caressed his
shoulder on the way out of the apartment.

- Alerting Chino to Isaac Davis: "He's in here."
  She was alert and fully cooperating. Defendant kept comparing her level of culpability
  to Nestor DeJesus, in front of him. She rejected his suggestion of suicide. She spoke
  freely. Paula did not deny that Chino said,
  "You never said this was going to happen."

- Chino went through mood swings during
  hostage standoff, but was never physically or
  emotionally abusive to Paula.

- Maher testified that Paula wasn't forced to
  enter the bank.

- Inconsistencies in Officer Shepler's testi-
  mony. He said, "I am totally focused on him."
  (So he had no idea what defendant is doing.)
  "I wanted to get the bastard for what he did
  to Lois." Showed he was emotionally affected.
  "I didn't have a chance to be affected by it,
  I had to stay alive."

- Paula wasn't controlled. Defendant went to
  the gym and worked out, had her hair done,
  went into the pool, went to the park. Defendant wrecked the new car they couldn't afford
  and Nestor DeJesus never got mad at her.

- Defendant had spent her whole life trying to
  punish her parents for sending her to Colombia and for forcing her to have an abortion.
  Nestor DeJesus was the ultimate act of rebel-
  lion. Her parents didn't like him and they
  couldn't stop her from seeing him.

- Each time authorities were called, when

Chino was in a rage, he had a predictable reaction. He calmed down and complied, until the one time his confrontation with authorities threatened Paula. Then he shot an officer dead to try and get his true love to safety.

- Defendant refused Chino's demands to move to New York, refused his proposals of marriage, refused his requests that she socialize with his sister during Thanksgiving. Went to New York against his wishes and stayed for prolonged visits with her family. Refused his request that they live together during her pregnancy. Took him to task for looking at other women. Apparently had convinced him finally, after just eighteen months in Florida, to return to New York because she wanted to be close to her family. How does agreeing to move back to New York and into the basement of her parents' home coexist with an intent and pattern of isolation?

- Because defendant was depressed and missed her family, Chino bought her a brand-new, very expensive car so she could go out. Got her a gym membership. Encouraged and paid for her trips to New York.

- When Chino did abuse her, she didn't hesitate to let him know she was angry, giving him the silent treatment.

- Defendant felt comfortable calling police/ security when she didn't want Chino around. Said she stopped getting out of bed about June 6, 2001. Isaac Davis moved into his apartment in May and saw them in the pool after that date.

- Defendant said it never occurred to her that cops were chasing her, but unlike the flower shop robbery, they ditched the car, changed clothes, showered, kept the gun, and were quickly on the move again. And she grabbed her wallet from the car.

Ober said, "There's just no way she wasn't a willing participant in both robberies. She wasn't a battered, abused woman. I don't doubt that they had their fights, but she gave as good as she got. Nestor DeJesus's first thoughts were to take care of her and Ashley."

Now the jury had heard all the testimony. The state and defense had one more chance to influence the jurors, with their closing arguments. Those would come the next day. Paula changed from her pretty white blouse and skirt into a baggy orange jumpsuit and waited in her eight-foot-by-eight-foot cell.

Chapter 24

Almost two years after the bank robbery and the murder of Officer Lois Marrero, Paula's trial was winding down. It was May 21, 2003, and court convened for final arguments by both sides. The jury would receive instructions after the final arguments and would begin deliberations to decide whether Paula was guilty or not guilty of the charges.

This was crunch time for Paula. If convicted of first-degree felony murder, she would spend the rest of her life in prison with no chance of parole. The judge had no discretion in the sentence. There was absolutely no doubt about it. She faced the possibility of a lifetime behind bars.

Pruner rose to make the final argument for the state. The state had to prove Paula's guilt beyond a reasonable doubt, and he intended to argue that Paula was never under duress, and that she had not reached a place of safety before Lois was killed by Chino.

Pruner briefly reviewed the case, and said Paula and Chino had dumped the yellow SUV because they were still running from the police. He pointed out that the SUV's motor was still warm when found at the

Regency Apartments. Paula and Chino, he said, had committed robbery and "wanted to get out of Dodge."

Although Paula and Chino had reached their apartment at the Crossings without seeing a police car chasing them, Pruner said, the police were in hot pursuit. He argued that Paula knew that because she barely had time to take a shower before they were on the run again. In fact, she and Chino left the apartment so soon, Pruner said, that Paula didn't even have time to put on underwear.

"That's the most telling about the brief time she was there before they left," Pruner said. "That's how brief; that's how hectic. So if you hear an argument about them being safe or in a safe haven in that apartment, think about how soon they left, and think about why they left.

"They left because they heard helicopters overhead and because they knew that the dragnet was being tightened."

Pruner presented a more detailed timeline to show that the police were in hot pursuit even while Paula was in her apartment. He verified the timeline with telephone calls, radio traffic, helicopter searches, and police activities from the time the bank was robbed until Lois was killed.

The assistant state attorney insisted that police pursuit began with the first 911 call as the robbery was taking place at 10:41 A.M. At 10:42 A.M., bank surveillance cameras record the robbery and two radio transmissions were made by the Tampa police. Two minutes later, Barbara Oppenheim telephoned about money being thrown from a car. She gave a description of the Xterra.

"Why were they driving the bright canary Xterra?" Pruner asked. "Logic tells you they were going to head out of Dodge. Bags were packed, money in hand, and it didn't matter if they were driving a Goodyear blimp down Kennedy Boulevard, they were going to get out of Dodge before they could be apprehended. Only the dye pack explosions prevented this," Pruner said.

Officer Scudder arrived where money was "raining" at 10:48 A.M. At 10:55 A.M., just fourteen minutes after the first robbery report, a helicopter was in the air searching for the Xterra. About thirty minutes after the robbery, the Xterra was found at the Regency Apartments with the engine still warm. Police then began looking specifically for Chino, who owned the SUV. They knew where Chino lived.

Lois reported at 11:23 A.M. that she was chasing Chino. Other police units hurried to help. Within sixty seconds Lois was back on the radio saying that she still was in hot pursuit. "Even less than a minute later," Pruner said, "there's the fatal broadcast, 'Officer down. Officer down.'"

Pruner argued that "Paula Gutierrez was on the run with Mr. DeJesus each and every step of the way."

There were many contradictions between Paula's actions and the defense's claim that she acted under duress, Pruner argued. He noted that Paula had the gun in the bank, she carried it into their apartment at the Crossings, and she carried it when she left the Crossings. Pruner argued that Paula was the only person seen with the MAC-11 until Lois was shot.

"What the evidence has demonstrated to you," Pruner said, "is an unbroken, continuous series of events that constituted the escape from the immediate scene of the robbery. They didn't leave the apartment because they were doing anything illegal. They left because they knew what they did in the bank. So they could escape and continue to escape from that immediate scene of the bank robbery," Pruner said.

Paula had never found a safe haven, Pruner said. "She was on the run every step of the way." In committing a robbery, Pruner said, "flight" is part of the crime. The evidence showed continuity, he said. "There is no abrupt ending, no safe haven at any point."

Athan objected, claiming that Pruner had misstated the law. Padgett overruled.

The flight continued even after Lois's death, Pruner contended, when Chino kicked down the door to Isaac Davis's apartment and he and Paula took Davis hostage. Pruner asked the jury to return a verdict of guilty "for the highest degree of crime that you have found has been proven beyond a reasonable doubt."

Deeann Athan approached the jury to make her closing argument. In her dark suit and red blouse, she was all business. She was a passionate advocate throughout a trial that seemed to be an uphill climb for the defense. Undaunted, Athan fought for Paula, who she believed was not guilty of the crimes with which she was charged.

She began by saying the trial wasn't as simple as Pruner wanted them to believe, and cited a movie entitled *Twelve Angry Men,* where all evidence pointed to the defendant's guilt. One juror, played by the late Henry Fonda, convinced the other eleven jurors to vote for acquittal because the evidence was not what it seemed to be.

On the surface it appeared that Paula might be

guilty, Athan said, but jurors had to look deeper. "I tell you without hesitation that if you follow the law," Athan said, "she is not guilty."

She mentioned that both the state and defense psychiatrists agreed that Paula suffered from mental illness and that her ability to make decisions was impaired. The only question between the two diagnoses, Athan said, was when the impairment began. Paula suffered abuse and was terrorized by Nestor DeJesus for three years and had learned how to stay alive with a man who threatened to kill her and her family, she said. Sure, Paula made an independent decision not to kill herself, but that was consistent with how Paula had learned to adapt.

"Ladies and gentlemen, duress is not about being robotic, although at times she felt that she was a robot," Athan said. "It is about making decisions. The question is why she made them."

Athan said the evidence proved that Paula acted out of duress. "Can anybody say that [Chino] was not a danger to her?" Athan asked. "Dr. Maher told you about this choking, the kind of thing that is life-threatening. Imagine being held up against the wall by this six-foot, two-hundred-pound weight-lifting maniac. The threat and harm was significant to her."

The randomness of Chino's attacks on Paula was what made it so devastating, Athan said. If you were beaten every day at 2:00 P.M., you would expect it, she said. After 2:00 P.M. passed, she said, you wouldn't have to worry. With Chino, Paula never knew when he would explode. "That's what makes it so scary," Athan said. "You never knew when it was coming. That was her pathological, sick world with Nestor DeJesus."

The introduction of Paula's confession to the flower shop robbery had been devastating and Athan tried to soften the effect during her closing argument. "She's not on trial for the flower shop robbery," Athan said. "She had no reasonable means to avoid danger except being in the flower shop or being in the bank."

Athan said no one had been injured at the flower shop and that there had been no pursuit by the police. That gave Paula reason to believe there would be no pursuit after the bank robbery, Athan maintained.

Athan said Paula had resigned herself to the horrible life she had with Chino. Paula had called the police twice, she said, and both times Chino had been released without being arrested. Each time he had threatened to kill her. "She had decided that she would bear whatever horror he wanted to give her, because she had brought this maniac into their (the family) lives and she took responsibility."

At the bank, Athan said, Paula told people to keep their heads down because she was afraid of what Chino would do. "She had seen his rage. Was he capable of hurting anyone in the bank without a gun? You bet he was."

Athan told the jury they had to look at Paula's mental illness. She told them they had to look at things from Paula's perspective. Paula did not act as a reasonable person because she was impaired, Athan argued.

Athan again stressed that both psychiatrists had diagnosed Paula with post-traumatic stress disorder, brought about by fear, helplessness, or horror. Paula, Athan said, suffered from all three.

Athan was unable to use the battered spouse syndrome as a defense, but she argued that Paula's PTSD was based on ongoing domestic violence.

"Physical violence associated with verbal threat," Athan said. "What did he say? You heard it from her. You heard it from many witnesses: 'I will kill you. If you leave me, I will kill you. If you weren't pregnant, I would kill you. I will hunt you down. I know your mother's Social Security number. You can't hide from me. Not only will I hunt you down, I will hunt your family down and I can find you. Even if you go to Colombia, I will find you.'"

Athan reminded the jury that Chino had said the same thing to Hadaad during the flower shop robbery: "'I have your driver's license. Don't call the police. I will hunt you down.'"

The goal of domestic violence was accomplished by physical and verbal abuse, along with psychological components, to break down the will of the abused partner, Athan said. This gave the abuser control of the partner, who adapted to the escalating violence. Both psychiatrists agreed this was what happened to Paula, Athan said.

The defense attorney argued that Paula was so beaten down that neighbors barely noticed her. She rarely said hello and kept her eyes averted, Laura Kent didn't think Paula spoke English, Athan said, and Isaac Davis, who had a nickname for everyone, including Chino and Ashley, did not have one for Paula. "She didn't exist," Athan said. "She was withdrawn and did not interact. She was a nonentity."

Athan knew that juries didn't like a duress defense. In fact, they rejected it more than 90 percent of the time. Still, she had to show Paula's state of mind. Also crucial to Paula's defense were Athan's contentions that she had reached a safe haven and that she didn't get an attorney before being interviewed by Detective Black, even though she had made a request.

Athan said that "flight" was *the* issue in this case. Lois's murder didn't occur in the bank or while they were attempting to rob the bank, she said, which would have made it felony murder. If the murder occurred while Paula was fleeing the immediate scene of the robbery, that would be felony murder, too. Athan argued that Paula had reached a safe haven and had stopped running. The flight, she said, was marked by a series of interruptions in the series of events.

There was a break, Athan said, before Lois was killed. When Paula left the bank, police were not pursuing the Xterra getaway vehicle, Athan said. "They got away, but they hadn't reached their safety yet," she said. The defense attorney argued that the police did a fantastic job, but they were never in pursuit of the SUV: it had been abandoned when police found it.

"Paula Gutierrez was home taking a shower," Athan said. "She had reached a place of safety. That is what breaks the chain. That is what tells you she's no longer escaping from the scene. She's home."

The law, Athan argued, held the home sacred, and that a person in her home was protected by the Fourth Amendment of the Constitution. "It says the police, the government, cannot come into your home without a search warrant signed by a magistrate," Athan said. "Your home is your sacred place. Your home is your castle. And that's how the law views it. . . . It is your place of sanctity, your place of safety."

Athan insisted that Paula believed it was over and that she cried with relief. "She thought it was over," Athan said. Paula told Black that she heard helicopters, but that she was mistaken. Remember, the interview was "torturous at the end of a long, torturous day."

Paula testified in court that she wasn't sure about

hearing the helicopters, Athan said. Athan pointed out that on her cross-examination, Davis, Kent, Tatum, Forney, and Officer Metzgar did not hear helicopters. Paula was taking a shower, Athan said, and all she heard was Chino ordering her to get dressed and run.

Athan reminded the jury that when Chino's mother dropped them at the Crossings, they wanted to take Ashley. If they were escaping, would they put Ashley in peril? she asked. "The child is precious to everyone," Athan said, "even this monster, Nestor De-Jesus. He's going to take this child and put her in danger in the middle of a police pursuit? I don't think so."

Athan expected the state to present a large blowup of the devastating photograph showing Paula with the MAC-11. There was little she could do except try to take some sting out of it. "This picture means nothing," she said. "They put this picture in and then we put the whole roll in . . . family pictures. [Paula] is sitting on the sofa like a bump on a log, looking depressed, looking a lot like a victim."

Athan again talked more about Paula's statement to Detective Black. "I've made a lot of noise about her statement," Athan said. "Our constitutional rights are precious. She asked for a lawyer that day. The police say that isn't their job. You know what? It is their job."

She ended by asking the jury to look beyond the obvious. "Her escape was done," Athan said. "It's not felony murder. Nestor DeJesus is Lois Marrero's killer. Paula Gutierrez didn't kill anybody. She didn't help anybody kill anyone. She shouldn't be the sacrificial lamb because [Chino] took his own life and has robbed us all of the vengeance of getting a cop killer in this courtroom."

* * *

Athan took her seat next to Paula as Pruner rose to make his rebuttal. He intended to strip away the "revised" edition of Paula like layers of an onion and to show her as selfish, manipulative, and fully in control of her faculties. Just as Athan expected, Pruner displayed a larger-than-life photograph of Paula with the MAC-11.

Pruner attacked the defense contention that Paula had found a safe haven and that the flight from the bank robbery was over. That should be obvious, he said, because Lois was killed while Paula and Chino tried to steal a car to continue their flight.

"If they weren't fleeing," he asked. "why were they carrying the gun?"

To see the real Paula Gutierrez, Pruner said, all you had to do was look at what she said and did. Look at her as she is, he said, and not through a lens filtered by a psychiatrist or interpreted in a diagnostic manual. He turned his attention to the enlarged photograph so feared by the defense.

"This photograph was taken at a time when she is supposedly so depressed that she can't get out of bed," he said. "This picture tells you one of two things: either she wasn't that depressed or this gun gave her energy because she liked the way it felt.

"Look at her. She is radiant in this picture. This is a pose that you would see if it was an actress holding her first Oscar or a graduate from college holding a well-deserved diploma."

Pruner said the gun brought energy and comfort to Paula. The picture, he said, told more than any words or psychiatrist could tell about Paula's state of mind at that time. He asked them to listen to

Paula's words and voice when she talked with Batista during negotiations.

"She warns Detective Batista, not in timid, docile tones of a downtrodden, beaten woman, but in assertive warning tones: 'Don't come in here or there'll be a shoot-out.' She warns him that she's got Officer Marrero's gun."

And the only concerns Paula expressed, he said, were of going to jail, being raped in jail, having the police step on her neck, and having newspapers show her face. All of those statements show nothing but self-involvement, Pruner told the jury.

The jury listened to the portion of the tape Pruner had talked about and then he continued to talk about her self-involvement. She was afraid of incarceration, of what might happen in jail, and of publicity. "That's where her mind-set was," he said, "not in some deluded never-never land or nether region that Dr. Maher wants you to believe."

He said it was important for the jury to understand this so they could weigh the duress defense accurately, and whether Paula was forced to take part in the robberies and the armed burglary of Isaac Davis's apartment. The jury needed to understand the real Paula Gutierrez, he said, not the "new, revised" Paula.

Pruner produced Paula's wallet. Inside it was a smaller print of the photograph of her with the MAC-11. "Look at the photo there," he said, indicating the blowup. "That's your timid, docile, downtrodden, beaten, abused woman that she carried around. That's Paula Gutierrez."

Paula was a troubled girl long before she met Nestor DeJesus, Pruner said. The real Paula Gutierrez was a runaway who skipped school and became pregnant at thirteen. "She was so unmanageable she was sent to another country, to her homeland, by her parents," Pruner said. Paula learned how to manipulate people at age thirteen by threatening to kill herself if her parents didn't return her to New York.

Instead of being dominated by Chino, Pruner said, "she played him like a fiddle." He said Paula controlled when, and if, she would see Chino. She broke up with Chino many times and he didn't hurt her or her family. "She didn't fear violent repercussions of rejecting him and she didn't suffer any," Pruner said. Paula went to live with Chino, Pruner said, only after she had been dumped by a boyfriend, thrown an iron at her father, and demanded that her father leave his own house.

"She tells her mom, 'I can't live here with him anymore. You need to tell him to leave.' What does that tell you about her self-assurance? Mom doesn't back her. Paula calls Felix and he says, 'No, you can't stay here.' Who does she turn to? She turns to Nestor DeJesus when she needs him."

After Paula became pregnant, she defied Chino and moved into her mother's house, Pruner said, and she stayed there until she was ready to return on her own terms. She wasn't afraid to confront Nestor DeJesus if he insulted, offended, or disrespected her, Pruner said.

The small things in life can tell you volumes about a person, Pruner said. He asked the jury to take another look at Paula's wallet. This woman who never went anywhere. "What you see are credit cards, Household Bank, Visa, Bank of America Visa, Bank of America ATM, Target, Burdines, all in her name," he said. "Circuit City. You see cards to Tribeca Hair Salon, a doctor's card, pediatrician card, Busch Gardens passes, library cards, and health club card."

On July 6, Paula's bags were packed and she was ready to go to New York. Who was always going to New York? Pruner asked. It was Paula. But she needed a big score to leave town. Who had the motivation to rob a bank? Pruner asked. Paula.

Pruner debunked the notion that Paula was mentally ill and in such a disassociative state that she didn't know what was happening on July 6, 2001. During the interview with Black, Paula was asked if she had done any other robberies in Tampa. She answered no. Pruner said Paula followed that by specifically denying involvement in the flower shop robbery. She denied it a third time to Detective Hevel.

It was important to Paula not to be associated with the flower shop robbery, Pruner said, because that would show she had robbed before, and knew exactly what she was doing. This, Pruner said, struck at the heart of the defense claim that Paula was under duress.

Pruner showed the videotape of the bank robbery and described Paula's movements. "Look where she's standing. Look where she's looking. You know where she's standing, ladies and gentlemen?" he asked. "She's standing at the right apex, the only location in this bank where she can see the front door and where she can see Nestor DeJesus, who is robbing."

It was important for the jury to see that, Pruner said, because it didn't jibe with the revised Paula. "If she was a downtrodden, abused woman who was forced by duress to do that," he said, "as a timid, docile young puppy would do, wouldn't you expect she would carry the gun and follow him directly to the teller window if there wasn't any preplanning?"

Paula staked out the only area where she could cover everything, Pruner said. He called it an orchestrated, takeover robbery that she knew was going to happen, and she intended to participate in it. She told Batista about the bank surveillance tapes before he knew about them. "Does that show you a level of sophistication and awareness of what was going on in the bank?" Pruner asked. "Sure it does."

He said Dr. Maher's diagnosis of Paula was based on "sloppy science." Maher didn't have all of the facts, Pruner said, and he took what Paula said at face value. There was no critical investigation as to whether or not she told him the truth. Only Paula's side of the troubled relationship was heard, Pruner said. "This trial is not a referendum on whether domestic violence is ever justified or is to be excused," he said. "I'm not suggesting to you that any abuse she may have suffered at the hands of Mr. DeJesus should be minimized or excused, but it doesn't rise to the level of duress, which excuses her criminal conduct."

Pruner said he was not suggesting that none of the abuse occurred, but, he said, nobody heard much about it until after Paula was told by a psychiatrist, who was there to help her and her attorneys.

"Mr. DeJesus was the type of person that you would expect would kill a cop," Pruner said. "I'm not going to portray him to you as anything but that." But Paula, he said, saw something in him that she loved, and which offered her a better and safer life. That's why she always came back to him.

Pruner played part of the videotape recorded by the police when Paula and Chino were in Davis's apartment. He said it would show the true nature of their relationship.

"'What do you want me to do?' he (Chino) says to Paula. 'Tell me,'" Pruner quoted. "That was crunch time. That's the true nature of their relationship."

Pruner said that when all the facts were studied, the only conclusion was that Paula was guilty as charged on each of the three crimes. He asked the jury to deliver that verdict. "The law allows it and simple justice demands it," he concluded.

Chapter 25

Following the closing arguments, the judge gave the jury instructions on how to deal with the charges against the defendant. The instructions were hammered out through considerable debate between the judge and both sides. The defense objected to the instruction the judge would give on "collateral" crimes—in this case, the flower shop robbery.

Padgett's instructions took about twenty-five minutes and the jury retired to consider its verdict at 1:45 P.M. About 4:00 P.M., court was called back in session. The judge had received a note from the jury foreman requesting the testimony of Lissette Santiago. Her testimony took about an hour.

At a bench conference Padgett told the attorneys he would deny the request, but he asked if the jury wanted particular portions read back. Padgett said he would reconsider the request then.

Goins objected, for the defense, to having just portions of the testimony read to the jury. That would not give the jury an opportunity to view it in context with the entire testimony.

"If they don't need her whole testimony, then

we're not going to read her whole testimony," Padgett said.

Goins said she understood. "I'm saying if the court is going to allow read-back, then we would ask the entire testimony, not just the portion the jury is asking for, be read back."

"Why? Because you can, right?"

"Because I can," Goins said.

"Because you can."

"Yes, Your Honor, I can. I think it's true that if you try to portion up the testimony, the jury's not going to have the opportunity to assess that in context with the entire testimony because many things can interrelate."

"We'll let the jury decide that," Padgett said.

The jury returned to the courtroom and Padgett addressed Julie Gordon, who had been elected foreman. He declined the jury's request, but said he would reconsider if only specific portions were needed. Padgett said that would be difficult because testimony was scattered between direct and cross-examination.

Gordon said the jury also wanted to know if there were two video cameras in Isaac Davis's room. The judge said there were two cameras, but only one recorded anything that was relevant. One camera did not record any people in the room, he said.

The jury was sent back to deliberate and court was recessed, pending a verdict.

"Were you going to say anything, Mrs. Athan?" Padgett asked.

Athan looked surprised. "Was I going to say something?"

"Yeah. You looked like you were getting ready to say something."

Athan replied, "I think I said enough."

* * *

Padgett called the court back in session at 6:00 P.M. There was still no verdict from the jury. When the jury entered the room, Padgett told them that if they were close to a verdict, they could continue to deliberate. If not, court would recess and they would continue deliberations at 9:00 A.M. the next day.

"I would say we're very close," Gordon said.

"Do you really? Fine."

Court was recessed again, pending a verdict.

Deliberations went on inside the jury room for another forty-five minutes. The jury had not reached a verdict and wanted to go home. Padgett recessed court and said it would reconvene at 9:00 A.M.

The next morning, a less than monumental decision had to be made regarding two jurors who were smokers. The attorneys huddled at the bench to consider this breathtaking issue.

"I just want to tell you people what we've done," he said. "We did it yesterday and we're getting ready to do it now and want to see if you have any objection. Better safe than sorry, Padgett's rule."

He said two jurors smoked. They were escorted out to a balcony, accompanied by a deputy, who stayed with them. "No talking about the case," Padgett said. "They just smoked. Anybody got a problem with that?"

No one did.

Having solved the problem to everyone's satisfaction, court was recessed, and the jury sent back to continue deliberations, after the two jurors had their smokes.

* * *

At 11:00 A.M., word came that the jury had reached a verdict. Padgett called the court back into session and asked the bailiff to return the jury. Paula sat at the defense table, her hands knotted on the table, her features tense and fearful.

Padgett asked Gordon if the jury had reached a verdict. She replied that it had and gave it to the clerk. Padgett ordered the clerk to publish the verdict.

Paula was found guilty of felony murder in the first degree. As she heard the first "guilty" ring out, Paula burst into tears and buried her face in her hands. She would spend the rest of her life in prison with no possibility of parole. The jury found her guilty of armed burglary and armed robbery, both in the first degree. Paula's shoulders shook and a wail came from the gallery. A woman cried so hard that it took two men to hold her upright as she stumbled out of the courtroom.

Padgett polled the jury and each one acknowledged the verdict of guilty. Padgett thanked the jury and discharged the members. The judge ordered a presentence investigation and set sentencing for June 23 at 9:00 A.M., just short of a month away.

On June 23, 2003, Paula Gutierrez sat in the courtroom, flanked by her two lawyers, and waited to hear Judge Padgett pronounce sentence on her. Paula was obviously nervous and choked back tears on occasion. She would have a chance to speak to the judge before sentencing, but first the court heard from Lois Marrero's life partner, then her sister.

Mickie Mashburn, who had married Lois twelve

years ago, was the first to speak. Mashburn had sat through every day of the trial. No matter how bad it had made her feel, she almost always had a kind word or a hug for Deeann Athan, the defense attorney.

Mashburn said, "We spent the three weeks listening to how bad her day was on July 6, 2001. We are here today to speak on how bad Lois Marrero's day was on July 6, 2001."

Mashburn said she looked at the case as a police officer, domestic partner, and a former domestic violence detective. She spoke of the painful loss, not just for herself, but for Lois's friends, family, and the Tampa Police Department. Mashburn said it was especially wrenching for officers to investigate the case because so many of them were close to Lois.

As for herself, Mashburn said: "Half of me died that day. All I'm able to do is either have the memories or go out to a plot of land that I look at that she's not really there. Paula's family is able to see her. I will never have that. Neither will the family. She (Brenda Marrero) has lost a sister. Her parents have lost a daughter." Mashburn said she could not imagine the pain of parents who lose a child.

Lois, Mashburn said, was a "very happy person" who loved to run, and who was bright and cheerful the moment her feet hit the floor in the morning. When they left for work in the morning, Mashburn said, she and Lois told each other they loved one another more than yesterday. "I'm not able to say that anymore."

Mashburn told Paula that she could have stopped the robbery, which led to the murder, at any time, but she chose not to. "I blame you for it and I do hold you responsible because you are guilty for those circumstances," Mashburn said.

The former domestic violence detective drew upon her experience in that field and told Paula that she was not a victim. "You may try to portray yourself as a victim, but you're not. These are the victims standing here today," she said.

Mashburn asked the judge to sentence Paula to life in prison. "Every day when she gets up, I want her to be told when she can go to the bathroom, when she can eat, what she can do, what she can't do," Mashburn said. "We will never have peace from this brutal killing."

Brenda Marrero, Lois's sister, was beautiful in spite of the grief that could be seen in her eyes. She told the judge that she was there as "the voice for all who knew and loved" Lois. Marrero told Paula that no matter how much she wished everything were just a bad dream, Lois's loved ones wished it even more. She said there was only one real victim and that was "my sister, Lois, the person Nestor and Paula killed."

Paula was never a victim, Marrero said, insisting that Paula had made other people victims all her life. Marrero said that Paula was heartless. "I wish upon you years of sorrow, grief, and continuous unsettling of your soul."

Marrero asked for a life sentence. "We beg the court [to] put Paula where she belongs, away, away for the rest of her erratic and irresponsible life. . . ."

Mark Ober argued for the prosecution, saying that the bank robbery was unique because the sole motivation was sheer greed. Most of the time, he said, such robberies were committed by people trying to support a drug habit.

Paula lived beyond her means, Ober said, and wanted to keep doing it. The state attorney said she had alternatives to robbing a bank: "She could have asked her family. She could have sold the Nissan Xterra. She could have sold the gun or—perhaps, even the unthinkable—get a lawful job and not put this community at great risk."

Paula had choices that could have spared Lois Marrero's life, Ober said. He said Paula had the ability to make sound decisions. She could have returned to New York. She could have told Chino no. She could have surrendered to Lois when the police officer approached. Paula could have warned Lois that Chino had a gun.

"Her choices were endless," Ober said. "Yet she chose to reunite with her beloved Chino, not only to terrorize Isaac Davis, but again to place a multitude of Tampa police officers and citizens of this community in great peril." Ober added that the defense claim of Chino dominating Paula was not credible.

"The state joins the Marrero family, Ms. Mashburn, the Tampa Police Department, Isaac Davis, and Pam Merin, of the Department of Corrections, in urging this court to sentence the defendant to life in prison on all counts."

Athan acknowledged that the judge had no choice but to sentence Paula to life in prison without the possibility of parole on the conviction of first-degree murder. She hoped that he would give her less than the minimum sentences for the other counts.

Paula regretted Lois's death, Athan said, but noted that Lois was killed by Chino, not Paula. It was interesting for Athan to hear excuses for Chino, she said. "He was a violent, despicable man. Judge, there is no question that Paula Gutierrez was a battered woman, and that's not to gain the court's sympathy. That is something the court should consider in determining the proper sentence."

The defense attorney pointed out that Dr. Donald Taylor, the psychiatrist appointed to examine Paula for the state, reported that Paula suffered some symptoms that go with battered spouse syndrome. Athan noted that the court did not allow her to explore battered spouse syndrome in her defense of Paula.

"Your Honor, the battered woman syndrome . . . really does explain why Paula Gutierrez acted as she did . . . that cycle of violence," Athan said. "Frankly, she is a textbook case. It explains why she stayed with Nestor DeJesus. It explains why she failed to call authorities. It explains why she didn't feel that she had any options."

Athan noted that both psychiatrists agreed that Paula suffered from battered woman/spouse syndrome, which is a subcategory of post-traumatic stress syndrome. Again she criticized the police for taking a statement from Paula when she was under duress and had asked about getting a lawyer.

"It's his (Detective Black) [duty] to make his case and not to establish a defense," Athan said. "But when she asks for a lawyer, he didn't give her one." Athan noted that Paula said she was happier, and felt safer, in an eight-foot-by-eight-foot cell than she had in the years before she was arrested.

"What she means, Your Honor, is that she's now free of Nestor DeJesus," Athan said. "No matter how bad her life is, no matter how difficult it is, no matter what her punishment is going to be, at least she's free of that monster. And he was a monster and there is no excuse for him."

Athan said the appropriate sentence for armed robbery and armed burglary was ten years, to run concurrently with the life sentence for first-degree murder.

* * *

Melba Henoa, Paula's mother, made a heart-wrenching appeal for leniency. She told the judge that Chino not only changed Paula's life, he changed the entire family.

"My daughter is not a bad child," she told the judge. "My child, my daughter, she's got a good heart, a clean and good heart. This man changed my life and my daughter's life. I beg you under Jesus Christ to please feel mercy and compassion for my daughter."

Henoa said that Paula was terrified of Chino and that she, her husband, and two other daughters were also terrified of the man.

"Your Honor, I beg you, I beg you, my daughter is not a bad person. She's not a criminal. I beg you in the name of God have mercy on my daughter. I beg you humbly."

When Henoa took her seat, it was time for Paula to speak. Hers would be the last plea heard before the judge passed sentence. She sat at the podium, her shoulders hunched, hands folded in her lap. Paula's voice was soft and she spoke with an accent.

Paula apologized for the lost lives and pain inflicted, and said that Lois died a tragic death by Chino's hands. "I suffer as a victim, too," she said. "I didn't take part in Officer Marrero's murder in any way. I'm not a coldhearted murderer as portrayed."

Paula said she was angry that Chino killed Lois and that she understood the hatred felt toward her by Lois's family, friends, and coworkers. "I repeat again," she said, "I took no part in her death."

Paula said she knew women who were abused,

including her aunt, and wondered why they never left the man who abused them. Having lived with Chino, Paula said, she now understood. Paula said she was immobilized by terror of what Chino would do to her and her family.

"People say I should have stayed in New York. I believe he would have killed me and my family. I knew the rage inside him and I couldn't take the risk, like my aunt did. She lived with her abusive husband and finally one day she left him. But, you know what? He kept his word. He kidnapped her and he tortured her to death. I know that was my fate if I stayed away."

Paula ended her plea by asking the court for mercy.

Judge Padgett had read and heard numerous reports and motions. He sat through the testimony and he listened to the jury and their sentencing recommendations. There would be no more testimony or pleas.

The judge looked at Paula and pronounced sentence: "Miss Gutierrez, it's the judgment, order, and sentence of the court that you be confined in the Florida State Prison for the remainder of your natural life on each of these three offenses. Any questions about that?"

Paula muttered no.

"Fingerprint the defendant, please," Padgett said.

Paula was fingerprinted and escorted from the courtroom.

Deeann Athan appealed the conviction to the Fourth District Court of Appeals. Athan asked for a new trial for her client, arguing that Paula had been denied a lawyer, the flight from the robbery was over when Lois was killed, and that she had not been allowed to use the battered woman/spouse defense. On March 15, 2006—the Ides of March— the court affirmed and confirmed the conviction.

By letting the verdicts stand without comment, the court slammed the door on Paula's right to appeal to a higher court. The only thing Paula could do was ask for postconviction relief, which would mean she would file a petition that claimed Athan did an inadequate job of defending her. This rarely occurred and, even more rarely, succeeded. Barring a miracle, Paula Gutierrez will spend the rest of her life in prison.

On the positive side Paula looks and feels better than she has in years. At the Lowell Correctional Institute in Ocala, Florida, she is active in several faith-based programs. Paula, in prison, feels safer and happier than she ever did during her time with the monstrous Chino DeJesus.

The effects of a murder spread far beyond the death of the victim; a murder is like a rock dropped in a pool that creates scores of concentric ripples. In this case of Lois Marrero's murder, Ashley will never know her father and will see her mother only behind bars. The Gutierrez family has lost a sister and a daughter. Lissette Santiago lost a son she loved, and Chino took his life. Mickie Mashburn lost her life companion and the person with whom she planned to spend her retirement. Had Lois lived, she and Mickie would have been retired almost three years now.

On August 17, 2001, just over a month after Lois was killed, Mashburn and Lois's family became engaged in a legal battle over Lois's pension benefits. Lois earned about $55,000 a year and the pension benefits would have been approximately $28,000 a year for the rest of the beneficiary's life. The Marrero family opposed Mashburn's petition, claiming that she and Lois were more like roommates than spouses, and that Lois intended to leave Mashburn because she had fallen in love with another woman.

The nine-member Tampa Fire and Police Pension Board (TFPPB) unanimously rejected Mashburn's claim. Florida doesn't recognize same-sex marriages and Chairman Tom Singleton said that the TFPPB had no other choice. Lois had also died without a will and her estate would go to her closest blood relatives.

Before her petition was turned down by the TFPPB, Mashburn had held gay rights groups at arm's length because she didn't want to become a cause célèbre. But dozens of gay and human rights groups from across the nation were outraged by the decision and offered to help once again. This time Mashburn welcomed them.

Mashburn was granted a second hearing on August 28, 2001, and her claim was again unanimously rejected. The pension benefits were placed in the Marrero Estate, whose primary beneficiaries were Lois's mother, Maria, and sister, Brenda. The name of Lois's alleged new love was never revealed and no one stepped forward to identify herself.

On July 1, 2003, the Family and Estate of Lois Marrero filed a wrongful death suit against the City of Tampa, in Hillsborough County Circuit Court, alleging that police didn't give Lois the support she needed. The suit, which sought almost $3 million in damages, stated that the police should have established a perimeter around the Crossings and that Lois should not have confronted Chino and Paula by herself. This was a hot pursuit, the city argued, and Lois didn't wait for backup or for a perimeter to be formed. Several police officers testified that Lois had not done well in previous training for similar situations and had to repeat parts of the training several times.

The suit also claimed that the police were negligent by having only one man in the search helicopter. The TPD had no clear guidelines on this issue when Lois was killed, but have since changed its directives to make it mandatory for two men to be in a support helicopter. The suit alleged that radio communications between police officers were flawed. On January 29, 2006, a six-member jury found in favor of the city. The jury deliberated less than two hours before reaching a verdict.

The lawsuit and death benefit conflicts among the family and friends Lois left behind was a sad ending to the even sadder story of Lois Marrero's murder. May she rest in peace.